AF800403

Research Series on the Chinese Dream and China's Development Path

Project Director
Xie Shouguang, President, Social Sciences Academic Press

Series editors
Li Yang, Vice president, Chinese Academy of Social Sciences, Beijing, China
Li Peilin, Vice president, Chinese Academy of Social Sciences, Beijing, China

Academic Advisors
Cai Fang, Gao Peiyong, Li Lin, Li Qiang, Ma Huaide, Pan Jiahua, Pei Changhong, Qi Ye, Wang Lei, Wang Ming, Zhang Yuyan, Zheng Yongnian, Zhou Hong

Drawing on a large body of empirical studies done over the last two decades, this Series provides its readers with in-depth analyses of the past and present and forecasts for the future course of China's development. It contains the latest research results made by members of the Chinese Academy of Social Sciences. This series is an invaluable companion to every researcher who is trying to gain a deeper understanding of the development model, path and experience unique to China. Thanks to the adoption of Socialism with Chinese characteristics, and the implementation of comprehensive reform and opening-up, China has made tremendous achievements in areas such as political reform, economic development, and social construction, and is making great strides towards the realization of the Chinese dream of national rejuvenation. In addition to presenting a detailed account of many of these achievements, the authors also discuss what lessons other countries can learn from China's experience.

More information about this series at http://www.springer.com/series/13571

Huaide Ma · Jingbo Wang

Building a Government Based on the Rule of Law

History and Development

SSAP

Springer

Huaide Ma
School of Law-Based Government
China University of Political Science and Law
Beijing, China

Jingbo Wang
Research Center for Government by Law
China University of Political Science and Law
Beijing, China

Translated by Jun Qi

ISSN 2363-6866 ISSN 2363-6874 (electronic)
Research Series on the Chinese Dream and China's Development Path
ISBN 978-981-13-0997-7 ISBN 978-981-13-0999-1 (eBook)
https://doi.org/10.1007/978-981-13-0999-1

Jointly published with Social Sciences Academic Press, Beijing, China

The printed edition is not for sale in the Mainland of China. Customers from the Mainland of China please order the print book from Social Sciences Academic Press.

Library of Congress Control Number: 2018945093

© Social Sciences Academic Press and Springer Nature Singapore Pte Ltd. 2018
This work is subject to copyright. All rights are reserved by the Publishers, whether the whole or part of the material is concerned, specifically the rights of translation, reprinting, reuse of illustrations, recitation, broadcasting, reproduction on microfilms or in any other physical way, and transmission or information storage and retrieval, electronic adaptation, computer software, or by similar or dissimilar methodology now known or hereafter developed.
The use of general descriptive names, registered names, trademarks, service marks, etc. in this publication does not imply, even in the absence of a specific statement, that such names are exempt from the relevant protective laws and regulations and therefore free for general use.
The publisher, the authors, and the editors are safe to assume that the advice and information in this book are believed to be true and accurate at the date of publication. Neither the publisher nor the authors or the editors give a warranty, express or implied, with respect to the material contained herein or for any errors or omissions that may have been made. The publisher remains neutral with regard to jurisdictional claims in published maps and institutional affiliations.

Printed on acid-free paper

This Springer imprint is published by the registered company Springer Nature Singapore Pte Ltd.
The registered company address is: 152 Beach Road, #21-01/04 Gateway East, Singapore 189721, Singapore

Series Preface

Since China's reform and opening began in 1978, the country has come a long way on the path of Socialism with Chinese Characteristics, under the leadership of the Communist Party of China. Over thirty years of reform, efforts and sustained spectacular economic growth have turned China into the world's second-largest economy and wrought many profound changes in the Chinese society. These historically significant developments have been garnering increasing attention from scholars, governments, and the general public alike around the world since the 1990s, when the newest wave of China studies began to gather steam. Some of the hottest topics have included the so-called "China miracle," "Chinese phenomenon," "Chinese experience," "Chinese path," and the "Chinese model." Homegrown researchers have soon followed suit. Already hugely productive, this vibrant field is putting out a large number of books each year, with Social Sciences Academic Press alone having published hundreds of titles on a wide range of subjects.

Because most of these books have been written and published in Chinese, however, readership has been limited outside China—even among many who study China—for whom English is still the lingua franca. This language barrier has been an impediment to efforts by academia, business communities and policy-makers in other countries to form a thorough understanding of contemporary China, of what is distinct about China's past and present may mean not only for her future but also for the future of the world. The need to remove such an impediment is both real and urgent, and the *Research Series on the Chinese Dream and China's Development Path* is my answer to the call.

This series features some of the most notable achievements from the last 20 years by scholars in China in a variety of research topics related to reform and opening. They include both theoretical explorations and empirical studies, and cover economy, society, politics, law, culture, and ecology, the six areas in which reform and opening policies have had the deepest impact and farthest-reaching consequences for the country. Authors for the series have also tried to articulate their visions of the "Chinese Dream" and how the country can realize it in these fields and beyond.

All of the editors and authors for the *Research Series on the Chinese Dream and China's Development Path* are both longtime students of reform and opening and recognized authorities in their respective academic fields. Their credentials and expertise lend credibility to these books, each of which having been subject to a rigorous peer-review process for inclusion in the series. As part of the Reform and Development Program under the State Administration of Press, Publication, Radio, Film, and Television of the People's Republic of China, the series is published by Springer, a Germany-based academic publisher of international repute, and distributed overseas. I am confident that it will help fill a lacuna in studies of China in the era of reform and opening.

Xie Shouguang

Acknowledgements

After a relatively short gestation period, the *Research Series on the Chinese Dream and China's Development Path* has started to bear fruits. We have, first and foremost, the books' authors and editors to thank for making this possible. And it was the hard work by many people at Social Sciences Academic Press and Springer, the two collaborating publishers, that made it a reality. We are deeply grateful to all of them.

Mr. Xie Shouguang, president of Social Sciences Academic Press (SSAP), is the mastermind behind the project. In addition to define the key missions to be accomplished by it and setting down the basic parameters for the project's execution, as the work has unfolded, Mr. Xie has provided critical input pertaining to its every aspect and at every step of the way. Thanks to the deft coordination by Ms. Li Yanling, all the constantly moving parts of the project, especially those on the SSAP side, are securely held together, and as well synchronized as is feasible for a project of this scale. Ms. Gao Jing, unfailingly diligent and meticulous, makes sure every aspect of each Chinese manuscript meets the highest standards for both publishers, something of critical importance to all subsequent steps in the publishing process. That high quality if also at times stylistically as well as technically challenging scholarly writing in Chinese has turned into decent, readable English that readers see on these pages is largely thanks to Ms. Liang Fan, who oversees translator recruitment and translation quality control.

Ten other members of the SSAP staff have been intimately involved, primarily in the capacity of in-house editor, in the preparation of the Chinese manuscripts. It is time-consuming work that requires attention to details, and each of them has done this, and is continuing to do this with superb skills. They are, in alphabetical order: Mr. Cai Jihui, Ms. Liu Xiaojun, Mr. Ren Wenwu, Ms. Shi Xiaolin, Ms. Song Yuehua, Mr. Tong Genxing, Ms. Wu Dan, Ms. Yao Dongmei, Ms. Yun Wei, and Ms. Zhou Qiong. In addition, Xie Shouguang and Li Yanling have also taken part in this work.

Ms. Liu Xiaojun is the SSAP in-house editor for the current volume.

Our appreciation is also owed to Ms. Li Yan, Mr. Chai Ning, Ms. Wang Lei, and Ms. Xu Yi from Springer's Beijing Representative Office. Their strong support for the SSAP team in various aspects of the project helped to make the latter's work that much easier than it would have otherwise been.

We thank Ms. Qi Jun for translating this book and Ms. Sonia Jia Song for her work as the polisher. We thank everyone involved for their hard work.

Last, but certainly not least, it must be mentioned that funding for this project comes from the Ministry of Finance of the People's Republic of China. Our profound gratitude, if we can be forgiven for a bit of apophasis, goes without saying.

Social Sciences Academic Press
Springer

Contents

About the Authors

Huaide Ma was born in Xining, Qinghai province, in 1965. He is the vice president of China University of Political Science and Law, president of the Research Center for Government by Law—a Key Research Base of Beijing Social Science; professor; advisor of doctoral students; vice president of the academic committee of China University of Political Science and Law; president of China Behavior Law Association; standing director of China Law Society; vice president of China Supervision Society; vice president of the Chinese Society for Academic Degree and Graduate Education; guest consultant for the Supreme People's Court of the People's Republic of China; expert consultant for the Supreme People's Procuratorate; member of the Coordination Committee of National Judicial Examination and; consultant or expert consultant of National Development and Reform Commission, Ministry of Housing and Urban-Rural Development, Ministry of Civil Affairs, Ministry of Health, and the people's governments of Beijing, Shandong province, Fujian Province, and Hunan province. He graduated from Beijing University and obtained a Bachelor of Law in 1988. He received his doctoral degree in China University of Political Science and Law in 1993. He became the first person to earn a doctorate in Administrative Procedure Law in China. He was a visiting scholar at Yale University, Boston University, University of Sydney, and the University of Melbourne.

He has published more than 20 academic books including monographs such like Studies on the Construction of Administrative Law System and the Cases, Theories and Practice of the State Compensation Law, Administrative Permission, and 100 academic papers on the key academic journals such as Chinese Legal Science, Jurisprudential Study. He has been in charge of a number of major projects and planning projects funded by National Social Science, key research projects of the Ministry of Education, and research programs of the Ministry of Justice and Beijing Municipality. He directly participated in drafting laws including State Compensation Law, Administrative Penalty Law, Legislation Law, Administrative Permission Law, Administrative Law Enforcement Law.

He lectured in the 27th collective study of the Political Bureau of the Central Committee of the CPC on the subject of Reform on Administrative Management System and Economic Law System in December, 2005, and gave lectures on administration according to law to Ministries and other local governments on many occasions. He was the candidate at the state level for the New Century Talents Project sponsored by seven ministries including the Ministry of Personnel. He is the winner of several national prestigious awards, including the Fourth China Ten Outstanding Young Jurists, Eminent Young Teachers under the auspices of Fok Ying Tung Education Foundation, Capital Labor Medal, and Talents of Beijing Municipality for Outstanding Contributions to Science, Technology, and Management. He is also the receiver of government special subsidies approved by the State Council.

Jingbo Wang received her Bachelor's degree of law from Northwest University of Political Science and Law in 1993, a Master's degree of Law from Northwest University of Political Science and Law in 1996, and a doctoral degree of Law from China University of Political Science and Law in 2005. She is now the vice president of the Law-Based Government Institute of China University of Political Science and Law; professor; and advisor of doctoral students. Her representative publications are Studies on the Issues of Administrative Law in Higher Education, Studies on EU Administrative Law, Urban Management and Administrative Law Enforcement, and others. She has also edited a number of textbooks, including Introduction to State Compensation Law, Administrative Law, and Law of Administrative Procedure. Professor Wang has published more than 50 academic papers in journals such as Jurisprudential Study, Political and Legal Forum, Administrative Law Review, and so forth.

She has been in charge of over 10 R&D projects such as National Social Science Fund, Researches on Social Society of the Ministry of Education, Researches on the Legal Construction and Theories of the Ministry of Justice, Philosophy and Social Science of Beijing. She once went to University of Paris I and Yale University as a visiting scholar. She was awarded the third prize of the National Teaching Materials of Jurisprudence and Achievements in Scientific Research of the Ministry of Justice, the first prize of the First Outstanding Achievements in the Science of Law. In 2011, she was selected as the New Century Elite of the Ministry of Education.

Abstract

The book on a government based on the rule of law summarizes and analyzes China's experiences and lessons as it strives to build a government based on the rule of law. It takes an in-depth look at what the country has achieved, problems it has faced and still does, and direction for future development in this area. The contents of the book mainly include: the historical development, achievements, and motivation mechanism of the construction of the government based on the rule of law; the development of administrative legislation, survey of administrative legal system in China, and the characteristics of the administrative legislation development; reform of the administrative examination and approval system and reform of the administrative permit system; reform of Chinese social security system, welfare state and government benefits, and the development of Chinese administrative law; sources of due process concept, the experience in and the development trend of administrative procedure legislation in China; government information and its elements, disclosure, problems, and development trend; history and current situation of emergency response management, reform of the public emergency response mechanism, and improvement of emergency requisition laws and regulations; development of administrative review system, problems encountered in practice, causes and improvement; development and improvement of administrative litigation system, achievements, and current situation; and historical development of state compensation system, responsible government, and development of administrative accountability system. In the book, the authors base their studies on the practice of administration according to law in China, absorb and draw lessons from a large number of relevant research results at home and abroad and, on the basis of profound analysis of the construction of the rule of law in China, put forward targeted countermeasures and suggestions which accord with the developing trend of the construction of the rule of law in China.

Chapter 1
Building a Government Based on the Rule of Law in China, 1949–Present: A Historical Review

At its core, a government based on the rule of law is subject to regulation by law in its exercise of power. A government's mode of operation is closely related to the country's political system, especially, the governance model of the ruling party. In the early time of New China, the ruling party did not have a definite goal of constructing the rule of law. Instead, it adopted the rule of policy for a considerably long time. It is not until China carried out the reform and opened up to the outside world that the government stepped onto the path of the rule of law under the boost of the market economy. The development of government administration mode, therefore, basically consists of two stages: from 1949 to the time of reform and opening up, and after the reform and opening up.

The Chinese government began in earnest to build a government based on the rule of law soon after the founding of the People's Republic of China. "The Common Program of the Chinese People's Political Consultative Conference", which had been passed in September 1949, served as the symbol of this historical endeavor. This document called in no uncertain terms for abolishing all oppressive laws, regulations and statutory system put in place by the Kuomintang (KMT) reactionary government, and replacing them with those that serve to protect and work for the people. However, it is much easier to abolish an old system than to establish a new one. At the time, the ruling party could ill-afford—philosophically, methodologically or practically—to give priority to the construction of a legal system. In 1954, the Constitution of the People's Republic of China was passed and released. However, the gradual development of rule of law was undermined by the Anti-rightist Movement, the Cultural Revolution and many other political movements. In an era when such mantras as "Rebellion is always justified" and "Destruction unto the legal system" held sway, the idea of the rule of law had no chance for survival.

The tragedy of the Cultural Revolution has taught the Chinese people a lesson, which is that safeguarding democracy calls for the strengthening of the rule of law, and establishing democratic institutions and systems of laws that can withstand changes in national leadership, or the personal opinions and focus of attention of the leaders.

© Social Sciences Academic Press and Springer Nature Singapore Pte Ltd. 2018

H. Ma and J. Wang, *Building a Government Based on the Rule of Law*,
Research Series on the Chinese Dream and China's Development Path,
https://doi.org/10.1007/978-981-13-0999-1_1

1.1 The Development in China of the Government Based on the Rule of Law

The development in China of the government based on the rule of law can be divided into three stages since 1978.

1. Embryo: 1978–1988.

The third Plenary Session of the 11th Central Committee of the Communist Party of China (CPC) held in 1978, which marked the beginning of reform, opening-up and modernization, also ushered in a new era of the construction of the rule of law in China. The idea was embodied in the Constitution of 1982, according to which the fundamental task of the country is to bring together all and any available resources and invest them toward the construction of a modern socialist country, that China would be committed to developing a socialist democracy and improving a socialist legal system, and that "all state apparatus, armed forces, political parties, social organizations, enterprises and institutions shall abide by the Constitution and laws."[1] Even though it had been written into the Constitution that all the state organs are bound by it, law scholars realized that the rule by law and the rule of law are inherently different: the rule by law refers to the combination of static laws and system, and leaves open the possibility of interference by human agents while the rule of law refers to the various aspects of the operation of the legal system, including its status, mode and process. The latter offers more protection against dictatorship and the whims of any individual or group of individuals. In the late 1970s and into the early 1980s, a national debate began on the relative merits of "the rule of man" and "the rule of law". The debate played an important role in propelling the country's senior leadership toward announcing in the Report of the 15th CPC Central Committee the government's fundamental and long-term commitment to building a socialist country based on the rule of law. This commitment was codified into the Amended Constitution at the 2nd Session of the 9th National People's Congress in 1999.

Meantime, as it guided the country's efforts to reform the economic system, the government tried to define its own role and proper place in the nation-building endeavor. Reform and opening-up and attracting foreign investment were issues of top priority. Legislation in the areas of foreign investment and foreign trade, therefore, was the main task of the legal system. Since the reform aiming at free trade and relaxation of rules and restrictions, imposing limits on the power of the government was a notable feature of legislations related to China's international cooperation, joint venture, and sole proprietorship using foreign capital. In 1988, senior party leadership clarified at the 13th National Congress of the CPC that administrative legislation must be improved and basic norms and procedures for administrative work must be established to consolidate the achievements of structural reform and

[1] Deng Xiaoping, Emancipating the Mind, Seeking Truth from Facts, Looking Ahead in Unity, *Selected Works of Deng Xiaoping*, Vol. 2, People's Publishing House, 1978, p. 146.

advance the institutionalization of administrative management. We should improve current regulations governing administrative organs and introduce rules specifying their size in order to subject their establishment and staff scale to legal and budgetary constraints. A multi-level administrative responsibility system is needed to improve work quality and efficiency. An administrative procedural law is needed to strengthen supervision over administrative work and personnel and investigate cases of neglect or dereliction of duty and other breaches of law or discipline by administrative personnel. Although the Report proposed to enact a series of legislations regarding administrative work, policies remained the primary regulative instrument in this area.

2. Concerted efforts and rapid progress: 1989–2003.

Enactment and promulgation of the Law of Administrative Procedure of 1989 marked the beginning of a new chapter in the country's efforts to build the rule of law in China. The 1989 Law and the Regulations on Administrative Review of 1990 have played an important role in ensuring the rights of citizens, regulating administrative conduct, and supervising administrative organs, and have laid a solid foundation for the administration according to law. The administrative procedure system facilitated the establishment of the principle that the government is subject to the rule of law in its administrative acts. Ren Jianxin from the Supreme People's Court proposed in the Report of the Supreme People's Court delivered to the 4th Session of the 7th National People's Congress (NPC) on April 3, 1991, that efforts should be made to guarantee fairness and justice in the trial of civil and administrative disputes, that the legitimate rights and interests of the citizens and legal persons should be protected, and that the government should discharge its administrative duties and responsibility in accordance with the rule of law." And again in 1992, the Supreme People's Court proposed, echoing the earlier statement, that "through the trial of the administrative disputes and the enforcement of the judgments thereof, the rights and interests of the citizens, legal persons and other organizations are protected and the government's performance of its administrative duties based on the rule of law should be supervised and strengthened." On the 1st Session of the 8th NPC on March 15, 1993, to meet the needs of the administrative procedure system, then on behalf of the State Council, Premier Li Peng pointed out in the Government Work Report delivered that "governments at all levels should abide by the law while performing their duties and handling affairs." On Nov. 14, the sentence "the governments at all levels should abide by law in performing their duties and handling affairs" was written into Decision of the Central Committee Regarding Some Issues of the Socialist Market Economy.[2] "The principle of administration based on the rule of law was proposed after the establishment of the administrative litigation system, which is the legal foundation thereof."[3] This indicates that, rather than acting proactively, the government took up

[2]The words in the document of the Communist Party of China are, "To enhance and improve the judicial and administrative law enforcement and law enforcement supervision, maintain social stability, guarantee the economic development and the legitimate rights and interests of citizens. Governments at all levels shall abide by law in performing their duties and handling affairs."

[3]Ying Songnian, The Outline of Administration Based on the Rule of Law, *China Legal Science*, Issue 1, 1997.

the issue of administration based on the rule of law largely because of the pressure it had come under. Recollection by legal scholars who participated in drafting the Law of Administrative Procedure in those early years also serves to corroborate this.[4]

The Interim Regulations on State Civil Servants of 1993 has changed the situation that a civil servant who once got promoted can never be demoted or removed from his position and established a system of selection, appraisal, rewards and punishment, resignation and dismissal of civil servants. The State Compensation Law of 1994 established the state compensation system under which any citizens, legal entities or other organizations injured by the exercise of the state power shall be compensated. The Law of Administrative Punishment of 1996 provides that the rights and interests of the concerned person shall be guaranteed when administrative punishment is imposed. The State Council passed and released the Decision on Comprehensively Promoting Administration based on the Rule of Law in November, 1999, requiring governments at all levels and their departments to enhance the system construction, strictly abide by law in administration, strengthen the supervision thereof, and constantly improve the capability and level of handling affairs according to law. The 16th National Congress of the CPC set the development of socialist democracy and politics and construction of the socialist political civilization as one of the important goals of building a moderately prosperous society in all aspects in China. And it explicitly required "enhancing the supervision over law enforcement and promote

[4]Jiang Ping, Professor of the China University of Political Science and Law, said when he recalled on drafting the *Administrative Litigation Law* in the book entitled *Legislation on "Citizens Suing the Government"*: "in 1986, 'market economy' was not explicitly proposed in China, but a tendency of a shift to market economy appeared. It, therefore, is significant to limit the power of the government. In April, 1987, to celebrate the first anniversary of the *General Principles of the Civil Law*, the NPC Law Committee, the Supreme People's Court, the Propaganda Department of the Central Committee, the Ministry of Justice, and so forth held a seminar attended by Wang Hanbin, the secretary general of the NPC Standing Committee and the Director of the NPC Legislative Affairs Commission, Tao Xijin, the chief of the drafters of the old civil code, and the consultants and professors, including me, who participated in drafting the *General Principles of the Civil Law*. The seminar was evidently more than a celebration. It also looked into the future of the legislation of the civil law and other pertinent laws in China. Honorable Mr. Tao's remarks drew great attention from the participants. He asserted that about 40 years had passed since the founding of New China, but the legal system had not been established in China. There was "System of Six Laws" in the Kuomingtang period, then how many laws should be included in the new system? He suggested to establish a "New System of Six Laws", namely the criminal law, criminal procedure law, civil law, civil procedure law, administrative law, and administrative procedure law under the Constitution, among which the first four are available while the latter two are absent. Laws regarding administration, therefore, should be enacted as soon as possible." Wang Hanbin said in his concluding remarks that Mr Tao's advice should be given a serious consideration, but we were in lack of the knowledge and experience of legislation of administrative law. He, hence, suggested that a research group of legislation of administrative law, composed of law experts, scholars, the Legislative Affairs Commission of the Standing Committee and the specific entities, including the Supreme People's Court and the legislative affairs bureaus, be established under the leadership of Mr. Tao, and with the Legislative Affairs Commission taking charge of the specific jobs and expenses. Wang said that he would be the director of the group, while Luo Haocai and Prof. Ying Songnian the deputy directors thereof and that the other members would be Jiang Ming'an, Zhu Weijiu, Jiang Bixin, Xiao Xun from the Legislative Affairs Commission, and the people from the Legislative Affairs Office of the State Council and other departments thereof. It was decided later that making the Administrative Procedure Law be the priority task.

administration in line with the rule of law". The amendment of "the rule of law" to the Constitution has ushered in China a new era of building a socialist country based on the rule of law in all aspects. The Law of Legislation of 2000 regulates legislative activities, expressly prescribing the fundamental principles and procedures of legislation, which is of great significance for improving the quality and level of legislation and promoting democratic and scientific legislation. The year of 2003 saw the government transforming from "the rule by law" to "the rule of law". That the 17th National Congress of the CPC set the goals of putting people first, scientific development and that more attention paid to social fairness marks a further transformation of the role of the government. China's access to the WTO also has contributed to the transformation of the Chinese government in administrative mode.

The idea of administration based on the rule of law was established and gradually took root in the government with the passage of the Law of Administrative Procedure. However, to perfect the administrative legal system is still the main task for the government.

3. Rapid development: 2004–present.

In 2004, that the State should respect and safeguard human rights of the individuals was written into the Constitution. Putting people first and respect for human rights have become the principles of government administrative acts. In the same year, the State Council released the Implementation Outline of Comprehensively Promoting Administration Based on the Rule of Law (hereinafter the Implementation Outline) more explicitly put forward the concept of the government based on the rule of law, set building a government based on the rule of law as the ultimate goal of promoting the administration according to law in all aspects, and made a ten-year plan for it. The Implementation Outline also pointed out the necessity and urgency, and provided the guiding ideology, goals, fundamental principles, requirements and main content of promoting the administration in accordance with the rule of law. The establishment of the goal of building a government based on the rule of law is the prerequisite for the Chinese government implementing the strategy of rule of law and building a country under the rule of law, and the outcome of its practice of the rule of law for a period of time. It indicates that the Party had achieved better understanding of the rule of law. The Administrative Permission Law of 2004 aims at promoting the transformation of governmental functions and creativity of the administration mode. In 2007, the Report of the 17th National Congress of the CPC included improving the construction of a government based on the rule of law into the requirement for realizing a well-off society in all aspects, and put forward more definite and specific requirements. The Report mentioned two main tasks: fully implementing the basic principle of the rule of law, and speeding up the construction of a socialist country based on the rule of law. "Fully" and "speeding up" here further clarified the direction and tasks of building a government based on the rule of law.

The Emergency Response Law of 2008 regulates the government in responding to unexpected events and strengthens the protection of civil rights and freedom. The Regulations on the Government Information Disclosure, effective since May 1, 2008, requires the government to disclose information to the public so as to guarantee the citizen's right to know, which marks China had made a substantial progress in building a transparent and open government. The Opinions on Deepening the Reform of the Administrative System passed at the 2nd Plenary Session of the 17th National Congress of the CPC in Feb., 2008, once again stressed enhancing the construction of administration based on the rule of law and the construction of the administrative system, regulating power, business and people in accordance with law, improving the supervision mechanism, strengthening accountability system, and ensure that power go with responsibility and be subject to supervision and that anyone who misuses the power be held responsible." The Opinions also made specific requirements for regulating administrative decision making, enhancing and improving legislation of the government, the administrative law enforcement system and procedure, the system of administrative review, administrative redress and administrative compensation, the system of government performance management and administrative accountability system, the system of supervision over the executive power, and the construction of the team of civil servants.

In May, 2008, in order to fully boost the administration in accordance with law and build government based on the rule of law, given the significant position of city and county governments in the political system in China and the urgency to improve their capability and level of administration in line with law, the State Council released the Decision on Strengthening the City and County Governments' Administration According to Law, stressing such important goals as vigorously raising the awareness and capability of administration according to law of the personnel in city and county governments, perfecting the decision-making mechanism of the city and county governments, establishing and improving the supervision and control system of regulatory instruments, strictly implementing the administrative law, enhancing supervision over administrative acts, and strengthening the social autonomous function and so forth.

In October, 2010, the State Council passed and released the Opinion on Strengthening the Construction of a Government Based on the Rule of Law considering the effect of the Implementation Outline. The Opinion consists of 29 subtopics, such as raising the awareness and capability of administration according to law of government workers, particularly leading cadres, strengthening and improving the system construction, adhering to democratically and scientifically making decisions according to law, strictly regulating and justifying law enforcement, fully promoting the openness of government affairs, strengthening administrative supervision and accountability, legally resolving social conflicts and disputes, and enhancing institutional leadership, supervision, inspection and so forth. In addition, the Opinion also stresses the tasks and priorities of administration according to law in the following period.

1.2 Achievements Made in the Construction of a Government Based on the Rule of Law in China

Since 1978, China has made significant achievements in reform and opening-up. In the past more than 30 years, China has made profound transformation and rapid development in all respects: transformation from planned economy to socialist market economy, and from an omnipotent and all-controlling government to a limited and service-oriented government based on the rule of law. To build a government based on the rule of law is a key but difficult task. The past 30-year development indicates that the concept of administration according to the rule of law has been rooted in people's mind, that the theories of government based on the rule of law have kept developing, that governments' capability and level of administration according to law have been improved constantly, and that the supervision over administration has been increasingly perfected. The remarkable achievements made in the construction of a government based on the rule of law in China are mainly as follows:

1. The government and civil servants understand the idea of administration according to law better now than ever before, and are fully committed to the goal of building a government based on the rule of law in China.

Since the reform and opening-up, an increasing number of people have accepted modern administrative and associated concepts, such as administration according to law, government based on the rule of law, due process, that rights constitute the ground for demanding compensation, and that the exercise of any power must be subject to independent oversight. The Report of the 16th National Congress of the CPC stressed the need to enhance oversight for law enforcement, and to improve administration according to law. The Report of the 17th National Congress of the CPC called for enhancing the enforcement of the Constitution and the laws, ensuring that all citizens are equal before the law, striving for social fairness and justice, safeguarding the uniformity, dignity and authority of the socialist legal system, and promote administration according to law". The governments at all levels and their personnel at large, particularly CPC members and its leaders, are now more aware of the importance of administration according to law, and more capable of meeting relevant requirements in their work. The concept of administration according to law has become the fundamental principle for the majority of government organs. In particular, the government officially declared in the Implementation Outline passed and released by the State Council in 2004 the construction of a government based on the rule of law to be a key task for the nation. This declaration provided efforts to build administration according to law with both direction and theoretical support.

2. A large number of laws and rules and regulations have been enacted and promulgated, and legislation has greatly improved both methodologically and in terms of quality.

In the three decades of reform and opening-up, China has made tremendous progress in legislation and enacted and promulgated a great number of laws and rules and regulations regarding administrative work. The socialist legal system is now basically in place. The State Council has enacted and promulgated 3668 rules and regulations since 1979, 3087 of which are in effect.[5] These administrative laws and rules and regulations regulate the governments' administrative conduct, secure and promote reform and opening-up and socialist modernization. In recent years, the administrative organs that have been given legislative power have been improving their legislative work with respect to methods and mechanism, introduced higher-order rules governing the formulation, review and assessment of and record keeping for first-order rules and regulations, and made great strides toward establishing a uniform and scientifically-sound procedures for making rules and regulations. Legislation has become increasingly transparent and enjoyed growing involvement of the public. The open government legislation has become prevalent, and a system has been established for the government to hear the people's voice in various ways. For those bills that are of particular significance or potentially have large impact on people's lives, hearings, forums and seminars are held. Other times the bills are made public so that stakeholders can voice their opinions. These measures have done much to ensure that the legislative process is as adequately informed by and accord proper weight to the opinions, wills and fundamental interests of those who are concerned and the society at large.

3. Governmental function has been changing, capability of administrative law enforcement has been strengthened, and the service mentality has taken roots.

Since the beginning of reform and opening-up, the government has been adjusting its role and function, especially in the areas of economic regulation, market supervision, social management, and public services. The governments at all levels acknowledge that the market should be given the space it needs to regulate itself, that social intermediaries and trade organizations should be allowed to practice self-governance based on the rule of law, and that citizens, legal entities and other organizations should have the right to make decisions on some particular matters so as to reduce unnecessary government intervention on economic and social affairs. The governments at all levels should make every effort to establish an administrative law enforcement mechanism with definite powers and responsibilities, code of conduct, effective supervision and strong security, and abolish such "the chronic illnesses" as abusive or lackadaisical law enforcement. Pursuant to the Administrative Punishment Law, and the Administrative Permission Law, in many places, the local governments have experimented with comparatively consolidated the powers of administrative punishment, administrative permit and comprehensive law enforcement; clarifying the subjects of the administrative law enforcement and the administrative permit matters. The phenomena such as multiple law enforcement agencies doing the same thing, needless repetition, and laxity in law enforcement have largely been eliminated. Governments at all levels and the departments thereof have gradually established and completed

[5]The above data are from the Laws and Regulations—Chinalawinfo, URL: http://www.pkulaw.cn/cluster_form.aspx?Check_gaojijs=1&menu_item=law&EncodingName=&db=chl, last access on May 10, 2014.

the review, evaluation and record keeping systems for administrative law enforcement, accreditation system for administrative law enforcement entities, system of accountability, and the system of the administrative discretion. The administrative law, therefore, has seen a high degree of compliance. The Working Rules of the State Council of 2008 expressly provides that building a "service-oriented government", further enhancing the government's role as a service provider and strengthening the service mentality of civil servants, simplifying public service procedure, reducing public service fees, and reforming the administrative model. To better serve the people, more local governments and the departments thereof have introduced measures meant to increase the efficiency and quality of services and so forth.

4. The system and mechanism of supervision over the administrative review and administrative procedure have been improving.

Absolute power leads to absolute corruption. Supervision mechanism, therefore, is vital to guarantee that the government exercises its power properly, and that the powers of the government correspond to its responsibilities. In the past 30 years, a mechanism of inner-outer combined supervision over the administration has been established. The National People's Congress and its Standing Committee supervise the government by questioning and "file for record" of rules and regulations while The Chinese People's Political Consultative Conference did it by giving opinions or advice. The supervision made by the organs such as the monitory and audit organs have been enhanced. The governments at all levels are willingly subject themselves to the supervision of the particular supervisory organs. Meanwhile, the inner system of the administration has been improving the supervision mechanism, and building and perfecting the mechanism of supervision over the rules and regulations and other regulatory instruments. The role of the hierarchical supervision of the administrative review system has become increasingly apparent. Courts enhance supervision over administration by administrative procedure. In recent years, the courts have expanded their jurisdiction over the administrative disputes. The governments at all levels actively appear before the court to answer the complaint or defend themselves, and willingly enforce the judgments or rulings entered by the people's courts.

Throughout history of China's administration according to law, enormous progress has been achieved. However, we should also notice that due to the unique history and tradition of China, the administration according to law and the government based on the rule of law is driven from up to down. This up-to-down driving will usually undermine or damage the executive capability of the governments at all levels, which make the writs held back and enforcement thereof unsmooth. Nowadays, the administrative legal system has been improving in China, and the achievements in legislation are universally recognized, but the implementation of many administrative acts is far from satisfactory for the reason that governments are not fully motivated to promote rule of law. Therefore, only by inner-and-outer regulation and up-and-down interaction internalizing the concept of administration according to law into the work directive of the government and conduct rule of the government officers can the goal of building a government based on the rule of law be realized as soon as possible. As far as the current situation in China is concerned, for the purpose of building a government based on the rule of law, it is necessary to establish a continuous driving system with the ruling party, government and society combined. Particularly, to achieve this, the following jobs should be done:

(a) Fully understand that the administration according to law and the construction of the government based on the rule of law is of great significance to the improvement of the Party's ruling capability and the maintenance of the Party's ruling authority. The administration according to law is the specific channel to realize the rule of law and maintain the stable and harmonious society. The Party and government organizations and their leaders should increase their awareness of the rule of law, understand that the government power is vested by the people whose rights are protected by law, improve the consciousness, capability and level of the rule of law and administration according to law, guarantee the peoples' political, economic, cultural, and social rights and interests, promote social fairness and justice, protect the people's legitimate rights and interests, and ensure that people benefit from the reform achievements.
(b) Deepen the market economy reform and legalizing the government functions at the same time. Since the beginning of the economic reform and opening-up, China has carried out government institutional reform six times. Since 1988 when it was decided to transform the governmental functions, a vicious circle has been formed, namely streamlining, expanding, streamlining again, and expanding again. Because the transformation of the governmental function has not been in place, the government has not switched its function to economy regulation, market supervision, social management and public service. The government still intervenes in the micro-economic operation in a large scope, which hinders the market economy development. To step out of the vicious circle of the prior government institutional reform and transformation of the governmental functions, it is critical to legalize the governmental functions. The law of the government institution, which provides the government power restriction and operation, is available in all the countries advanced in the rule of law. In China, the current government institutional system and its powers are in flux. There are difficulties in legalization of the governmental functions, which is impossible to accomplish by one-time legislation. But it is suggested to provide the part of powers which are relatively ascertained into the laws and regulations. It is not a scientific approach to simply rely on the program of three regulations (the program of making the regulations on the powers and responsibilities, the internal institutions, and the staffing levels), which in fact directly caused overlaps and conflicts of functions in the institutions.
(c) Enacting the Law of Administrative Procedures, normalizing procedures of administrative act, and prohibiting the abuse of power. The Administrative Permission Law and the Administrative Punishment Act have been enacted and promulgated in China. The Act of Administrative Law Enforcement and the Act of Administrative Charge are under discussion. These legislations are aimed at regulating specific types of administrative conduct, and are often misunderstood

or avoided by executive organs. For instance, many executive organs will state that their approvals are not made for the matters which are not subject to the Law when they do not want to apply the Law of the Administrative Permission. Or when they want to evade the Administrative Penalty Law, they will state that their decisions are not for administrative penalty. It is impossible to exhaust all the administrative acts by law, so it is obviously crucial to enact and promulgate a uniform law of administrative procedures to establish the principles and procedures for the exercise of the administrative power.

(d) Incorporating the idea of administration according to law into rules of conduct for government officials and include the capability for the administration according to law an important criterion used for performance evaluation for government officials. To motivate the governments, especially the local governments, and arouse the passion of the government officials to carry out the rule of law so as to transform passive promotion of rule of law into active one and make it government officials' rational choice, the level of legal knowledge and the capability of administration according to the rule of law should be included as criteria into the government officials' performance evaluation system. Governments at all levels should make the legal knowledge and the capacity of administration according to law the qualifications for recruit and promotion of the government officials. Those who are found liable for severe misconduct will never get promotion.

(e) Modifying the State Compensation Law and supervising administration according to law. The amendments and modifications to the legal systems, including expanding the jurisdiction of the people's courts over the administrative disputes by adding the cases of public interests, enlarging the scope of national compensation, and raising the standard of national compensation, has pushed the government to strengthen the administration according to law and the idea that powers and responsibilities should correspond to each other.

(f) Enhancing the social autonomous function, encouraging and guiding the public participating in political affairs. The ruling party, government and the society should coordinate with each other so as to effectively and continuously promote reform. The government should make efforts in building the social autonomous system and improving the consultation and communication mechanism in decision-making and implementation so as to greatly reduce the costs of public policy implementation.

1.3 The Motivation Mechanism of the Construction of the Government Based on the Rule of Law

The strategy of governing the country according to law derives from the reflection of the whole society of China on the Cultural Revolution and the lessons learned from the rule of men. To choose the path of the government based on the rule of law is inevitable in China and is consistent with the strategy of governing the country according to law. The grounds for the Chinese government to adopt the rule of law are as the following:

1. The system of market economy is the economic foundation of the construction of the government based on the rule of law in China.

Since 1978, the reform of market economy and political system in China have contributed to various degrees to the choice of administration according to law as China's governance strategy, but economy is the most direct reason. After the Cultural Revolution, the Chinese economy was on a blink of breaking. Economic development was the top priority of the country. Under the system of planned economy, economic development mainly relies on the plan and intervention of the government, and the executive powers are mainly vested in the government, while under the system of market economy, the government has to make room for the market subjects. There is a big difference between the two systems in position and responsibility of the government. But in the early period of reform and opening-up, the reform of the economic system was not carried out along a pre-paved path. Instead, the path was explored and paved one stone by another, developing from "plan-oriented economy supplemented with market regulation" to the "planned commodity economy", and finally to the "socialist market economy". The governmental functions have been constantly adjusted with the improvement of the economic system. The market economy is more demanding for the transformation of governing idea and the law enforcement mode of the government. The government has transformed its functions from direct control of economy under the planned economic system to the control of service fields such as education and medication, withdrawing from the economic field. The government act mode has been gradually transformed from compulsory measures including regulations to combination of compulsory measures and services. The norms of the government acts have been made more and more in accordance to laws and regulations so that arbitrary acts can be avoided.

2. Awareness of civil rights is the social foundation of the construction of the government based on the rule of law in China.

The maturity of the market economy and the wealth increase of individuals made the individuals aware of the economic rights first, then the human rights and social rights. The awareness of civil rights causes the change of the space for civil rights and powers of the government. The space for civil rights has been enlarged, while the space for government powers has been narrowed. Meanwhile, the government must change the mode of management, and legally act so as to prevent civil rights violations by public powers.

3. The reform of the political system is the logical extension of the construction of the government based on the rule of law in China.

The reform of the political system is extremely sensitive. Moreover, the reform and opening-up occurred in a transformation period in which various social conflicts emerged. For fear that the reform of the political system might cause turbulence of the society, policies should be made more cautiously, and measures taken more steadily. In 20th century, the guidance thought of the Chinese political system reform centered on the key issue of the Party's leadership and ruling ability. The basic idea was to steadfastly take the course of democracy legalization. As Jiang Zemin stated in the Report of the 16th National Congress of the CPC that to develop socialist democratic politics, it is essential to organically unify upholding the Party's leadership, people being the masters of the country and governing the country according to law. The Report of the 15th National Congress of the CPC stated that the ruling of the Communist Party means leading and supporting the people in exercising the power of running the state, carrying out democratic election, democratic decision-making, democratic policy-making, democratic management and supervision, ensuring the people have extensive rights and freedom according to law, and respecting and protecting human right.

4. China's access into WTO is the international pressure imposed on China in building up a government based on the rule of law

WTO rules aim at establishing an international trade mechanism for fair and free competition and eliminating trade barrier between member states. The requirements made by the WTO Agreement to the governments are embodied in the nation treatment principle, transparency principle, the principle of uniform law enforcement, administrative fairness principle, and the principle of administrative supervision and relief. These rules promote the transparency of the government information and legalization of the administrative management, reduce the conflicts of law, stress the fairness of administrative act, and normalize the law enforcement methods and procedures. Meanwhile, The WTO establishes uniform act principles, which sets an international reference for the Chinese government.

Both the market economy and the democratic politics require the Chinese government to transform from an omnipotent government with absolute powers to a government based on the rule of law with limited powers. For 30 years since the reform and the opening up to the outside world, the reform of the market economy has almost been completed, but the reform of the political system has been comparatively lagging, which will not only adversely affect the ultimate establishment of the market economy, but also hinder the development of rule of law to some extent.

Chapter 2
The Legislative Process of Administrative Law in China

China has established an integral socialist legal system with the Constitution as its core and laws as its mainstay. China's legal system consists of seven bodies of law, each subdivided into three tiers, including administrative regulations, departmental regulations, local government rules, regulations by autonomous governments, special regulations and other regulatory instruments.[1] The administrative legislation which mainly consists of administrative laws and regulations has become an important part of the socialist legal system with Chinese characteristics.

2.1 The Development of Administrative Legislation

The development of China's administrative legislation can be divided into the following stages:

1. The embryonic stage from 1949 to 1981.

In the early period of new China, the national legislation focused on the constitutional instruments, including the Constitution and the organic law. The Constitution of 1954 established a highly consolidated legislation system, stipulating that the National People's Congress is the only law-making body in China. Although the Constitution did not vest the executive organs with the power of legislation, the regulatory instruments which regulated the operation of the country were actually issued by the State Council and subordinate departments. The administrative legislation in fact functioned effectively. Particularly, in the first five years after the People's Republic of China was founded, the State Council and local governments at all levels functioned as legislative bodies. The legislation by administrative bodies was sus-

[1] The Speech of Wu Bangguo, the Chairman of the NPC Standing Committee, at the second plenary session of the 11th National People's Congress on March 8, 2008.

© Social Sciences Academic Press and Springer Nature Singapore Pte Ltd. 2018

H. Ma and J. Wang, *Building a Government Based on the Rule of Law*,
Research Series on the Chinese Dream and China's Development Path,
https://doi.org/10.1007/978-981-13-0999-1_2

pended because of the Cultural Revolution and other political movements. It was not resumed to work until 1978.

2. The establishment of the administrative legislative power from 1982 to 1986.

The economic development and reform and opening-up demanded for protection of a sound legal system. The Constitution of 1982 vested the State Council and its subordinate departments with the legislative power, stipulating that the State Council has the power to formulate administrative regulations pursuant to the Constitution and the laws, and the departments under the State Council have the power to formulate departmental regulations. Moreover, The Organic Law of the State Council defines the statutory duties of the State Council and its departments to make administrative and departmental regulations.[2] The Organic Law of the People's Congress at All Levels and Governments at All Levels also provides that the people's governments of provinces, autonomous regions, municipalities, capital cities where the people's governments of autonomous regions are based, and other comparatively big cities designated by the State Council are empowered to formulate regulations pursuant to laws and regulations of the State Council. The provisions of the Constitution and the Organic Law lay a constitutional basis for the administrative legislation power and establish the legislative power in the legal system. The reform and opening-up and the economic development have brought about enormous social changes. The advantages of the administrative legislation being highly efficient and professional were prominent in the legal system. A large number of administrative laws and regulations tailored to the demand of economic and social development were formulated. Meanwhile, to adapt to the reform of the economic legal system, the National People's Congress pioneered the delegation of legislative power in 1984. The Standing Committee of the National People's Congress authorized the State Council to draft the regulations on taxation. In 1985, the National People's Congress authorized the State Council to formulate interim rules or regulations regarding the reform of economic system and opening up.

3. The institionalization of administrative legislative procedure from 1987 to 1999.

After the administrative legislative power was established, attention turned to administrative legislative procedure. In 1987, the State Council issued Interim Regulations on the Enactment Procedure of Administrative Laws and Regulations, which established the principles and procedure of administrative legislation, including planning, drafting, approval, issue and others and so forth. The institutionalization of administrative legislative procedure was primarily accomplished. In the following decade, a large number of administrative laws, such as the Law of Administrative Procedure, the Administrative Review Law, and the Administrative Penalty Law, had been released and so were the regulations pursuant to the aforesaid laws. Particularly the establishment of the principle of administration according to law, which requires that there must be laws to go by, the laws must be observed and strictly enforced, and

[2]Art. III of the *Organic Law of the State Council*.

law-breakers must be prosecuted, radically sped up the process of administrative legislation and increased the number of administrative laws. Meanwhile, a great number of administrative rules and regulations regulating the exercise of the executive powers were issued. The demand for local development, to a certain degree, boosted the expansion of administrative legislation scope of the local government. Governments of Shenzhen, Xiamen, Shantou, and Zhuhai were authorized to implement rules and regulations applicable to their special economic zones in 1992, 1994 and 1996. The Organic Law of the People's Congress at All Levels and Governments at All Levels modified in 1995 expanded the administrative legislation scope of local governments and, meanwhile, provided the filing system and other legislative supervision systems.

4. The formation of the administrative legislative system from 2000 till now.

The Legislation Law of 2000 is the first specific law on legislation, expressly stipulating the legislative system, powers of legislative bodies, and legislative principles, procedures, supervision and other aspects and so forth. In 2001, the State Council issued the Rules of the Legislative Procedure of Administrative Laws and Regulations, the Rules of the Legislative Procedure, and the Rules of Putting Laws and Regulations on Record, which symbolizes the comprehensive institutionalization of the administrative legislative procedure and the perfection of the legislative supervision system.

2.2 Survey of the Administrative Legal System in China

After thirty years of development, China's administrative legal system has been established preliminarily and administrative legislation has made prominent achievements.

1. Main administrative laws have been enacted and promulgated.

The National People's Congress and the Standing Committee thereunder have successively enacted and promulgated nine basic administrative laws: the Law of Administrative Procedure, the State Compensation Law, the Administrative Penalty Law, the Administrative Supervision Law, the Administrative Review Law, the Legislation Law, the Administrative Permission Law, the Civil Servant Law, and the Emergency Response Law (see Table 2.1). The aforesaid laws constitute the main framework of the administrative legal system in China, and boost the development of administration according to law and construction of a government based on the rule of law. The main rules and systems established by the laws are of great significance in promoting democracy and rule of law in China.

2. Rapid increase of administrative legislations.

During the thirty years of reform and opening-up, China has enacted and promulgated a great number of laws and regulations that reflect the process of the reform and opening up and play an active role in ensuring and promoting the smooth and healthy

Table 2.1 Number of regulations introduced by the government, 1978–2010

Date	Title of the Law	Doctrines and systems established
Oct.1, 1989	Law of Administrative Procedure	• The system of citizens suing government officials • The doctrine of the burden of proof on the defendant in administrative litigations
Jan. 1, 1995	State Compensation Law	• The state liability for compensation • Normalized compensation procedures
Oct. 1, 1996	Administrative Penalty Law	• Doctrine of statutory punishments and rule of double jeopardy • Protection of the rights of concerned persons • Hearing process
May 9, 1997	Administrative Supervision Law	• Doctrines and systems of administrative supervision
Oct. 1, 1999	Administrative Review Law	• Expanded scope of administrative Review • Doctrines of public convenience and other doctrines
July 1, 2000	Legislation Law	• System of legislation • Normalized legislation procedures
July 1, 2004	Administrative Permission Law	• The doctrine of trust protection • Scope of administrative permit
Jan. 1, 2006	Civil Servant Law	• The scope and classifications of civil servants • Civil servant appointment system • Compensation system for the rights of civil servants
Nov. 1, 2007	Emergency Response Law	• Emergency response system • Scientific response procedures of public emergencies • The doctrine of proportionality

development of the reform and opening-up and the construction of the socialist modernization. In terms of the quantity of legislations, only 8 administrative laws and regulations were issued in 1978. Until 2010 did the total quantity of the legislations reach 971 with over 600 legislations still effective, increasing over 120 times, at the rate of 375% per year. The chart below showed the result of a study made by the author on the number of laws and regulations released from 1978 to 2017.[3]

[3]The data are obtained at the http://pkulaw.cn/Search/SearchLaw.aspx?rdoType=1. Pursuant to the *Interim Regulations Concerning the Procedures for the Formulation of Administrative Regulations*, released on April 21, 1987, the administrative regulations refer to the regulations promulgated by the State Council or the controlling departments under the State Council subject to the approval by the State Council. However, the *Regulations Concerning the Procedures for the Formulation of Administrative Regulations* effective on Jan. 1, 2002, provides that the administrative regulations are those signed by the Prime Minister and promulgated by the State Council. In addition, in terms of the manner of promulgation, pursuant to the *Notice of the State Council General Office Concerning the Improvement of Administrative Regulations Promulgation Work* effective on May 31, 1988, the State Council promulgates administrative regulations subject to the ordinance signed by the

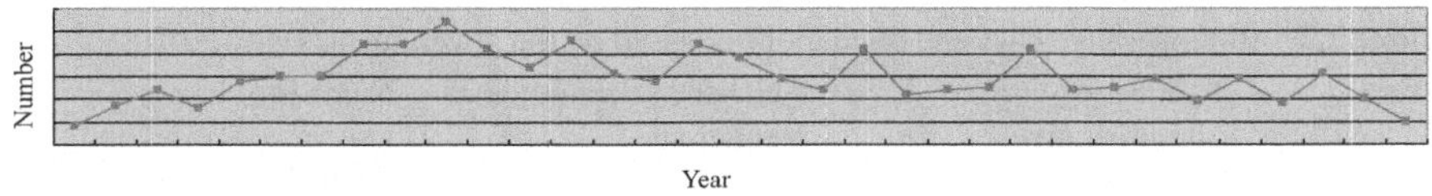

Fig. 2.1 Number of regulations introduced by the government, 1978–2010

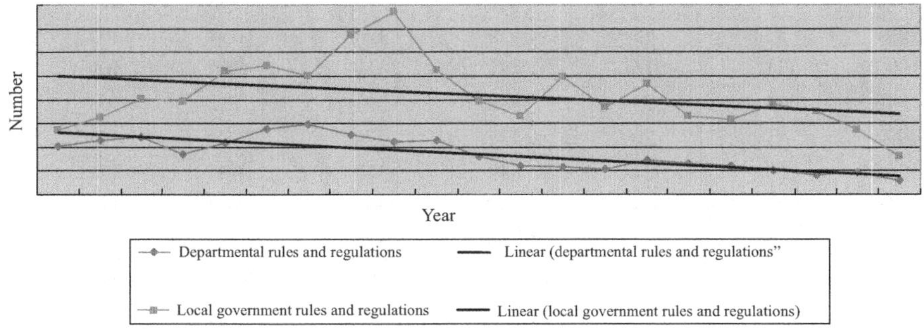

Fig. 2.2 Number of regulations introduced by the government, 1990–2010

Figure 2.1 shows that, since 1978, the number of the laws and regulations has been increasing steadily. A rapid increase occurred from 1978 to 1987, from fewer than 10 laws and regulations per year to over 50 in 1987, during which China was undertaking the reform and opening up to the outside word and in great demand of legislations to ensure the economic development. In the next more than 20 years, although there were several small ups and downs in the quantity of the laws and regulations released, the increase rate of 20–30 laws and regulations annually has been maintained.

The information regarding the administrative laws and regulations formulated respectively by the State Councils, departments and the local governments from 1990 to 2010 is summarized in Table 2.2.

To study the development of the administrative legislation, we did a linear analysis of the number of regulations introduced by the departments and the local governments each year from 1990 to 2010 (see Fig. 2.2). The author noticed that the departmental regulations and the local government regulations were roughly consistent in the up and down tendency during this period. The local government regulations reached its peak in 1998 while the departmental regulations did in 1997. Afterwards, both were in gradually downward trend. The administrative legislation slowed down when a perfect socialist legal system was accomplished.

Prime Minister of the State Council; the departments, including the divisions, committees, banks, directly-controlled agencies, and state bureaus, promulgate administrative regulations signed by the chief leaders of the departments and subject to the approval of the State Council.

Table 2.2 Administrative laws and regulations released by the government, 1990–2010

Year	Number of administrative regulations released by the State Council		Number of departmental regulations		Number of local government rules and regulations	
	Total	Effective	Total	Effective	Total	Effective
1990	47	28	408	276	543	231
1991	32	15	459	324	654	307
1992	31	16	481	319	809	400
1993	45	23	338	221	781	363
1994	41	20	437	274	1034	445
1995	29	24	549	340	1090	521
1996	24	18	587	360	999	498
1997	45	27	506	325	1350	737
1998	22	14	443	284	1538	925
1999	27	17	457	300	1047	662
2000	26	22	319	216	787	473
2001	48	35	243	166	664	412
2002	23	23	235	157	989	681
2003	28	25	215	154	741	555
2004	33	32	295	232	934	759
2005	23	21	266	233	662	608
2006	30	29	243	222	631	582
2007	36	36	206	198	753	732
2008	32	32	167	161	699	685
2009	22	21	182	182	541	539
2010	14	12	118	108	318	300

3. Increasing expansion of the scope of administrative legislation.

In the early time of the reform, to meet the needs of the economic system reform and the opening up to the outside world, the government put the legislative focus on economic legislation, mainly concerning the reform, opening up to the outside world, and invigoration of the economy. Economic laws and regulations carry great weight. With the gradual transformation of the economic system, administration according to law has been put on the agenda. More attention from the legislators has been paid on regulating and controlling administrative acts. In recent years, the government has continued its legislative efforts in enhancing the economic adjustment and market supervision and control. Meanwhile, more emphasis has been put on the legislation regarding social administration, and public services, and increasing efforts have been made in the legislation regarding improving people's livelihood, strengthening social construction, energy resources conservation, environmental protection, improving supervision and monitoring, safeguarding the citizens' legitimate rights and interests, and so forth.

2.3 The Characteristics of the Administrative Legislation Development

1. Value of administrative legislation: from pure administration to multiple targets.

In the early period of the administrative legislation, more emphasis was put on authorizing by law the government to administrate the society. However, since the principle of administration according to law was established, particularly since the goal of a government based on the rule of law was set, the administrative legislation had attached more importance to securing the legitimate rights and interests of citizens, legal persons and other organizations and regulation on government powers. In the early days of administrative legislation, the executive organs governed the society mainly through the examination and approval power and penalty power. Most provisions were formulated to bind the concerned person and the public while fewer were made to regulate the exercise of the administrative power. The provisions of obligations were formulated, to a great extent, for the concerned person. The executive organs limited or deprived the concerned person of the rights by setting myriad penalties. However, they seldom imposed obligations on themselves by legislation.

In recent years, with the development of the perception of administration according to law and the regulation on the administrative legislative power by the administrative laws, including the Administrative Penalty Law and the Administrative Permission Law, the administrative legislation has laid more emphasis on the boundary of the administrative power. And the manner of administration shifted from resorting to mandatory means including pure sanction and examination and approval to paying more attention to the protective and incentive functions of laws and regulations. Administrative acts were performed more by non-mandatory measures including the administrative guidance, administrative rewards, and administrative relief.

2. Administrative legislative techniques: from the general and abstract to the scientific and specific.

At the beginning of the reform and opening-up, legislation was a tedious job with a heavy workload, and the society was undergoing a rapid change. Therefore, a legislative policy was proposed that administrative laws and regulations should be more general than specific. This policy was, to a large extent, tailored to the situation and based on the understanding at that time. However, it was actually of great benefit to stress the speed and framework of legislation instead of sticking to the detailed content thereof, which enabled us to take a big leap in legislation and made remarkable achievements in the construction of legal system. It took China about twenty years to establish a socialist legal system with Chinese characteristics, covering nearly all aspects of the country and social life. It should be noticed, however, that the policy that the legislations shall be more general than specific is only a matter of expediency for the legislation in a particular historical period rather than a scientific legislative policy. Excessively general and vague law caused difficulties in law application. Nowadays when the socialist legal system has been established, attention should be paid to not only the quality but also the speed and quantity of legislation.

The increasing maturity of the administrative legislation technology not only requires the laws, rules and regulations, and other regulatory instruments be specific and definite in content, but also the provisions be inherently logically rigorous in pattern and regulatory, brief and accurate in language so as to crease the applicability of laws and regulations. The government gradually realized the importance and necessity of studies on the cost of legislation and law enforcement, and social costs and, hence, laid more emphasis on the economic function of legislation. The governmental legislative institutes have been actively exploring the system of expert consultation and argumentation on the government legislative projects, particularly the system of argumentation on "cost-efficiency" of the economic legislative project.

3. The administrative legislation process: from executive dictatorship to public participation.

With legalization speeding up, the Chinese government legislation were gradually institutionalized and standardized. In 1987, the General Office of the State Council issued the Notice on Improving the Promulgation of the Administrative Rules and Regulations, which expressly provided that the administrative laws and regulations shall be promulgated by the State Council with the ordinance of issuance signed by the Prime Minister; and the rules and regulations shall be promulgated by a department with an approval of the State Council and a writ of issuance signed by the person in charge of the department. The Legislation Law passed at the third plenary session of the Ninth National People's Congress on March 15, 2000, is the basic law regulating the legislation in China and provide the principles on legislation by the government. On Nov. 16, 2001, pursuant to the Legislation Law, the State Council released the Regulations on the Process of Enacting Administrative Laws and Regulations and the Regulations on the Process of Enacting Administrative Rules and Regulations, which specifically provide for legislative procedure for administrative rules and regulations by the State Council, administrative regulations made by the departments under the State Council, and the rules regulations made by the local governments. These laws and administrative rules and regulations expressly empower the governments to formulate rules and regulations, standardize legislative procedures and ensure the governments to formulate rules and regulations legally and orderly.

For thirty years after the reform and opening up, the government has become increasingly transparent and the public has got more involved in legislation. In order to get the public more involved in legislative process, the State Council, its subordinate departments, and the authorized legislative institutes under the local governments have established mechanism, procedures and methods of expert argumentation and public involvement in the process of drafting and review of bills of administrative laws and regulations or in the process of drafting rules and regulations. Especially for the bills which were of great significance or which concerns public interests, a system has been established to explain how the opinions from all walks of life were heard and accepted by holding hearings, argumentation conferences or seminars, or publishing the bills to the public and presented to the public. These activities in exploring and creating systems have increasingly widened the channel for public involvement in the government legislation, greatly advancing democracy.

4. Resolving legislative conflicts: from nearly blank to increasingly perfect.

With the increase of the legislative achievements, the conflicts of laws more frequently occurred, particularly in legislation between the departments under the State Council, the interests of the Central Government and the local governments. It is urgent to establish a perfect resolution mechanism of legislative conflicts.

(a) To establish a system of filing administrative rules and regulations filed to the Standing Committee of the NPC for record.

To maintain a uniform socialist legal system, on March 7, 1987, the General Office of the State Council issued Notice on Filing the Rules and Regulations by the Local Governments and the Regulations by the Agencies under the State Council to the Standing Committee of NPC for Record, symbolizing the establishment of system of filing the rules and regulations to the Standing Committee of NPC for record in China. Pursuant to Article 100 of the Constitution of the People's Republic of China and Article 7 and Article 43 of The Organic Law of the National People's Congress and the Local People's Government at All Levels of the People's Republic of China, and the Notice of Putting on Record the Local Rules and Regulations issued by the General Office of the Standing Committee of the National People's Congress and the General Office of the State Council, the "file for record" system of the local regulations have been established. On Feb. 18, 1990, based on the experience gained in the practice of filing for record the rules and regulations, the State Council promulgated the Rules and Regulations on Filing for Record the Rules and Regulations. On April 29, The General Office of the State Council issued the Notice on Enforcement of the Regulations on Filing for Record the Rules and Regulations, expressly providing the "file for record" scope of the rules and regulations, the content and procedure of review. The "file for record" system of the rules and regulations were improved thereby. The Art. 89 of the Legislation Law of the People's Republic of China passed by the third plenary session of the 9th National People's Congress on March 15, 2000, provides comprehensively for the "file for record" system of rules and regulations.[4] It is provided that within 30 days of its promulgation, an administrative rule or

[4]Article 89 of *The Legislation Law of the People's Republic of China* provides: "Within 30 days of its promulgation, an administrative regulation, local government regulations, autonomous decree or special decree, or any administrative or local rule should be submitted to the relevant body for filing in accordance with the following provisions: (i) An administrative regulation shall be submitted to the Standing Committee of National People's Congress for filing; (ii) A local regulation enacted by the People's Congress of a province, autonomous region, or municipality directly under the central government and the Standing Committee thereof should be submitted to the Standing Committee of National People's Congress and the State Council for filing; a local decree enacted by the People's Congress of a major city and the Standing Committee thereof should be submitted to the Standing Committee of National People's Congress and the State Council for filing through the Standing Committee of the People's Congress of the province or autonomous region in which the city is located; (iii) An autonomous or special decree enacted by an autonomous prefecture or autonomous county should be submitted to the Standing Committee of National People's Congress and the State Council for filing through the Standing Committee of the People's Congress of the province or autonomous region in which the prefecture or county is located; (iv) An administrative or local rule should be submitted to the State Council for filing; a local rule should be concurrently

regulation, local regulation by a province or autonomous region, special rule or regulation, or any other administrative or local rule should be filed to the relevant organization for record, which makes a stricter requirement. After China got access into WTO, we were required to further improve the system of "file for record" and review. On Dec. 14, 2001, the State Council modified the Regulations on the System of Filing the Rules and Regulations for Record, which, to a large extent, modified and amended the original "file for record" system, forming a comparatively perfect legal system of "file for record" and review of the rules and regulations.

Nowadays, all the rules and regulations enacted and promulgated are timely filed for record every year. The legislative affairs office of the State Council has established a database of the rules and regulations filed for record. A "file for record" system of the regulatory instruments has been established in thirty one provinces, autonomous regions or municipalities. Almost all governments at the provincial level have established specialized governmental rules and regulations. Over ninety percent of the governments at the level of city with districts and over eighty percent of the county governments have established the review system of the regulatory instruments. In overwhelming majority of provinces (regions or cities), an institutional framework with four-level governments (province, city, county and town levels) and three-level "file for record" system has been established. The local governments at the level of county and above are authorized to review the regulatory instruments formulated by its subordinate departments and the governments at lower level. It is estimated that, from Jan., 2003 to June, 2007, thirty one provincial governments had received 29,752 regulatory instruments from its subordinate departments and the governments at the level of city with districts, 1741 of which, through intense review, were found problematic and corrected in different ways so that the regulatory instruments were made legal and valid, the legal system maintained uniform, and the governmental rules and regulations implemented smoothly.

(b) To clear up the administrative rules and regulations.

Up to now, the New China has intensively cleared up rules and regulations for ten times,[5] among which two times were for comparatively big and thorough clearing up, and six times were for specialized ones. The first big clearing up started in 1983 during which every region and department cleared up all the regulatory instruments made from 1949 till 1984, including over 3298 administrative rules and regulations and other regulatory instruments, over 20,000 departmental rules and regulations, over 20,000 local rules and regulations, various kinds of technical rules, and so forth. As a result, 661 rules and regulations formulated since the founding of the People's Republic of China remained effective, the other 2637 instruments were degraded

submitted to the Standing Committee of the local People's Congress for filing; local rules enacted by a major city should also be concurrently submitted to the Standing Committee of the National People's Congress and the People's Government of the province or autonomous region for filing; (v) An administrative regulation or local decree enacted pursuant to an enabling decision should be submitted to the body specified therein for filing.

[5]Wu Jing, Ten Consolidated Clearing up of Rules and Regulation, *People's Daily*, 13th ed., March, 28, 2007.

into routine documents, abolished or modified to a great degree. The said clearing up was carried out under a situation that China's socialist modernization construction entered into a new era and the socialist legal system was being strengthened. It was a comparatively complete clearing up since the founding of the People's Republic of China and created favorable conditions for the legislation and law enforcement thereafter.

The General Office of the State Council issued the Notice of the General Office of the State Council on Clearing up the Currently Effective Administrative Rules and Regulations on Jan. 15, 2000. Pursuant to the Notice, in 2001, the Legal Affairs Office of the State Council cleared up 756 administrative rules and regulations which were effective prior to the end of 2000. On Oct. 6, 2001, the State Council made the Decision of the State Council on Abolishing Some of the Administrative Rules and Regulations released before the end of 2000. The Decision abolished 71 administrative rules and regulations which conflicted with new laws, modified laws, new policies of the Party or the State, or modified policies of the Party or the State, or had been replaced by new laws or administrative policies; annulled 80 administrative rules and regulations which had expired, the subject matters of which no longer existed, or which had ipso facto been ineffective; and reinstated 70 laws and administrative rules and regulations which has been annulled from 1994 to the end of 2000.

On Feb. 25, 2007, to maintain the unity of the legal system and smooth implementation of the governmental rules and regulations, protect the legitimate rights and interests of the public, better satisfy the demand of speeding up the construction of a government based on the rule of law and comprehensive promotion of the administration according to law, the General Office of the State Council issued the Notice of the General Office of the State Council on Clearing up the Administrative Rules and Regulations, deciding to comprehensively clear up the administrative rules and regulations. The General Office of the State Council was in charge of comprehensively clearing up the administrative rules and regulations while the People's governments of provinces, autonomous regions, municipalities and comparatively large cities and the departments under the State Council are in charge of the rules and regulations. The clearing up ended up satisfactorily after 10 months. On Jan. 15, 2008, the Decision of the State Council on Abolishing Some Administrative Rules and Regulations was issued, which abolished 49 administrative regulations which conflicted with new laws or administrative rules and regulations; annulled 43 administrative rules and regulations which had been expired, or the subjects of which had disappeared. On Dec. 31, 2008, the State Council abolished the instruments including the Provisional Regulations Governing Urban Real Estate Tax (The Decree of the State Council No. 546), and the Provisional Regulations Governing Urban Real Estate Tax, Yangtze River Waterway Maintenance Fee Collection Methods, and the Inland Waterway Maintenance Fee Collection Methods and Usage. On Nov. 19, the State Council issued the Decision of the State Council on Modifying and Abolishing Some Administrative Regulations, abolishing five administrative regulations, on Feb. 19, 2014, the State Council issued the Decision of the State Council on Modifying and Abolishing Some Administrative Rules and Regulations, abolishing two administrative regulations, the main content of which were replaced by the new laws or administrative regulations. The abolished or annulled administrative rules and regulations totaled 102, taking 15.3% of the total administrative rules and regulations. Nowadays, the rules-and-regulations clearing up conducted by the local governments and departments under the State Council has achieved great progress.

In spite of the considerable achievements made in the Chinese administrative legislation, problems exist mainly in the following aspects: (1) The positioning and aims of the administrative legislation are defective. Due to the influence of the traditional ideas about administrative mode and the system of planned-economy, the previous administrative laws, rules and regulations and other regulatory instruments did not contain sufficient provisions on protection of the public rights and interests while attaching excessive importance to the control over the public and the empowerment of the government. (2) A uniform system of the administrative laws and regulations is lacking. Due to the unclear and unspecific division of the legislative scope between the administrative rules and regulations, conflicts occurred between the rules and regulations and the inconsistence existed between the departmental and local government rules. (3) Poor use is made of the administrative legislative sources. The poor quality of the administrative legislation, and the conflicts between and the infeasibility of the regulatory administrative instruments incurred enormous expenses of the administrative legislation. (4) The administrative legislation is insufficiently supervised. The government supervision power over the administrative legislation is not definite. The administrative subject made the supervision over itself formally rather than substantially, while the supervision power vested with the judicial organs was limited extremely to selecting applicable administrative rules and regulations and dismissing the unconstitutional and illegal administrative ones. The restriction of the Law of Administrative Procedure hindered the judicial supervision. To enhance the judicial supervision will, therefore, help improve the efficiency of the administrative legislation.

Chapter 3
The Reform of Administrative Examination and Approval System and Administrative Permission

For a long time, the Chinese government, as an omnipotent government, has interfered in all aspects of social life. Especially, the planned economic system requires the government to comprehensively interfere with the economic development, and the overuse or even abuse of administrative examination and approval system is somewhat a manifestation of an omnipotent government. One of the purposes of Administrative Permission Law, therefore, is to fixate the achievements made in the reform of the administrative examination and approval system.

3.1 Transformation of Governmental Functions and Reform of the Administrative Examination and Approval System

Governmental function is a specific embodiment of the state function. The government is delegated functions to meet the needs of the state and the society in a certain period of time. The functions delegated, therefore, do not remain unchanged. The government should constantly adjust its functions to the demand of the society.

1. The goals and direction of the transformation of governmental function.

For a considerably long period of time since the founding of the People's Republic of China, China had adopted the planned-economic system, under which the government controlled the economy and society by administrative orders. The government, like an omnipotent housekeeper, managed and controlled all the fields of the country. With the reform and opening up gradually developing from a single project to the whole system, the social structure has been transforming from being closed to open up, from planned economy to socialist market economy, and from agricultural society to industrial society, building up a political system which attaches much importance to democracy and a dominant social value of social productivity develop-

© Social Sciences Academic Press and Springer Nature Singapore Pte Ltd. 2018
H. Ma and J. Wang, *Building a Government Based on the Rule of Law*,
Research Series on the Chinese Dream and China's Development Path,
https://doi.org/10.1007/978-981-13-0999-1_3

ment, which symbolizes the beginning of transformation in all aspects of the society in China. In the process of transformation, the governmental functions have been faced with challenges in all aspects from both internal and external sources. On one hand, China is undergoing transformation, coinciding with the wave of the economic globalization, which brought both reform and challenges. Due to the comparative inferiority of domestic enterprises and private economic strength, the government must take the reform and renovation of the system seriously and, in the process of the system transformation, act as system designer, reform promoter, and so forth. The government should define the scope of functions of the government, enterprises and non-governmental organizations so as to establish the resultant force of the state, society and individuals in the aspects of public services and social administration and promote the economic system reform and transformation. On the other hand, the Chinese government, which is in the process of social transformation, must ensure the government smoothly transform from the traditional and charming authority to legal and rational authority while maintaining and promoting the economic development.[1]

To ensure the governmental functions effectively and meet China's social economic development needs during transformation, the transformation of governmental functions has been given high priority in the reform of the administrative system since reform and opening-up. In 1987, the 13th National Congress of the CPC clarified the prominent position of the transformation of the governmental functions in the reform and opening-up. In the past over thirty years, reform in the transformation of the governmental functions has been carried out in the government structure, power assignment and personnel system of the government officer system. Since 2000, the governments at all levels have started another round of governmental function reform, taking the reform of the administrative examination and approval system as its breakthrough.[2] In short, efforts by the Chinese government to transform its own functions have been guided by an idea of service that is thoroughly new, democratic and scientifically-sound, and sustainable. (1) to limit the power of the government, that is, to release the control of government as much as possible over those matters that citizens, legal persons or other organizations can handle by themselves; the government should stay away from matters the market can do competently; it should not interfere in matters which can be dealt with by ordinary citizens through self-discipline; and make great efforts to overcome offside, default, and disposition of government administration; (2) to develop a rule-of-law government which should function according to law and be found liable for any of its misconducts; (3) to develop a service-oriented government which, in addition to governance, should serve and provide convenience to the people and apply the principle of serving the people to practice; (4) to develop a transparent government, publicizing in a timely manner the grounds, procedure and process of the operation of administrative power so as to guarantee the right to information regarding the administrative affairs, push the

[1]Yang Jianshun, The Aims of the Governmental Function Transformation and the Rationales of its System, *China Legal Science*, issue, 6, 2006.

[2]Zhang Wei, *The Transformation of the Government Functions from the Perspective of the Administrative Approval System*, The Thesis of Degree of Northwest University, 2012.

government to abide by the law strictly in administration, and build a clean and honest government; (5) to develop a government with high credibility. The government should ensure that the information disclosed should be true and reliable and that its decisions and policies should be relatively stable rather than change too frequently.[3]

2. The inherent relationship between transformation of governmental functions and reform in the administrative examination and approval system.

In China, administrative examination and approval is one of the main means by which the government exerts influence on economic development. The government handles public affairs through administrative examination and approval which, while a strong and effective management instrument under a planned economy, is a poor fit with the country's current drive to transform the governmental functions. With the establishment of the market economy, the administrative examination and approval system has shown serious drawbacks. For example, it is unclear at which level of government administrative examination and approval-related powers should rest. In some places, it is the town governments or county governments that has and exercises this power. But in other places, the power rests with particular departments within the administrative bodies. Since no uniform criteria exist for deciding which matters should be subject to such requirements, examination and approval has been offered as a stock solution whenever problems of administration are discussed. The process is heavy on paperwork, procedurally complicated and time-consuming. Everything is handled in a "black box", lacking transparency. It is common for people to see examination and approval either as a replacement for or as more important than supervision and monitoring. This has on one hand made it difficult for new players to enter the market while on the other hand left those who have managed to do so largely unsupervised and unmonitored. Some administrative organs take administrative examination and approval as a means of rent seeking, which encourages corruption. For all the powers they are endowed with and can exercise administrative organs are usually not subject to a corresponding system of accountability and constraints.[4] Under this system, it has become increasingly common for the government to end up doing either more than it should, or less than it should, or something other than what it should altogether. Therefore, to achieve the goal of establishing a market economy and completing the transformation of society and economy, efforts should be made to transform its functions so the government acts within constraints, follows the rule of law, is committed to serving the people and to transparency and integrity. However, the transformation of governmental functions requires a reform in the system of administrative examination and approval, which applies to the whole process of the political and economic development in China. Thus, the system of administrative examination and approval is critical to transformation of governmental function. Therefore, the system of administrative examination and approval is

[3] Wang Li, The Administrative Permission Law and the Transformation of the Governmental function, *Journal of Zhengzhou Party School of the Central Committee of C.P.C.*, vol. 3, 2005.

[4] Yang Jingyu, *On the Administrative Permission Law of the People's Republic of China (Draft)*: at the 29th Plenary Session of the Standing Committee of the 9th National People's Congress, The Communiqué of the Standing Committee of the National People's Congress, issue 5, 2003.

the breakthrough point of the transformation of governmental function. The key to the transformation of governmental function is the reform in the administrative examination and approval system.

3. The development of the administrative examination and approval system.

Since the reform and opening-up, the conflict between the aforesaid administrative mode and the market economy has gradually become obvious. The Notice on Reducing the Authority of the Administrative Examination and Approval over the Investment in Fixed Assets and Simplifying the Examination and Approval Procedures, issued by the State Council on March 30, 1987, states that in the administration of investment of fixed assets, the authority of examination and approval is excessively consolidated and the procedures thereof is so complicated that it is hard to find out who should be liable for the problem occurring. Solving these problems permanently should rely on the reform in the economic and political system. At present, further efforts should be made in streamlining administration and delegating power to the governments at the lower level, reducing the authority of examination and approval and simplifying the examination and approval procedures on the basis of enhancing macro-administration and strictly controlling the scale of fixed asset investment.[5] Meanwhile, the local governments at the forefront of the reform and opening up have also launched the reform on administrative approval system in terms of business registration. In March 1993, for instance, the Rules of Shenzhen on Business Registration was released. According to the document, for business registration purposes, the examination and approval system is replaced by the verification and approval system; it is up to the business itself to decide which matters are to be included in its registration record (e.g. scope of business, mode of operation, new projects and initiatives, and so forth) and the organs charged with granting approvals and issuing registration should make their decisions based on the principles of legality (whether the business is in full compliance with the law of the land) and of effectiveness (whether it is consistent with relevant industry policies and optimal efficiency in resource allocation). This new system helps businesses reclaim some of its prerogatives that would allow it to exercise greater control over its own operations.[6]

Decision of the CCCPC on Some Major Issues Concerning Building Socialist Market Economic System passed by the Third Plenary Session of the 14th Central Committee of the Communist Party of China passed on Nov. 14 1993, put forward specifically that efforts should be made to deepen the reform on investment system and substitute the administrative examination and approval system with project

[5]See *Notice on Reducing the Authority of the Administrative Examination and Approval over the Investment in Fixed Assets and Simplifying the Examination and Approval Procedures*, March 30, 1997.

[6]Li You, From "Examination and Approval System" to "Approval System": Theories and Practice of the Reform in Business Registration System of Shenzhen Special Economic Zone, *Economy of Special Economic Zone*, issue 5, 1993.

registry or record system.[7] To achieve the market function of basic configuration, a comprehensive reform on the administrative examination and approval system has been carried out in some places. In early 1998, the Shenzhen government enacted and promulgated the Implementation Plan of Shenzhen Municipal Government for Examination and Approval System Reform and comprehensively began to carry out reform on the examination and approval system. The Guangdong province also carried out comprehensive cleaning and reform on the matters of examination and approval in over 70 departments under the local government. Specifically, the measures taken by the government are:

1. Adhering the reform principle: Letting the market play a decisive role in resource allocation; allowing the government to retain, in accordance with the law, control over examination and approval in relation to such important matters as public security, public finance and environmental, but making sure it stays out of everything and anything that is more effectively and more efficiently handled by the market, intermediary organizations, or enterprises;
2. Reviewing and updating the list of matters subject to examination and approval. The number of matters subject to examination and approval of the Shenzhen municipal government has decreased by 463, or 42.2%, from 1091 to 628; For the Guangdong provincial government, the numbers dropped by 878, or 63%, from 1,392 to 514;
3. Establishing a uniform set of rules and standards for examination and approval and improving the modus operandi. Depending on the purposes for which approval is sought, the exact matters for which approval is needed and the specific requirements for eligibility and for approval should be clearly defined. Simplifying the procedure and reducing paperwork. For instance, the Shenzhen municipal government used to have several different departments handling different types of approval applications. Recently, however, as it pushed reform forward, the government consolidated this work into the hands of no more than two departments. In addition, the logistics have also been simplified so that, to submit their application materials applicants need only to pass them through a window to a staff member, who will process the application according to a uniform set of internal procedure rules;
4. Enhancing supervision and monitoring of the examination and approval and the follow-up thereof, shifting the focus of government administration from routine examination and approval to the supervision and control in accordance with law so as to ensure the implementation of the matters approved.[8] Similar reform mea-

[7] See *Decision of the CCCPC on Some Major Issues Concerning Building Socialist Market Economic System* (passed by the Third Plenary Session of the 14th Central Committee of the Communist Party of China on Nov. 14, 1993).

[8] Tang Xiaoyang, Reforming the administrative examination and approval System and Normalizing Government Examination and Approval: the Enlightenment Gained from the Reform of Guangdong Province and Shenzhen City on the System of Examination and Approval, *Journal of Guangdong Administration Academy*, vol. 3, 2000.

sures have been put in place in Beijing, Shanghai, Zhejiang, Shandong, Jiangsu, Fujian, Liaoning, Heilongjiang, and so forth.

After 2000, as the market economy matured gradually, reforming administrative approval system took on increasing urgency. It was explicitly pointed out at the Fifth Plenary Session of the 15th Central Committee of the CPC that was held in October, 2000, that advancing administrative approval system reform called for a clear understanding of the specific needs of a socialist market economy and must involve transforming governmental functions and separating government administration from corporate management. The government should focus on macroeconomic regulations, and control and create a favorable market environment, refrain from intervening directly in business operations and management, ease requirements for administrative approval in economic affairs, promote the reform of investment and financing system, continue to reform and to downsize the government, and establish an administrative system to secure professional conduct, high efficiency and coordinated operation[9] In December, 2000, Jiang Zemin stressed at the Fifth Plenary Session of the Central Commission for Discipline Inspection on the importance and inevitability of the reform on the system of administrative approval.[10]

In September, 2001, the sixth plenary session of the 15th Central Committee of the CPC explicitly proposed to establish a mechanism of power operation with reasonable structure, scientific configuration, rigorous procedures, and effective restriction, ensure that powers are operated on the track of institutionalization and legalization, which is the fundamental measure to prevent influence peddling, reform the system of administrative examination and approval, and regulate the behaviors of administrative examination and approval.[11] In the same year, the State Council established the leading group of the reform on the system of administrative examination and approval of the State Council, in charge of directing and coordinating the reform of administrative examination and approval in China, study and propose the matters which should be removed from or remain in the list of matters subject to examination and approval of the departments under the State Council and draft relevant provisions, supervise and ensure the various departments under the State Council, clean and dispose the items subject to administrative examination and approval properly,

[9]*Proposals of the Central Committee of the Communist Party of China on the Outline of the Tenth Five-Year Plan for National Economic and Social Development*, approved at the Fifth Plenary Session of the 15th Central Committee of the CPC.

[10]Xia Changyong, The Reform of the Administrative Examination and Approval System is to be Intensified: Remarks of He Yong, the Deputy Team Leader of the State Council Work Leading Group of the Reform of the Administrative Examination and Approval System, *China Daily*, Jan. 9, 2003.

[11]*Decision of the Central Committee of the CPC on Enhancing and Improving the Construction of the Work Style of the CPC*, approved by the Fifth Plenary Session of the 15th Central Committee of the CPC on Oct. 11, 2000).

and study and dispose other important issues concerning the reform of the administrative examination and approval system.[12]

Afterwards, the State Council approved and issued the Notice on the Opinion Regarding the Implementation of the Reform on the System of Administrative Examination and Approval, officially deploying and carrying out the reform on administrative examination and approval system. The Notice made clear the guiding ideology and general requirement for the reform of administrative examination and approval system; established the principles for the reform of administrative examination and approval system and implementation procedures thereof and pointed out the problems for attention. The Notice played a significant role of guidance in the national reform of the administrative examination and approval. It explicitly pointed out that any administrative examination and approval which hinders open market development and fair competition and actually rarely functions effectively shall be canceled; all the matters which can be handled through the market mechanism shall be left to the market mechanism; and matters which cannot be handled through the market mechanism but by righteous and normal intermediary organizations and through industry self-discipline should be left with the said organizations and industry. Laws, administrative rules and regulations, local government regulations and the rules which are enacted in accordance with law and in legal procedures may delegate administrative examination and approval powers. Given the fact that the relevant legislation still has room for improvement, the departments of the State Council may, in accordance with the decisions, decrees and requirements of the State Council, delegate and publish in the form of document of the departments the administrative examination and approval powers; and the administrative examination and approval powers established by other organs or in accordance with other documents shall be revoked." The above principles regarding the establishment of administrative examination and approval power are embodied in the relevant provisions of the Administrative Permission Law.

Since 2011, in accordance with the arrangements of the teleconference on deepening the reform of administrative examination and approval system and to meet the requirements of the reform of administrative examination and approval system, the joint conference of the ministries on the reform of administrative examination and approval system, in accordance with the Administrative Permission Law and relevant rules and regulations, cleaned up for six batches of the items subject to the administrative examination and approval of the departments under the State Council. After strict scrutiny and argumentation, the State Council made a decision to cancel and adjust administrative approval of 314 matters of the sixth rounds. In 2012, the State Council made and issued the Decision of the State Council on Cancellation and Adjustment of the Sixth Batch of Administrative Approval Items (State Issuance (2012) # 52) (Hereinafter the "Decision"). Firstly, it requires that the government continues to cancel and adjust administrative approval of matters that can be decided independently by citizens, legal persons or other organizations, effectively adjusted

[12]See *Notice of the General Office of the State Council on the Establishment of the Leading Group of the Reform on the System of Administrative Examination and Approval of the State Council, No. 71*, issued by the General Office of the State Council, 2001.

by the market competition mechanism, and regulated and controlled by industry groups or agencies. Where the items can be supervised or controlled afterwards or indirectly, the upfront examination and approval should not be applicable. Any administrative permit established in the form of departmental rules and regulatory instruments in violation of the Administrative Permission Law should be corrected prior to a fixed time. Efforts should be made in establishing a dynamic mechanism of cleaning up items subject to administrative examination and approval. Secondly, the Decision also requires that efforts should be made to actively promote the normalization of administrative examination and approval. The new items subject to examination and approval should be established in accordance with law, and be subject to review and argumentation in terms of legality, necessity and reasonableness. Absent of legal grounds, any local governments or departments may not set items subject to administrative examination and approval in the form of rules or other regulatory instruments. Methods of establishing and managing the matters which are not subject to administrative permit and approval should be standardized. Thirdly, the Decision requires the government to speed up the reform in the management of institutional and social organizations, hand over the administrative work which can be handled by the public institutions and social organizations to the said organizations by trust, bidding, contract, and so forth, intensify efforts to cultivate related industry groups, and promote the said groups to work in a standard, public, efficient, fair and honest way. Fourthly, the Decision requires the government to improve the service system of the administrative examination and approval, continue to push forward the construction of government affairs centers, perfect government affairs service system with an interaction at the level of the provinces, cities, counties and townships and gradually extending to the village and community, enhance performance management of administrative approval, promote on-line examination and approval, joint or united examination and approval (for a matter which involves two or more authoritative agencies, examination and approval is conducted by one agency with the opinions provided by other agencies), make commitment publicly to guarantee service quality, and raise the service level of administrative examination and approval. The departments which have a heavy workload of examination and approval should establish halls of government affairs or service windows. Fifthly, the Decision requires pushing forward the work of anti-corruption in administrative examination and approval, deepening openness of examination and approval, implementing "sunny examination and approval", accelerating the promotion of electronic supervision system of administrative examination and approval, and taking stern actions against violations of law and discipline by abuse of the power of examination and approval. Sixthly, the Decision requires tightly combining the reform of administrative examination and approval system with investment system, fiscal、taxation and financial system, social system and reform of administrative system, further straightening out and normalizing relationship between the government and enterprises and relationship between the government and society, standardizing the relationship between the governments at different levels, further optimizing the government institutions and functions, improving administrative efficacy and service quality of public administration.

In May, 2013, in accordance with requirements set out in the Plan of the State Council for Institutional Reform and Functional Transformation that was approved at the First Session of the 12th National People's Congress, the State Council issued the Decision of the State Council on Cancelling Administrative Examination and Approval Requirement or Replacing Requirement for Central Government Approval with Requirement for Provincial or Local Government Approval in regard to Select Matters (State Issuance (2013) No. 19), affected areas include investment, production and business operations, administrative examination and approval accreditation and certification of professional qualifications, the collection of administrative charges and fees that were never fully justified, and contribution toward governmental funds. The State Council decided, on the basis of study and argumentation, to cancel or delegate administrative approval power for a batch of matters, totaling 117, including 71 matters with administrative approval power being canceled; 20 matters with administrative approval power being delegated to the lower administrative agencies; 10 appraisal award matters, 3 matters of administrative fees; 13 matters of internal affairs of administrative organs or involving confidential information (separate notifications were given in accordance to provisions). In addition, another 16 matters for which administrative approval power was to be canceled or delegated were established pursuant to relevant laws which the Standing Committee of the National People's Congress would modify at the request of the State Council.

In November, 2013, the State Council, in its the Decision of the State Council on Cancelling Administrative Examination and Approval Requirement or Replacing Requirement for Central Government Approval with Requirement for Provincial or Local Government Approval in regard to Select Matter (State Issuance (2013) No. 44), decided to further cancel and delegate administrative approval power for 68 matters (two of them are confidential and the notifications therefore were given separately in accordance to relevant provisions). In addition, it also made a proposal to cancel and delegate administrative approval power for 7 matters established pursuant to relevant laws, which would be modified by the Standing Committee of the National People's Congress at the request of the State Council. Request to modify and promulgate the laws relevant to administrative approval power for 16 matters mentioned in the Decision of the State Council on the Issues Including Cancelling Administrative Examination and Approval Requirement or Replacing Requirement for Central Government Approval with Requirement for Provincial or Local Government Approval in regard to Select Matters (State Issuance (2013) No. 19) has been made to the National People's Congress. In January 2014, the State Council again issued the Decision of the State Council on Cancelling Administrative Examination and Approval Requirement or Replacing Requirement for Central Government Approval with Requirement for Provincial or Local Government Approval in regard to Selected Matters (State Issuance (2014) No. 5) and decided to cancel and delegate administrative approval power for another 64 matters and 18 sub-matters. The State Council also made a proposal to cancel and delegate administrative approval power for 6 matters established pursuant to relevant laws which the State Council would request the Standing Committee of the National People's Congress to modify, urged the local governments and departments to ensure canceling and delegating administrative approval power for the matters and the connection work fulfilled, and effectively enhance supervision and control during and after the fulfillment, continue to make great efforts in deepening the reform on the system of administrative approval so as to make streamline administration and delegate powers into a constant reformative action, improve the supervision and restriction mechanism, strengthen the supervision over the operation of the administrative approval power, and constantly raise the level of scientific and standardized administration.

Until May 15, 2013, the State Council had canceled or adjusted administrative approval power for seven batches of matters, totaling 2,507.[13]

4. Problems in the process of reform on the administrative approval system.

The number of matters subject to administrative approval has been radically cut in China, but the change in number does not necessarily mean a change in substance. From the perspective of social reality, particularly the entrepreneurs and the public, the reform of administrative approval system has made limited accomplishments. People are still running into difficulties in all respects in dealing with the government,

[13]On Nov. 1, 2002, the first batch of items subject to administrative examination and approval, totaling 789, were canceled. On Feb. 27, 2003, the second batch of the said items, totaling 406, were canceled, together with 82 items handed over to the industry groups or social agencies for examination and approval. On May 19, 2004, the third batch of items, totaling 409, were canceled, another 39 items were no longer subject to administrative examination and approval and, instead, put under the control of the industry groups or agencies, and 47 items were delegated to the lower-level administration, as the result of changing the management mode. On Oct. 9, 2007, the fourth batch of items were canceled or adjusted, totaling 186, out of which 128 items were canceled and 58 items were adjusted for administrative examination and approval (29 items were delegated to the lower-level administration; 8 items were transferred to other department for examination and approval; 21 items were merged into each other for the reason of same kind). Another seven items for which administrative examination and approval power was to be canceled or adjusted was establish in accordance with relevant law, which would be modified by the Standing Committee of the National People's Congress at the request of the State Council. In 2010, administrative examination and approval power was canceled and delegated for 184 items, including 113 items for which the said power was canceled while 71 items of which the said power was delegated. In 2012, administrative examination and approval power was canceled and delegated for 314 items, including 184 items for which the said power was canceled while 117 items of which the said power was delegated, and 13 items merged. In 2013, there were altogether 133 matters including administrative examination and approval power for items canceled and delegated. See *Decision of the State Council on Canceling Administrative examination and approval Power for the First Batch of Items [State Issuance* (2002) No. 24], *Decision of the State Council on Canceling Administrative examination and approval Power for the Second Batch of Items* [State Issuance (2003) No. 5], *Decision of the State Council on Canceling Administrative examination and approval Power for the Second Batch of Items and Transforming the Management Mode of Items Subject to Administrative examination and approval Power* [State Issuance (2003) No. 5], *Decision of the State Council on Canceling and Adjusting Administrative examination and approval Power for the Third Batch of Items* [State Issuance (2004) No. 16], *Decision of the State Council on Canceling and Adjusting Administrative examination and approval Power for the Fourth Batch of Items* [State Issuance (2007) No. 33], *Decision of the State Council on Canceling and Adjusting Administrative examination and approval Power for the Sixth Batch of Items* [State Issuance (2012) No. 52], *and Decision of the State Council on the Matters Including Canceling and Delegating Administrative examination and approval Power for a Batch of Items* [State Issuance (2013) No. 19].

and the administrative power has not been scaled back in spite of the radical reduction in the number of matters subject to the requirement. There are a number of factors which have hindered the reform of administrative approval system.

First, the power and interests of the governmental departments. The departments under the government will surely protect rather than give up their power and interests. Even under the high pressure of being compelled to cut the matters subject to administrative approval, these departments will try by every means to protect their powers and interests, which, consequently, has turn a few of reform of administrative approval system into phony ones. Generally speaking, the biggest problem in the process of reform of administrative approval system is that the government vested with the power and interests is reluctant to give up its power and interests even under heavy pressure. Therefore, the problems exist, such as phony reform, increase while decrease is made, overtly decreasing but covertly increasing, and falsely decreasing but actually increase, and so forth.

Second, during the reform of administrative approval system, there are many disguised permissions. Although permission has been abolished, something new has emerged, such as "核准 (approval)", "备案 (file for record)", "指标 (index)", "计划 (plan)", "验收 (inspection and acceptance)", "审评 (review)", "考核 (assessment)", and "评估 (appraisal)". Chinese Language is abundant in Chinese characters. In addition to "许可 (permission)", there are many other characters meaning or implying the meaning of permission. Subsequently, many administrative organs maintain or increase permission in a disguising way by using different characters or terms. For instance, there used to be thirteen matters of educational permissions established in accordance to laws and regulations. Only six of the matters remain after radical cut of matters made by the State Council. However, the recruit plan is still subject to the approval of educational departments although it is not permission. The disguised permission as such has made administrative approval power continue to exist for the matters despite of the fact that the administrative approval power for many matters has been abolished on the surface.

Third, the prerequisites for permission are requisite. Permission may require several prerequisites. If the prerequisites are required by the administrative organs, they themselves are permission. For instance, a land developer should satisfy a dozen prerequisites for land planning permit. A majority of the prerequisites are obtained from the relevant administrative organs, including the land use permit and land use permit issued by Land and Resources Bureau, the quality inspection opinion provided by the quality inspection department, and so forth. These permits constitute the prerequisites for the planning permit. Meanwhile, each permit is independent.

Fourth, the Administrative Permission Law is inherently flawed. It provides that administrative permit hereby referred to the permission, given by the administrative organ after examination at the request of citizens, legal persons or other organizations, of carrying out particular activities. It also provides that this Law is not applicable to the examination and approval by the relevant administrative departments of such matters as personnel, financial and foreign-related affairs of other departments or of the institutions directly under the administration of the said departments. In another word, the Administrative Permission Law is not applicable to internal permissions of administrative organs. Subsequently, many people tried by every means to put their applications in the list of non-administrative permit matters. Therefore, at that time, the Administrative Approval Reform Office created a new concept, that is, an approval of matters which are not subject to administrative permit. The number of the aforesaid matters therefore increased radically. Many matters which are statutorily subject to administrative approval are not bound by the Administrative Permission Law.

5. The path of administrative approval system reform.

With regard to the further reform of the administrative approval system, the State Council has taken correct measures, generally speaking: further reducing the matters subject to administrative approval and scaling back the government power, making more market space available, and transforming functions and raising efficiency of the government by reducing the matters subject to administrative approval. In the process of the following administrative approval system reform, more measures should be taken[14]:

First, the government should redefine the scope of administrative permit the matters which are subject to administrative approval but not administrative permit should be included in the scope and be subject to the Administrative Permission Law.

Second, declaration should be made explicitly that all the procedures of administrative permit instituted by rules and the regulatory instruments thereunder are invalid and may not be enforceable. In the process of the administrative approval system reform, some administrative organs blatantly violated the Administrative Permission Law by formulating rules or other regulatory instruments to institute the procedure of administrative permit and, consequently, caused superficial decrease but essential increase of the matters subject to administrative permit. Therefore, a sweeping approach should be taken by announcing all procedures of administrative permit instituted by the rules and the regulatory instrument thereunder are invalid and may not be enforceable.

Third, Decree 412 should be repealed. Decree 412 explicitly provides that all the matters subject to the procedure of administrative permit are no longer valid except 500 matters subject to the procedure of administrative permit instituted by the rules and regulatory instruments. Decree 412 has not made an obvious impact since it took effect. Some administrative organs voluntarily promoted 21 matters which have no legal ground according to Decree 412 to the ones with such legal ground, and 28 matters subject to the said procedure to the ones with regulation ground. In the following six reforms of the administrative approval system, 104 matters were cleared out. But out of the 500 matters, 119 matters remained as they were, procedure of administrative permit for 138 items was re-instituted by modified or newly issued rules and for another six matters, the said procedure was instituted by regulatory instruments.

---

[14]Ma Huaide, Suggestions on the Reform of Administrative Approval System, *Legal Daily*, p. 12, Oct. 16, 2013.

Overall, in the process of implementing Decree 412, many administrative organs intended to evade the Administrative Permission Law by, for instance, re-formulating rules or regulatory instruments in accordance with Decree 412 and instituting procedure of administrative permit or curing the previous procedures of administrative permit. Decree 412, a decision of the State Council on temporary procedures of administrative permit, has turned out to be a long-term instrument. Decree 412, therefore, should be abolished as soon as possible, and so are the procedures of administrative permit instituted by the rules and regulatory instruments.

Fourth, the Administrative Permission Law should be revised when necessary. The Law has been in effect for nearly ten years, but has not produced a satisfactory effect. This is because the Law has a tight control over and covers a wide range of the administrative power so that the administrative organs tried hard to resist and circumvent the law. The author therefore suggests: (1) ensuring the Administrative Permission Law is effectively implemented, particularly strictly abiding by that examination should be made on the necessity and feasibility of instituting the procedure of administrative permit and that items instituted without legal ground should be cleared out or canceled in time; (2) revising the Law, that is, expanding the scope of application of the Law to include all the matters subject to administrative permit and approval, while specifying Article 13 of the Law which provides that, for the matters which can be decided independently by citizens, settled by the market, supervised afterwards or handled by intermediaries, the procedure of administrative permit may not be instituted. This Article is too general and abstract. The circumstances under which the procedure of administrative permit may not be instituted should be specified, so as to limit the institution of new matters subject to administrative permit to the maximum extent.

Fifth, the participation of the public should be ensured in the implementation of the Administrative Permission Law. The Administrative Penalty Law provides that an administrative organ, before making a decision on administrative penalty, including ordering for suspension of production or business, rescission of business permit or license or imposition of a comparatively large amount of fine, should notify the party that he has the right to request a hearing; if the party requests a hearing, the administrative organ should arrange for the hearing. The Administrative Compulsion Law also includes provisions regarding participation procedure. These measures have played a significant role in ensuring the effective implementation of law. However, the Administrative Permission Law lacks explicit and feasible provisions regarding public participation. Therefore, it should guarantee the participation of the public in the institution and implementation of administrative permit. For instance, any administrative permit which is not granted in accordance with laws or regulations is subject to administrative review and administrative litigation by the public. Corrections should be made, and punishment should be imposed in a timely manner. The persons in Charge should be held accountable. To supervise the regulatory instruments or rules granting new administrative permits, under the circumstances that the systems of filing for record regulations and other regulatory instruments still have room for improvement, the public supervision is necessary. The scope of cases subject to administrative review and litigation should be expanded and petitions are accepted for the review and litigation of the grounds on which administrative permits are granted, so as to tightly control the power of granting administrative permits.

All in all, during the past more than ten years, the reform of administrative approval system has made some achievements. Many problems remain. The reform task will be tougher in the next phase. With great attention paid to the transformation of the governmental functions by the new administration and the reform of the administrative approval system, it is believed that more practical solutions will be worked out.

3.2 The Development and Improvement of the Administrative Permit System

To consolidate the fruits of reform on the administrative approval system, the Standing Committee of the 9th National People's Congress put the Administrative Permission Law on the agenda of legislation and empowered the State Council to submit the bill. On June 19, 2002, The State Council held the 60th executive meeting and passed the Administrative Permission Law (draft) and, on Aug. 23, 2002, submitted it to the 29th Meeting of the Standing Committee of the 9th National People's Congress for deliberation.[15] On Aug 27, 2003, the 4th Meeting of the Standing Committee of the 10th National People's Congress passed the Administrative Permission Law and put it into effect on July 1, 2004.

Since the Administrative Permission Law was passed and released, extensive discussions aroused in the academia and practice field on the partially consolidated administrative permit power provided therein. So far, China has gained some experience in both theory and practice in this field. The system of partially consolidated administrative permit power is of significance in promoting the reform of administrative system, ensuring administrative organs function in accordance with law, and making it easy for concerned persons to obtain administrative permits.

1. The administrative permit legislation: from an omnipotent government to a limited government.

The Administrative Permission Law, which adopted the framework of the Administrative Penalty Law of 1996, mainly provides the institution, principles, procedures and others of permission and so forth. Particularly, the Administrative Permission Law is fairly similar to the Administrative Penalty Law in the legislation framework with the regard to the institution of administrative permit, but more advanced in terms of the concept of administration according to law.

[15] Yang Jingyu, On the Administrative Permission Law of the People's Republic of China (drafted): at the 29th Meeting of the Standing Committee of the 9th National People's Congress on Aug, 23, 2002, *The Communiqué of the Standing Committee of the National People's Congress*, issue 5, 2003.

First, the Administrative Permission Law has made the concept of limited government into truth through limiting the scope of administrative permit.

The Administrative Permission Law mainly aims at solving the problems that the scope of administrative permit is too wide and that the government controls too many matters. Which matters should be subject to administrative permit is a hot issue in the legislation of the Administrative Permission Law should. There is a tendency in reality: administrative approval is needed whenever administration is mentioned. Consequently, administrative permit is applied to all matters. To deal with this issue, the majority of the people solicited for advice believed that the bill should specify explicitly which matters may or may not be subject to administrative permit. Given the fact that the Chinese economic system is undergoing a transformation and the transformation of governmental functions has not been completed, and to leave space for further reform, the provision regarding the said issue should not be excessively specific so as to be exhaustive. Therefore, the bill has provided the principles regarding the matters subject to administrative permit, which mainly include matters directly related to the state security, economic security, public interests, and people's health and life and property guarantee, and matters which can hardly be redressed in either impact or compensation. Except for the said matters and matters for which the administrative permit is established in accordance with the treaties signed or the international conventions participated by the Chinese government, no other matters should be subject to administrative permit. Meanwhile, the administrative permit should be established on the basis of rational principle. Matters subject to administrative permits are not necessarily subject to administrative examination and approval. The bill, accordingly, proscribed that matters which can be handled through the market mechanism should be left to the market mechanism for resolution; matters which can be handled through self-regulation by normal and justice intermediaries should be handled through self-regulation by intermediaries; matters which cannot be handled by the said intermediaries through self-regulation and instead need the government control should be firstly subject to supervision afterwards".[16] However, during the process of deliberation by the Standing Committee of the National People's Congress, this generalized provision was criticized in all aspects for vagueness and infeasibility. It was considered too flexible and hard to achieve the goal of normalize and narrow down the scope of administrative permit. When the second draft was submitted for review to the 31st meeting of the Standing Committee of the 9th National People's Congress, the Law Committee proposed to remove the principle provision regarding the matters subject to administrative permit from Article 13.[17] Article 12 of the Administrative Permission Law passed at last proscribes six circumstances under which administrative permit may be established. Except the sixth circumstance which is miscellaneous, the other five circumstances

[16]Ibid.

[17]Qiao Xiaoyang, The Report of the Law Committee of the National People's Congress on the Revision of the Administrative Permission Law of the People's Republic of China (Drafted): at the 31 Meeting of the Standing Committee of the 9th National People's Congress on Dec. 23, 2002. *The Communiqué of the Standing Committee of the National People's Congress*, issue 5, 2003.

are actually the combination of the scope of administrative permit for which the procedure is instituted and the scope of administrative permit for which the procedure is instituted under the five circumstances provided in the Draft, and the latter is made the scope of administrative permit for which the procedure is instituted.

Related to the scope of administrative permit is the limited power of the institution for administrative permit, which is a key issue in the process of enactment of the Administrative Permission Law. And the debate centered around the limited power of institution of procedure for administrative permit delegated by the all-binding decisions and regulations made by the State Council. The Law Committee asserted at the fourth Meeting of the Standing Committee of the 10th National People's Congress on Aug. 22, 2003, that, where it is necessary for the State Council to, as an urgent or interim measure, institute procedure for administrative permit and it is too late or not necessary to enact laws, it is necessary for the Administrative Permission Law to empower the state Council to institute procedure for administrative permit by issuing decisions. In the reform of administrative approval, the State Council decided to revoke the power of the departments under the State Council of instituting procedure for administrative permit by formulating departmental rules for the reason that each department should not be self-empowered, neither should it establish nor expand power within its own department or system. The administrative permits which have been declared by the departments and are necessary to continue to implement should be certified by the regulations made by the State Council after the Law herein is put into effect. Therefore, the Law Committee suggested that this issue be tackled in accordance with the opinions of the State Council. As for the power of the rules and regulations made by the provincial government to institute procedure for administrative permit, the Law Committee stated, after deliberation, that because each of the provinces in China cover comparatively a large area and the economic and social development in this area is not even, the provincial governments, in comprehensively taking charge of the economic and social management work within the administrative region, need to take immediate measure of administrative permit whenever necessary. Where there is no relevant law or administrative regulations available and it is too late or unnecessary to enact local rules and regulations, it is necessary for the law to vest the regulations made by the provincial governments with certain power to institute procedure for administrative permit. Since the procedures for administrative permit instituted by the provincial governments are actually implemented by relevant organs delegated by the governments, there is no self-delegation, which is different from the rules and regulations made by the departments under the State Council. However, some members of the Standing Committee suggested in their review opinions that limitation should be imposed on the provincial governments in instituting procedure for administrative permit, that is, the administrative permit instituted by the said governments should be provisional, which was accepted by the ultimate legislation.[18]

Second, the Administrative Permission Law calls for the first time for the protection of legitimate expectations with an aim of building government credibility.

---

[18]See Article 14 & 15, *Administrative Permission Law*.

Credibility is critically important not only to private individuals but also to leaders in governing their countries. According to The Analects: Governance, credibility is a treasure of the State and a safeguard for the people. In Guanzi Shuyan, it says that credibility is what holds everything together. Its paramount importance in theory notwithstanding, credibility was severely damaged in the early years of the People's Republic of China, during which the scale of class struggle continued to grow, leading to escalating tension in interpersonal relationship, both within and beyond the Party, culminating in the Cultural Revolution. Since the beginning of reform and the opening up to the outside world, China's has been transforming from a planned economy to a market economy. On one hand, the market economy requires social trust to be the foundation and support, and a mature market economy should be a contract-based economy and a credit-based economy. The more market-oriented the economy is, the higher the requirement for trust. In a market economy, the government must be honest and trustworthy as well as market players such as individuals and enterprises. Under the systems of planned economy and rule of man, the government rules through coercion and not trust by the people, so both the idea and the institution of credibility and trust were largely absent. The Cultural Revolution did more than anything to destroy the basic value system of the whole society and trust between people. After the reform and opening up, China is in a transition period from a planned economy system to a market economy. In a market economy that has yet to reach maturity, such as what now exists in China, trust is still wanting in economic activities. Fraud, counterfeiting and so forth and other kinds of misconduct frequently occur. The government has yet to define its own role in the economy, especially in relation to the market. And as it tries to do so, it is inevitable for it to do either more, or less, or other than what its proper function calls for. This is a key reason for the inconsistency and discontinuity that are often seen in government policies, and the high frequency government actions that undermine its credibility among the public. Article 59 of the Interpretation on the Issues Regarding the Implementation of the Law of Administrative Procedure of the People's Republic of China passed by the Supreme People's Court in 1999 provides that pursuant to Sec. 2, Article 54 of the Law of Administrative Procedure, Those specific administrative acts deemed illegal should be revoked, and for those that have caused damage to the interests of the state, public or private individuals, the people's court may order the administrative organ being sued to take appropriate remedial measures. The said interpretation mainly addresses the practical issue of compensating those whose legitimate rights and interests have been hurt through the revocation of administrative acts in practice. While it does not make explicit appeal to government credibility or the protection of legitimate expectations, it is an expression of the respect for individual rights and interests. The principle of trust protection in the Administrative Permission Law[19] protects the legitimate reliance interests of the interested person to whom such permission is granted, which indicates that the principle of credibility has started to be followed in regulating the government acts in administration in China and that building a credible government has been one of the goals of the government in promoting the rule of law. The State Council made

[19]Article 8 & 69, *Administrative Permission Law*.

honesty and trust worthiness a basic requirement for administration in accordance with law in the Enforcement Outline of Comprehensively Advancing Administration according to Law in 2004. The application of the principle of honest and trust in the administrative law has set forth the specific requirements for the government, which functions as an administrative organ: the information disclosed by the administrative organ should be comprehensive, accurate and true; the government organs should not revoke or modify any effective administrative decision without any legal grounds or through law procedures; where the administrative decisions need to be revoked or modified for the reason of state or public interests or other statutory reasons, the revocation or modification thereof should be made within the statutory functions and powers and through statutory procedures, and the interested people therefore should be compensated for the damage incurred by them. With the construction of the rule of law government speeding up, it is of great importance to establish the principle of trust protection by legislation.

Although reform in the system of administrative approval has been conducted several times and the flood of administrative approval has been under control to a certain degree, no obvious achievement has been made. Many administrative organs tried to evade the regulation of the Administrative Permission Law by various means including confusing the administrative permit approval with non-administrative permit approval. The resurgence of administrative approval exists to various degrees in all fields of public administration. These problems indicate to some extent that further studies and practice should be made on the issues including the scientific establishment of governmental functions and powers and reasonable allocation of powers.

2. Partially consolidated power of administrative permit and the reform of super-ministry system.

The top legal ground for the system of partially consolidated administrative permit power is the Administrative Permission Law of the People's Republic of China. Article 25 thereof provides that upon approval by the State Council, the people's government of a province, autonomous region or municipality directly under the Central Government may, on the basis of the principles of simplification, uniformity and efficiency, decide to let one administrative department exercise the power of administrative permit which is exercised by relevant administrative departments. Article 26 provides that where matters of administrative permit need to be handled by more than one institution within an administrative department, the said department should decide on one of the institutions for accepting applications for administrative permit and for serving the decisions on such permission itself. Where administrative permit is granted separately by more than two departments of a local people's government according to law, the government may decide on one of the departments for accepting applications for administrative permit and for handling them itself after the relevant departments are informed of the matter and after they respectively put forth their opinions, or have the relevant departments to handle them jointly or in a consolidated way. How to understand the provisions of the Administrative Permission Law and what does partially consolidated administrative permit power refer to?

There is controversy over these questions. Some people believe that the partially consolidated administrative permit power refers to the power of administrative permit exercised by a relevant administrative organ subject to the approval of the statutory organs provided in Article 25 of the Administrative Permission Law. Article 26 provides the handling of applications for administrative permit instead of the partially consolidated administrative permit power.[20] Others assert that Article 25 and 26 of Administrative Permission Law establish the system of partially consolidated administrative permit power, which is practiced in the two types of modes and four ways."[21] Still others hold that "the one-stop examination and approval, one-window acceptance, online examination and approval, etc. bear some quality of partially consolidated administrative permit power and can be deemed as the exploration and practice of the construction of the system of partially consolidated administrative permit power."[22]

The core of partially consolidated administrative permit power is the exercise of consolidated power of administrative permit. In terms of permission procedures, the administrative permit power can be divided into acceptance, review, decision, and so forth. Decision is the core and key of the permission power. Whereas, procedures, such as acceptance and review, are also integral parts of the power, and closely related to the final decision. The partially consolidated administrative permit power can be both the consolidation of procedural powers for instance, consolidated acceptance and consolidated service, and consolidated substantive powers of administrative permit, such as review and decision. The two articles of the Administrative Permission Law provide for direct legal grounds for the partially consolidated administrative permit power. Article 25 stresses the consolidation of the substantive powers of the administrative permit among the administrative organs, while Article 26 emphasizes the consolidation of the procedural powers of the administrative permit including consolidated acceptance and coordinated handling.

Although, "based on the comparatively successful experience of partially consolidated administrative penalty power, the Administrative Permission Law also provide s for the system of partially consolidated administrative permit power with the same rationale."[23] Both the partially consolidated administrative permit power and the partially consolidated administrative penalty power are the horizontal configurations. Differences exist between them in feature and operation of power consolidation and its impact. The consolidation of administrative permit power more deeply affected

[20]Hu Zhenjie, et al., *Questions and Answers Regarding Practical Knowledge of the Administrative Permission Law*, Economic Management Press, July, 2006, pp. 51–53; Li Shasha, The Development of the Administrative Service Center and Construction of the System of Relatively Consolidated Administrative Permission in China, *Journal of Shenyang Carders*, 2011, vol. 13, issue 4.

[21]Li Lu, On Creativity of the System of Relatively Consolidated Administrative Permission Power and the Perfection of Legislation, *Journal of Socialist Theory Guide*, Sept., 2010.

[22]Zheng Chuankun, Yi Xuezhi, and Liu Jian, Studies on Construction of the System of Relatively Consolidated Administrative Permission Power, *The Forum of Constitutional Law and Administrative Law*, vol. 3, edited by Wen Zhengbang, China Procuratorial Press, 2007, p. 202.

[23]Qing Feng, The Sketch and Theoretical Analysis of the Reform of the System of Administrative Law Enforcement, *Journal of Shanghai University of Political Science and Law*, 2007, issue 1.

the system of power division between higher and lower levels and between different departments than the consolidation of administrative penalty power. Studies on the consolidation of administrative permit power are essential to the promotion of reform of the administrative approval system and practice of government public services. The consolidation of administrative permit power can be deemed, to certain extent, as a sample of horizontal configuration of administrative power. It also provides ideas for super-ministry reform. This paper tends to make a contrastive study on the different types of mode of operation of the partially consolidated administrative permit power through the analysis of the system of partially consolidated administrative permit power, discuss, from the theoretical perspective, the jurisprudential rationale and categorization of the relatively concentrative administrative permit power, and put forward suggestions on the solution to the legal problems with the partially consolidated administrative permit power and the direction of development.

(1) The practice of the system of partially consolidated administrative permit power in China.

The practice of the system of relatively consolidated administrative permit power in China and the one-stop public services in the world manifest the new public administration movement. Influenced by the ideological trend of new public administration which arose in the world in 1970s, the governments of the countries in the world have been making efforts in adjust the mode of public services so as to meet the needs of the public. For instance, the former British Prime Minister Margaret Thatcher carried out the reform of public-oriented one-stop services to raise government efficiency and effectiveness after taking office. To have matters handled, citizens only need to submit their applications to one agency or department or at one window and then can have all procedures done, saving the trouble of calling at one department to another.

In China, consolidated examination and approval which aims at raising the administrative efficiency appeared in 1980s–1990s. For instance, in 1983, the government of Kunming City issued Kunming Interim Measures for Protection of Groundwater Resources, aimed at protection of groundwater resources, provided that "the municipal planning and construction bureau and municipal water conservancy department jointly plan, review and approve the exploitation of groundwater resources, and manage it respectively."[24] Another example is Guangzhou City, which is in the forefront of the reform and opening up, establish an international trade street which consolidated all the international trade in 1985. In 1992, Kunming municipal government issued Measures for Examination and Approval of Foreign Investment, stipulating that "the municipal office of foreign investment unitarily handle and jointly review and approve the applications for establishing foreign-invested enterprises", aiming at "improving investment environment and simplifying the procedures of examination and approval of the applications for establishing foreign-invested enterprises."[25]

[24] Article 1, Kunming Interim Measures for Protection of Groundwater Resources, issued by Kunming municipal government in 1983.

[25] Article 1, *Measures for Examination and Approval of Foreign Investment*, issued by Kunming municipal government on Aug. 23, 1992.

In the same year, Heilongjiang Province implemented Regulations on the Transformation of Operational Mechanism of the State-Owned Industrial Enterprises, aiming at simplifying the procedures of examination and approval of the applications for foreign-invested enterprises, which provides that the planning commission and the economic commission are responsible for taking the lead and organizing banks and other authorities, including the departments of land management, city planning, urban construction, environmental protection, and so forth, to work jointly on a regular basis and deal with the concerned formalities in a consolidated manner."[26] In 1993, Jilin Province and the city of Tianjin Municipality, to grant enterprises the right of import and export, established consolidated examination and approval system and one-off approval pattern. In 1995, Shenzhen's government for the first time consolidate eighteen governmental departments concerned with the approval of applications for foreign-invested enterprises and established a specialized administrative service center for examination and approval, which is deemed as the rudiment of the specialized administrative service center in China. In 1999, in Jinhua city of Zhejiang province, forty-six departments which are empowered with administrative approval opened windows in the city business hall to handle the matters, establishing the first comprehensive administrative approval center in China and adopting one-stop service pattern and an operation pattern of one-window acceptance, one-off notification, a package service, one-off fee payment, and timely decision. To promote the transformation of the governmental functions, optimize the environment of economic and social environment, and raise the government efficiency and effectiveness, the local governments have explored a series of new types of administrative permit mechanism, various kinds of agencies which, in a consolidated manner, handle the matters of administrative approval and provide a part of public services, such as the center of administrative service, center of administrative affairs, service center for the public convenience, hall of the administrative affairs, have been established all over the country. Since 2000, some local government have started to write the provisions of consolidated examination and approval and jointly handling matters into the general rules of administrative approval. For instance, Article 8 of the Rules of Chengdu City on the Reform of the Administrative Approval System issued in 2000 provides that the matters for examination and approval should be joined and categorized and handled unitarily by a department which is in charge of the matter. Response should be made to the applicants by the department after consultation of all the relevant departments." Subsequently, in 2001 and 2002, Jinan city, Shandong province, Xining city, Shenyang city successively formulated rules of administrative approval which specifically provided for establishing the business hall for administrative approval and handling the applications for administrative approval in a consolidated manner.[27]

[26] Article 13, Rules of Heilongjiang Province on Implementation of the Regulations on Transformation of Operational Mechanism of the State-owned Industrial Enterprises, issued on Dec. 23, 1992.

[27] *Rules of Jinan City on the Reform of the Administrative Review and Approval System* (2001); *Rules on Shandong Province on Administrative Examination and Approval* (2001); *Rules of Xining City on Administrative Examination and Approval* (2002); *Rules of Shenyang City on Administrative Examination and Approval* (2002).

After the Administrative Permission Law took into effect in 2004, a large number of provisions on partially consolidated administrative permit, consolidated examination and approval, joint handling of applications have been written into local rules and regulations regarding the matters such as administrative permit, administrative law implementation, administrative procedures, administrative supervision, and so forth The aforesaid development indicates that the system of partially consolidated administrative permit power, including consolidated examination and approval and joint handling of applications, stem from the economic goals of pushing for economic and trade development, attracting investment, and quickening the state-owned enterprises ownership reform. The consolidated administrative pattern has been applied to administrative permit in economic sector and subsequently in other sectors, from administrative permit to more comprehensive government services, and has developed into a common mode of public administration.

Administrative service center, as the main form of partially consolidated administrative permit system, has undergone two stages of development. At the initial stage, the administrative service center, as a platform for handling affairs on behalf of the government, set up a window accepting the application and serving permission documents. The original administrative permit function and permission procedures remain unchanged. The physical consolidation makes the administrative service center into "the mail room" and "gate house" and the carrier of "serial approval"[28] of relevant departments. This approach, on the surface, gathered the relevant affairs regarding administrative permit to the administrative hall, obviated the need for applicants to visit many different department for either submission or pick-up; but on the whole, the power of administrative permit was not transferred. Due to the diversity of the matters for administrative permit, the powers, such as examination and approval, review, and decision, still remained in each department. Between the administrative service centers which aim at partial consolidation of the power of administrative permit and the original administrative organs, the boundary is unclear because power is indefinite, communication and coordination are not smooth, and effective coordination mechanism is lacking. Consequently, administrative expenses have been increased due to function overlapping of the multiple administrative organs and the one-stop services. In general, confusions abound in how administrative approval applications are actually processed once they are received by the government, exacerbating the existing tendency to treat the granting of permission ahead of time as either an adequate replacement of supervision and monitoring or a superior approach to management.

Two important measures have been put in place to streamline and simplify the administrative permit system. First, the number of offices responsible for processing administrative permit is reduced to one; and secondly, all matters related to administrative permit are handled at the service window open to the public at a service

[28]"Serial examination and approval" means that, after the administrative service center accepts the application, the principal department is designated to take the sole responsibility for acceptance, conclusion, and service of the files by the ways of serial review, jointly signing with relevant administrative departments, and so forth.

center. What these two measures basically do is to consolidate both the authority to exercise the power to process administrative permit and the provision of services to the public.[29] While they no doubt represent progress towards substantive downsizing of the number of offices and departments involved in handling permissions, these measures leave fundamentally unchanged how such powers are allocated according to the law. In other words, the power to handle these matters continue to rest with whichever government body to which such power has been given by the law, and it is only the authority to exercise such power and to provide related service to the public that has been consolidated and assigned to a single service center.

As early as before the Administrative Permission Law went into effect, it was suggested "to transform the existing local centers of administrative approval into administrative permit agencies which have substantive administrative permit power and unitarily handle the routine administrative permit affairs which were handled separately by the departments concerned."[30] In 2008, the Administrative Approval Bureau of Wuhou District was established, symbolizing an independent partially consolidated administrative permit authority coming into being. The District Administrative Approval Bureau shares out work and cooperates with the functional departments. The Bureau is responsible for the administrative approval, while the functional departments are responsible for supervision and management after permission is granted. The Bureau also has the duty to make annual inspection. In the process of specific examination and approval, on-site investigation, technology demonstration, public hearings required for examination and approval should be taken care of by functional departments, which, upon the notification from the Administrative Approval Bureau, should provide the Bureau with the results of on-site investigation, technical argumentation and social hearings within the provided time. This model consolidates the permission power from the original functional department to the Administrative Approval Bureau. It is the significant turning point at which the system of partially consolidated administrative permit developed from the procedural consolidation to substantive consolidation, directly touching the core of configuration of permission power. The priority, hence, is to solve the problem of how to consolidate the permission power and which mode of consolidation should be adopted.

(2) The operation mode and principles of partially consolidated permission power.

Judging by the current operation mode of the system of partially consolidated administrative permit adopted all over the country, different classification of operation modes can be made according to the different criteria. The first classification is procedural consolidation and substantive consolidation. Procedure classification is

---

[29] Implementation of these two measures is uneven across China. It is applied all over the provinces in Sichuan, Hainan, Ningxia, Tianjing, and so forth. However, in some provinces, it is applied only in some cities, such as Hohhot in Inner Mongolia, Weihai city in Shandong province, Zhuhai city in Guangdong province, Kunming city in Yunnan province, Xining city in Qinghai province, Quanzhou city and Longyan city in Fujian province, and so forth; and in the provinces such as Anhui province, it is applied in provincial employers.

[30] Wang Yongqing, *The Textbook of the Administrative Permission Law of the People's Republic of China*, China Legal Publishing House, 2003, p. 93.

the primary stage of consolidation of administration permission powers, which are consolidated at the procedures of acceptance and service. The procedural consolidation does not help to optimize the administrative permit system, nor does it actually improve the efficiency of administrative permit. But this mode can help to put the principle of convenience for the public into practice. Particularly, after the power is consolidated to the administrative service center, although the administrative permit is still under the control of the original administrative permit organ, it helps to raise the status of the administrative service center through the two "consolidations" and two "put in places". The strong point of the model is that the department handles administrative matters through one window, and the government does through one center. To reduce the points at which the public deal with the administrative organ can not only make things easier for the public but improve the administrative efficiency as well. Meanwhile, since the implementation subject of the administrative permit does not change in terms of system, there are fewer barriers to reform. The weak point of the mode is that it does not solve the long-standing problem of permission granting by multiple organs and hence cannot achieve the goal of reducing administrative permit matters.

The consolidation of substantive powers refers to exercising the administrative permit powers including acceptance, review, decision and service in a consolidated manner, particularly the powers of review and decision. The consolidation of substantive powers is the higher-level consolidation of administrative permit powers. To consolidate the powers of various departments to the Administrative Approval Bureau directly changes the implementation organ of administrative permit, replacing multiple organs to handle the administrative affairs by one organ so as to save high social costs caused by multiple organs handling the administrative affairs. The Administrative Approval Bureau is exclusively responsible for administrative permit, which greatly improves the administrative efficiency. Applicants only need to deal with one administrative permit organ, which makes things much easier for them. But this mode is the adjustment made to the macro scope of administrative functions, which involves many aspects and make it hard to reform. And monopoly may occur due to several administrative permit powers being consolidated to one organ and lack of supervision.

The second classification is vertical consolidation and horizontal consolidation according to administrative systems. The vertical consolidation refers to the consolidation of permission powers of the administrative organs at various levels. Many identical administrative permit matters are handled by administrative organs at various levels according to their significance. The advantages of vertical consolidation are: the same system, minor difference in specialty, and no separation of powers of planning, approval, supervision and penalty involved. And it is favorable to the administrative organs for comprehensive management with multiple powers. The drawback is it destroys the hierarchical administrative system. In case supporting systems is lacking and supervision proves to be unsatisfactory, a situation may be created that market failure occurs when control is tight and disorder arises when control goes loose.

Horizontal consolidation refers to the consolidation of approval matters of different departments at the same level. It maintains the hierarchical management system and can effectively reduce administrative permit affairs. But it may probably result in separation of powers of planning, approval, inspection, supervision and penalty, and adversely affect overall management and coordination of operation. It can be subdivided into specialized consolidation and general consolidation according to the extent of horizontal consolidation. Specialized consolidation, namely consolidated management by specialized departments, is the consolidation of approval matters of administrative organs in related fields including investment, construction, science, education, culture and health, commerce, municipal management. General consolidation is the consolidation of all the matters subject to the approval of the administrative organs at the same level. Compared with general consolidation, specialized consolidation is less inclusive, but is easier to practice because of strong correlation of and minor differences between the matters subject to administrative permit.

The third classification is internal consolidation and external consolidation of the administrative organs according to whether consolidation is made within or out of the administrative organs. The internal consolidation means setting up a special administrative permit agency within the administrative organ to consolidate the permission powers of the organ. The internal consolidation integrates the permission powers within the administrative organ, improving the administrative efficiency and helping the administrative organ enhance supervision and inspection after permission is granted. In addition, inside the organ, the administrative departments are familiar with their own business and, therefore, encounter fewer obstacles. The consolidation of matters subject to the permission of the administrative organs needs to integrate the matters of several organs. For instance, the power of administrative permit is deprived of from one administrative organ and delegated to another; or a special administrative permit organ is established to integrate the permissions powers of several organs.

The fourth classification is made according to hierarchy, namely consolidation of the county governments, consolidation of the municipal government, and consolidation of provincial government. Relatively speaking, the grassroots governments are more comprehensive in terms of administrative affairs. It is therefore easier, in a consolidated manner, to subject the matters to comprehensive law enforcement, including administrative permit and administrative penalty. The provincial governments handle comparatively more material and more specialized approval matters. And it is hard for the provincial government to consolidate such matters.

The mode of consolidation is affected by many factors, such as the changeable administrative affairs and adjustment of administrative management mode. Hence, the consolidation modes are not necessarily the same. To deal with the flexible mode of administrative management, a mechanism of regular evaluation should be established to evaluate the operation of the partially consolidated permission power in terms of the index of efficiency, effectiveness, and so forth.

Therefore, the ways of consolidation are different, and so is the scope of consolidated administrative permit power. Currently, the matters subject to administrative permit are consolidated into the service center under three circumstances: firstly, full consolidation without any exception, such as Jiling, Ningxia, and Sichuan; secondly, partial consolidation of the matters subject to administrative permit with some exceptions which vary from one province to another, roughly including matters concerning state confidentiality, security, trade secret, privacy, religion, and ideology; or matters which do not need to go through many procedures, or are not in a large number or with low coverage or relevance; thirdly, the matters subject to the decision of local governments due to lack of definite provisions therefore. Since the administrative service center does not adopt the substantial consolidation of the administrative powers, it does not matter much to the permission power which of the matters subject to administrative permit are handled in the administrative service center. But in terms of the mode of examination and approval of Administrative Approval Bureau of Wuhou District, the substantial consolidation of permission powers has changed the current integral system of review, approval and supervision, and must inevitably affect the configuration and exercise of administrative powers. Hence, a study in the rules of administrative power configuration should precede one in the principles of the consolidation of administrative permit powers.

The system of partially consolidated administrative permit power requires, in accordance with the principles of simplicity, efficiency and unity, adjustment and consolidation of administrative powers, re-configuration of powers among the departments, and streamlining government. This requirement is of great significance for handling the problems, such as several government organs getting involved in permission for an matter and repeated permission; establishing a mechanism of consolidated administrative permit power, reasonably delegate administrative powers, reducing the matters subject to administrative permit, simplifying administrative permit procedures, shortening the time of administrative permit, saving costs, regulating administrative permit, providing convenience for applicants, transforming administrative modes, increasing administrative efficacy. The system of partially consolidated administrative permit power has changed the rule of vertical division of administrative permit power on the basis of industry. Instead, it horizontally divides the powers of examination, approval, supervision and punishment on the basis of administrative procedure. Under the existing laws and regulations, the administrative organs adjust through statutory procedures the subject of administrative permit, re-delegate administrative permit power, and re-establish the operation mechanism of administrative power. Since it is the reconfiguration of administrative powers, theoretically some questions should be answered first: what is the power? how many powers can be consolidated? how to check and balance the powers after consolidation of powers? Which powers can be consolidated? These are the theoretical grounds for the system of partially consolidated administrative permit power. Putting too much emphasis on power consolidation probably is not helpful for the reform of the system of administrative approval. Moreover, it will hinder enforcement and coordination, increase administrative costs, and cause abuse of administrative powers. Hence, the principle of administrative power consolidation and the principles of separation of powers and checks and balances should be applied together. The partially consolidated powers should be reasonably delegated. Theoretically, when it comes to determine whether to consolidate administrative powers or to use the power separately, the following principles should be followed:

First, the specialized powers should not be consolidated. Powers or functions delegated to a certain agency by law should not be consolidated. For instance, the General Administration of Customs, the Internal Revenue Service, the authority of Financial Regulation and Supervision, and China Entry-Exit Inspection of Quarantine Bureau, and other authorities which are responsible for the state security and control of personal freedom have the powers and functions which are not subject to consolidation because of their special properties of law enforcement.

Second, there should be relevance among consolidated powers. The partially consolidated powers should be relevant, fall into the same category in terms of the object of administration, have basically same objectives, and rules of activity, since it is hard to handle the matters which are consolidated but with relevance with each other. It increases the difficulty of administrative management rather than improve the administrative efficiency.

Third, consolidation of powers should not influence the checks and balances of powers. The administrative permit is the middle of the administrative process. Administrative planning is at the beginning, and administrative supervision and punishment at the end. Some of the administrative permit powers are closely related to the existing administrative planning, such as land use permission and land use planning; others are closely related to administrative punishment; still others checks with each other. Consolidation of powers to one organ will have impact on check between each administrative power. To decide on the matters to be consolidated for examination and approval, the relationships between administrative permit, administrative planning and administrative punishment should be taken into consideration. Those which can hardly be clearly divided or of which the division may adversely influence checks between the powers should not be consolidated.

Fourth, specialized administration and general administration should be divided. Specialization is the inevitable result of social division of labor. Each industry has its own expertise and technologies. To consolidate the powers of administrative permit, analysis should be made of the extent of specialization thereof. Those that are highly specialized should not be consolidated for examination and approval. At present, the market economy of China still needs improving, and the government administration continues to change. The government still exerts significant influence in many areas. Under the circumstances, the specialized administration is still the main aspect of administration. The reform of consolidation of administrative power is the supplement to the specialized administration. It configures the relatively simple routine matters subject to examination and approval so as to accord with the principles of economy and efficiency.

Fifth, the consolidation mode and hierarchy of administrative power need to be considered. The administrative permit powers can be vertically divided into hierarchies. Local governments have relatively fewer matters to review and approve, and the matters are comparatively simpler and less specialized so that the powers can be easily consolidated. The higher governments handle the matters with great diversity, and, therefore, it is hard to set up a special department with a consolidated power to review and approve the matters. However, it does not hinder the consolidation of powers of the departments in the fields with high relevance. In the field with low relevance, spots or procedures for applying for administrative permit can be consolidated, rather than the substantive powers.

The fore-going analysis indicates that factors which affect the consolidation of the administrative powers, such as the matters subject to administrative permit, the relationship of the administrative permit power with other powers, and the levels of the administrative permit agencies, should be considered on a comprehensive basis when matters for consolidation are to be determined. The administrative permit powers are consolidated partially rather than completely insofar as it covers only the following aspects: firstly, the consolidation is limited since it is easier for the procedural powers to be consolidated than the substantive powers. The practice in different places also demonstrated that the procedural powers, including acceptance of the case and service, are much easier to be consolidated than the specialized powers, such as review and decision-making. Paper review is easy to be consolidated, compared with other types of review including field investigation, peer review, hearing and discussion. More specialized the power is, more difficult it is to be consolidated, especially when expertise, experts, specialized equipment, technical appraisement, and so forth are involved. Therefore, the specialized powers should not be consolidated at present. Secondly, the fields where the powers can be consolidated are limited since not all the fields are fit for having their matters subject to approval consolidated. It is not necessary to consolidate the matters which are sharply different. Finally, the level of administrative agencies for consolidation is limited. Not every agency is eligible for power. Nor is it necessary to consolidate the matters with big differences. The higher the level of the agency is, the more difficult for administrative powers to be consolidated.

The partial consolidation of administrative permit powers into a small number of agencies is closely related to the reform of the administrative approval system. It is stated in the Implementation Opinions and Notices Approved and Issued by the State Council on the Reform of the Administrative Approval System of 2001 that the reform of the administrative approval system should divide and adjust in a reasonable manner the powers and functions of administrative permit among the agencies in accordance with the principle of effectiveness and efficacy. In the same year, the leading group of the reform on the system of administrative approval of the State Council stressed the consolidation of administrative permit powers into the hands of a relatively small number of agencies again in the instrument entitled Issues of Carrying out the Five Principles of the Reform of the Administrative Approval System, asserting that the government at this level should create conditions, break departmental boundaries, and consolidate the matters subject to administrative approval which are scattered in different departments of the government. In 2008, the State Council issued the Opinions on Deepening the Reform of the Administrative Approval System released by the Ministry of Supervision, and so forth, stressing improving the system of relative consolidation of administrative approval. Deepening the reform of the administrative approval system, cutting the matters subject to administrative permit and reducing the levels of administrative permit are the prerequisite for consolidation of administrative powers. And the consolidation of administrative permit powers will necessarily bring about the integration of the matters subject to administrative permit. It could be said that the reform of administrative approval system is the prerequisite for survival and development of the system of relative consolidation of administrative permit powers while relative consolidation of administrative permit powers can also promote the reform of administrative approval. The system of relative consolidation of administrative permit powers cannot develop independently from the reform of China's administrative approval and reform of administrative management system. These three factors interact with each other.

Subject to the process of the reform of the administrative approval system and the reform of super-ministry, the relative consolidation of the administrative permit powers is unlikely to be accomplished overnight. In practice, it may be carried out step by step on a gradual basis or triggered in one particular place. The powers of administrative permit for ordinary, routine and less specialized matters may be firstly integrated. Permissions and services can be integrated and consolidated through delegation of power by administrative organs to township governments or community offices for the sake of convenience for the people and in accordance with the principle of proximity and dispersion. The development of relative consolidation of administrative permit powers can provide experience for the reform of super ministry. The reform of super ministry will involve the consolidation of administrative organs and integration of administrative powers, including the power of administrative permit. This will inevitably bring about consolidation of administrative permit powers. Meanwhile, the consolidation of administrative permit powers will also provide experiences and ideas for integration of other administrative powers and adjustment of administrative organs and ultimately promote the reform of super ministry.

Chapter 4
Welfare State and Government Benefits

4.1 Welfare State and Reform of the Chinese Social Security System

The welfare state is the outcome of the interactions between the state and the society. In China, the idea of poverty relief has its roots in ancient times. Poor relief theories proposed by various schools could be found in the Spring and Autumn and War periods more than 2000 years ago, among which the most well-known are the notions of primacy of people's interests, benevolent governance and universal harmony. In the time of natural economy, the idea of relief was executed mainly through saving surplus grains during the years of good harvest for use during years of poor harvest. Since the Han Dynasty, China has adopted a grain reserve system, namely *Changpingcang* (Grain Reserve Storage), which was established by the imperial government. In Sui Dynasty, *Yicang* (Charity Grain Reserve Storage) was introduced, which held grain donations solicited from the public by the local governments. In the Southern Song Dynasty, there was *Shecang* (Communal Grain Reserve), which partly served as a form of social security, and was managed by the local community and in which all local residents enrolled. In addition to the reserve system, there were other forms of charity such as poverty relief, old age care and childcare. During the Ming Dynasty, *Tongshanhui* (Commonweal Association) was established. It was a non-governmental grassroots charitable organization and the first of its kind. The Chinese traditional poverty relief or public assistance system developed under the influence of Confucianism. Even though there is a long history of state involvement in poverty relief, the basic premise of the aid system is still the idea that state aid is a form of charitable giving to those in need, and not something to which the people have a natural right or entitlement. Modern thinking in China about welfare has been an extension of the Confucian ideas and has, in addition, been influenced by the bourgeois-democratic revolution and the notions about welfare that originated in the west. Sun Yat-sen proposed the principle of the people's livelihood, believing that this principle matters the survival of people, the society and the country. The poverty

© Social Sciences Academic Press and Springer Nature Singapore Pte Ltd. 2018
H. Ma and J. Wang, *Building a Government Based on the Rule of Law*,
Research Series on the Chinese Dream and China's Development Path,
https://doi.org/10.1007/978-981-13-0999-1_4

relief was legalized in the Rules of Workhouses for Vagrants passed and released by the government of the Republic of China in 1915. In 1943, Public Assistance Law, the first national law regarding poverty relief, was released. The social security and public assistance systems were also provided in the Constitution of the Republic of China which took effect in 1947.[1]

The Constitution, including several of its amendments passed and released after the founding of the People's Republic of China all clarify that public assistance is not a gift but a basic administrative function of the government. It is the right of the citizens to obtain the public assistance.[2] The current Constitution of 1982 provides three-level guarantee of the citizens' rights of welfare. (1) The state should provide material assistance to a particular group of people. In accordance with Article 45 of the Constitution of 1982, the state establishes and develops the social insurance, public assistance and medical and health services that are required to guarantee citizens' right. The state and society ensure the livelihood of disabled members of the armed forces, provide pensions to the families of the war dead and give preferential treatment to the families of military personnel. The state and society help make arrangements for the work, livelihood and education of persons with disabilities. (2) The state protects the working people. In accordance with Article 42, using various channels, the state provides opportunities for employment, strengthens labor protection, improves working conditions and, on the basis of expanded production, increases remuneration for work and social benefits. In accordance with Article 44,

---

[1]Article 155 of the *Constitution of the Republic of China* of 1947 provides that the state should implement social insurance system to promote the social welfare, and provide with reasonable aid and relief to those aged, feeble, or disabled and the victims of big disasters.

[2]Article 93 of the *Constitution of the People's Republic of China of 1954* provides that working people in the People's Republic of China have the right to material assistance in old age, and in case of illness or disability. To ensure that working people can enjoy this right, the state provides social insurance, social assistance and public health services and gradually expands these facilities. Art. 92 of the *Constitution of the People's Republic of China* of 1954 provides that working people in the People's Republic of China have the right to rest and leisure. To ensure that working people can enjoy this right, the state prescribes working hours and systems of vacations for workers and office personnel, and gradually expands material facilities for the working people to rest and build up their health. Art. 27 of the *Constitution of the People's Republic of China of 1975* provides that citizens have the right to work and the right to education, and working people have the right to rest and the right to material assistance in old age and in case of illness or disability. Art. 48 of the *Constitution of the People's Republic of China of 1978* provides that citizens have to the right to work. To ensure the citizens enjoy the aforesaid right, the state arranges employment according to the principle of taking overall consideration of the situation, gradually raise the remunerations on the basis of development of production, improve the working conditions, enhance the work protection, and expand the collective welfare. Art. 49 of the *Constitution of 1978* provides that working people have the right to rest. To ensure that working people enjoy this right, the state prescribes working hours and systems of vacations, and gradually expands material facilities for the working people to rest and build up their health. Art. 50 of the *Constitution of 1978* provides that working people have the right to rest and the right to material assistance in old age and in case of illness or disability. To ensure that working people can enjoy this right, the state gradually develops welfares including social insurance, social assistance, public health services and cooperative healthcare system. The state takes care of and secures the life of the revolutionary disabled veterans and the families of the revolutionary martyrs.

the state provides by law the system of retirement for workers and staff in enterprises and undertakings and for functionaries of organs of state. (3) The state guarantees the basic welfare of all citizens. The amendments to the Constitution passed on March 14, 2004 clarifies that the state establish and develop a social security system compatible with the level of the economic development. With the addition of the right to social welfare in the Constitution, various social security systems have been gradually established and improved.

Throughout of the history of China's social security system, the aims, scope, the parties targeted, and the model have been progressing from treating poverty to preventing poverty, from creating contentment among the public to securing citizens' economic right, from helping a particular group of people to providing universal social security to all citizens. During the process, the call for raising the citizens' welfare right and the warning of the state welfare crisis appeared in turns, and so did the value of fairness and the value of efficiency, and the theory of freedom and theory of society and state. The disputes regarding the welfare state centered on the speed and ways of building a welfare state rather than on its necessity in nature and function. The Chinese decision makers were reminded repetitively that building the welfare state equals reconstruction of the society, and with the social transformation deepening in China, the social security system were also undergoing profound reform.

The protection of the citizens' welfare right is closely related to a country's economic and political systems. Both the market economy and democratic political systems require the Chinese government to transform from one that wields unbound power to one constrained by the rule of law, whose powers are subject to institutional checks. The social security system should consequently be changed in the following aspects:

1. The development from the urban-rural dual system to urban-rural integration system

Under the planned economic system, the urban-rural economy and divisions of the social institutions directly caused the unbalanced dual structure of the provision of social security. The social security system was divided into two completely different sub-systems: the state-working employer security system applied in towns and the collective-family security system applied in countryside. The urban-rural security system applied in towns mainly consists of the endowment life insurance and labor insurance medical system applicable to the workers of the state-run enterprises and the endowment life insurance system and the free medical care system applicable to the workers of the government institutions. In addition, it also includes the enterprise and institution welfare system and civil administration welfare system. Almost all the urban population is eligible for the welfare and security provided by the state itself or through the enterprises. The rural population mainly relies on the family or collective welfare and security. There is no social welfare and security system available to the rural population. The rural collective welfare and security system relies on the people's commune and mainly consists of the "five-guarantee" program, corporative medical care insurance, the system of public assistance mainly for the poor and feeble, and the system of care and preferential treatment for the families of the servicemen and service women on active duty, veterans, and the war dead. The welfare and security for the rural population are not comparable to those for the urban population in either quantity or quality. Since the end of 1970s, the rural economic system reform abolished the collective security based on the people's commune and left the rural population with no social welfare and security at all. With the development of the market economy, the rural people were faced with greater survival risks. Particularly, the problems of aging and poverty in rural areas became more and more serious, and rural migrant workers were threatened by work-related injuries and occupational diseases. With the construction of the new countryside which started in 1990s, to narrow the gap between the urban and rural areas and promote the integration of the social welfare and security system, the reform of social welfare and security system in rural areas was carried out: including establishing a new type of cooperative medical care system with a combination of individual contribution and government support, based on comprehensive arrangement of particular serious diseases, and covering all the rural residents; reforming the "five guarantees"[3]comprehensive method which requires the government rather than the rural collective pay for the expenses thereof, setting up the rural endowment life insurance system and subsistence allowance system in the rural area, and so forth. The reform of the social security has effectively expanded the coverage of the state welfare and security from the urban area to the rural area.

2. Shifting from complete reliance on the government to reliance on the government, non-governmental actors and private individuals

Under the planned economic system, the welfare is funded by the state and arranged by the employers, requiring no contribution from the individual. This reduced people's sense of individual responsibility and compromised their incentive to work. The welfare system of "low salary and high welfare" and "high or full employment" exceeds the level of economic development. High expenditure on welfare payments constituted a great burden on the enterprises and the state. As marketization progressed, non-governmental actors and private individuals gradually became involved as well as the government in welfare programs. The social insurance of endowment, medicare and unemployment are paid by the state, employer and individual respectively according to the different proportion of their shares

3. Comprehensive transformation from a uniform employment-based security system to a more diverse and multi-tiered system

The egalitarianism of uniform social security standard adopted under the planned economic system could not suit different forms of economic ownership. The social

[3]The Five Guarantees refers to the guarantees of food, clothing, housing, medicare and burial expenses (or education for the minors) provided, in accordance with the *Regulations on the Rural Five-Guarantee Work* released by the State Council in 1994, to the aged, the disabled and minors who are not able to work and hence have no source of income and have no caregivers designated by law, or whose caregivers have no capability to take care of him.

security system developed from providing everybody with the same welfare benefits to providing different group of people with different welfare benefits. The eligibility requirements for becoming a welfare recipient are stressed. Distinctions among the minimum security, basic security, and supplemental security are clarified. The standards have been shifted from a homogeneous one to one that provides different levels of welfare to meet the needs of different social classes. Managerially, social and professional organizations have replaced the employers as the bodies operating the social security system. The social fund insurance has been established. The National Social Fund Insurance Council, a non-governmental organization, has been founded. The administration of social security is separated from the management of funds. Welfare benefits are delivered to all members of the society and subject to management by the community.

With the past 30-year reform and development, China has preliminarily established a basic framework of social security with the social insurance as its core and the social welfare and public assistance system as its supplements. The framework mainly consists of three parts: (1) A variety of social insurance system applicable to laborers,[4] including the basic social endowment insurance, basic medical insurance, unemployment insurance, occupational injury insurance, maternity insurance, and so forth; (2) the public assistance system applicable to the poor or low-income group of people,[5] including the basic living allowance security system, the rural help-the-poor policy, disaster relief, and so forth; (3) a variety of social welfare system,[6] such as the endowment security, welfare for minors, welfare for the disabled, and various kinds

[4]The social insurance provided in the *Social Insurance Law of the People's Republic of China* are the endowment insurance, medical care insurance, occupational injury insurance, maternity insurance, and unemployment insurance. The costs thereof are paid jointly by the state, enterprise and individual, or by both of the enterprise and the individual.

[5]In accordance with the *Public Assistance Law of the People's Republic of China* (draft open to comments), public assistance refers to the material aids and services provided by the state and society to the citizens who can hardly support themselves independently. Its main content is to the basic living allowance. In addition, there are also special relief, natural disaster relief, temporary relief and other relieves provided by the state, dependent on the circumstances. The social insurance is a social security system established by the state through legislation and funded by the money paid by the people in the society for the purpose of aiding and subsidizing the laborers who temporarily or permanently lost working capability because of age, illness, work-related injuries, maternity, or unemployment.

[6]In a different and more broad sense, social welfare is a general term for the benefits, welfare facilities, and social services provided by the state for the purpose of improving the material and spiritual life of all the community members. The social welfare, in a narrow sense, refers to the basic living security provided by the state to the aged, minors, and disabled who need special care. The social welfare discussed in this book is the narrow one. This special social welfare, mainly provided to the aged, minors, disabled, army soldiers, martyrs, etc., is regulated by the laws and regulations, including the *Law of the People's Republic of China on the Protection of the Rights and Interests of the Aged*, the *Law of the People's Republic of China on the Protection of the Minors*, the *Law of the People's Republic of China on the Protection of the Rights and Interests of the Disabled People, the Regulations on the Military Pensions and Preferential Treatment, The Police Law of the People's Republic of China.*

of pensions and preferential treatments.[7] With the rapid development of the social security system in China, problems such as inadequate governmental involvement in providing social security, the absence of legal institutions safeguarding the social security system, the difficulty of expanding coverage, and so forth have become more pronounced. Bread-and-butter issues and providing public services have now become the primary function of the government.

"Public administration is not only a research topic for administrative law scholars but also something to whose practical development they should be responsive to. Developments in administrative law should stay abreast of those in administrative practices."[8] Under the planned economic system, the government runs enterprises, which in turn run the society. This model, to a certain extent, reduced the burden to provide relief and assistance on the government. But this also meant that the social basis needed for a full-fledged government benefit system was lacking. As a result, the administrative law presents a structure of a single line with the orderly administration as its central point. One example of simplifying the provision of government benefits into a specific administrative act is providing material aid to groups of people in need. The transformation of the economic system has broken the traditional welfare model. "With the development of civilization, there is a rising tendency of the government activities relevant to the public demands and, consequently, the number of the public services has been increasing."[9] The scope of the administrative relief has been expanded to match the concept of orderly administration. The academic study of administrative law, therefore, is tasked with developing a dual-line structure with both maintaining order and providing benefits at the core.

4.2 Government Benefits and Services

A service-oriented government should serve the people and perform public services through specific administrative acts. In other words, the government should actively provide various services so as to give proper living care to citizens and organizations. In China nowadays when transformation is undergoing, the living care as the core content of the construction of the service-oriented government does not merely refer to food, clothing, housing and travelling but also matters related to people's quality of life, including education, medical care, employment, environment, social security, public welfare, and income distribution. The Report of the 17th National Congress of the CPC gave high priority to bread-and-butter issues, including those related to education, employment, healthcare, old-age care and housing.

---

[7]Zhao, Chunling, et al., *The Welfare System and Development of the Social Security in China*, China Business Press, 2008, p. 130.

[8]Carol Harlow (U.K.) and Richard Rawling (U.K.), *Law and Administration*, translated by Yang Weidong, et al., The Commercial Press, 2005, p. 76.

[9]Leon Duguit, *The Transformation of the Public Law*, Translated by Zheng Ge, et al., Liao Hai Press & Chunfeng Literature and Art Press, 1999, p. 50.

1. Understanding the concept of government benefits

The system of government benefits refers to the act of public administration whereby the state provides aid, assistance and services in the forms of funds, material and labor for purpose of meeting citizens' basic survival and developmental needs, protecting their economic interests and promoting social public welfare. It is the basic task of the modern administration to continuously provide various types of relief to the citizens for survival and development. Administration should be the means by which the state welfare is provided so as to satisfy the demands of the society. The government should take various measures of administrative relief to ensure the citizens and organizations obtain proper living care. Living care as the core content of the construction of the service-oriented government does not merely refer to food, clothing, housing and travelling but also the matters related with the quality of people's life, including education, medical care, employment, environment, social security, public welfare, and income allocation.

The Concept of the provision of government benefits is derived from a German term Leistungsvervaltung co-translated by a Taiwan scholar and a Japanese scholar. It was first shown in an article entitled The Administration as the Provider of Services written by Ernst Forsthoff, a German jurist of public law, and published in 1938, in which, Forsthoff proposed the doctrine of living care, that is, to provide services for the purpose of living care to citizens is the core of the modern administration, and the obligation of living care should be performed through the provision of government benefits. Forsthoff asserted that governments should provide relief to those who have established a service relationship with them and whose lives rely on this relation.[10] With the increasing prominence of the idea of human right, the concept of the provision of government benefits has gradually fully developed in the west. Nowadays, the Japanese scholars have a consensus that "the provision of government benefits refers to the public administrative activities of positively promoting and improving people's welfare by the benefiting activities, including providing social economic and cultural services through the public relation facilities or enterprises, and protection and guarantee of livelihood and monetary support through social security and public assistance."[11]

The concept of the provision of government benefits was not introduced to mainland China until fairly recently, so we lag behind the above-mentioned countries and regions in the theoretical study of the subject. The provision of government benefits is still narrowly explained. The provision of government benefits is a general term of related administrative behaviors in China. Generally speaking, administrative relief, also administrative material assistance, refers to a specific administrative act that the relief subjects/providers grant certain property interests or property-related interests, in accordance with relevant laws, regulations, and policies and on the application of the applicants, to the citizens who are aged, ill or not capable of working, or who

[10]Yan Erbao, Reflections on the Provision of Government Benefits: Case Study on the German Administrative Laws of Germany and Japan, *Studies on the Administrative Law*, 2010, vol. 3.

[11]Yang Jianshu, *The General Analysis on the Administrative Law of Japan*, China Legal Publishing House, 1998, p. 329.

are laid-off, unemployed, poor, or suffering from disasters or accidents, no matter natural or man-made. According to this definition, administrative relief is a specific administrative act while the provision of government benefits is a generalization of a kind of administrative activities with the same nature, such as the social security, the offer of the public facilities, the operation of the public business, various kinds of administrative subsidies, and so forth. To carry out the administrative activities mentioned above, a specific administrative act may be done, that is, the administrative subject may perform an act of administrative relief; or, other kind of act may be done, such as rendering administrative agreements or civil contracts, and so forth.[12] To equate the provision of government benefits with administrative relief will directly narrow down the scope and the number of relief receivers of government benefits. Nowadays, the provision of government benefits in China is mainly applied to the poverty alleviation and disaster relief, and so forth the receivers are the poor citizens and the specially designated group of people. As for all the people in China, the provision of public facilities, public service and public welfare is just at the initial stage. Without the obligation of relief provided by law, the citizens' relevant rights and interests would not be recognized and protected by law. Therefore, those who study the provision of government benefits should distinguish between different ways in which such benefits are delivered.

The provision of government benefits corresponds with intervention administration. It is, therefore, remarkably different from the traditional intervention administration in the following aspects: (1) both are different in the theoretical basis. Compared with the traditional power control and order maintenance theories in the administrative law, the provision of government benefits is based on the theory of human right protection, and focuses on the provision of social services and the improvement of social welfare; (2) both are different in effect. The provision of government benefits usually benefits the targeted receivers in some way while intervention administration mostly limits and deprives the concerned person of rights; (3) both are different in the way of acting. The provision of government benefits is realized by means of supplying, securing, funding, and so forth, while intervention administration usually bring adverse impact on the concerned person through punishment, levy, and so forth.[13]

Of course, providing aid and assistance and intervention are not absolutely separated from each other. In fact, they are often intertwined. Just as German scholar Maurer put it, the two are closely linked in the following ways: (1) relief is often provided with the prerequisite of particular obligations, such as responsibility and damages, for instance, scholarship is granted on the condition of excellence in academic study; (2) a measure to be taken may bring damage and relief at the same time since it brings relief to the concerned person but damage to a third party, such as those who also applies for the relief but failed; (3) in some administrative field, the provision of government benefits and intervention administration can interchange

[12] Yan Erbao, Reflections on The provision of government benefits: Case Study on the German Administrative Laws of Germany and Japan, *Studies on the Administrative Law*, 2010, vol. 3.

[13] He Zhengrong, The Development of the Provision of Government Benefits and the Responses to the Theories and System in the Administrative Law, *Academic Forum*, 2007, vol. 11.

with each other, for instance, in terms of environment protection or the ancient town protection, on one hand, construction is limited; on the other hand, financial subsidies are provided; (4) in terms of particular goals, the administration may take the measure of relief or intervention.[14]

2. Principles governing the provision of government benefits

Different from the traditional intervention administration, the provision of government benefits has greater affinity and allure because of its benefit-conferring nature. But we should know that even though the provision of government benefits aims at increasing national welfare, it is part of the function of the administrative power. Hence power abuses and violation of the legal principles, such as principle of fairness, may occur. The provision of government benefits requires governments perform more actively their duties and governments, therefore, need more functions, powers and resources granted to achieve the goal. And this may probably cause the excessive expansion in government power.[15] In the public social space with the battles going on between the public power and the private right, the rights and interests of the citizens are infringed, and even the government becomes omnipotent again. Since governments have more powers in the provision of government benefits than order administration and are even harder to be controlled effectively, abuse of power and violation of the fairness principle in allocation of resources are likely to occur. The efficiency of the provision of government benefits is also an issue of great concern. The Chinese national economic development is in the "middle income trap". There is an obvious danger of the social "welfare trap", which means that the social welfare system exceeds the level of the economic development and become a burden of the finance and the taxpayers.[16] The provision of government benefits requires the government to invest enormous amount of manpower, material and financial resources, which definitely causes the radical increase of costs and, consequently, imposes heavier burden on the taxpayers.

To avoid the drawbacks of the provision of government benefits, there must be limitation and control set over its enforcement. The following policies should be abided by in the process of the enforcement thereof:

(1) The principle of the state subsidiarity, also named the principle of the state supplemental assistance. In accordance with the principle, the state should provide

[14]See Hartmut Maurer (Germany), *The General Theories of the Administrative Law*, Translated by Gao Jiawei, Law Press China, 2000, pp. 9–10.

[15]Jiang Bixin, How do Studies on the Science of Administrative Law Respond to the Practice of the Service-Oriented Government? *Modern Law Science*, 2009, vol. 3.

[16]The emerging-market countries will enter a take-off phase from \$1000 to \$3000 after getting out of the "poverty trap" of GPD \$1000 per person. However, when the GDP reach about \$3000 per person, the conflicts accumulating in the process of rapid development break out together, and the self system and mechanism are badly in need of updating. Many developing countries are plunged into the "middle income trap" due to the reason of unsolvable conflicts of economic development, mistakes in development strategy or external influence, and the economic growth dropping or prolonged stagnation.

the relief to the individuals who cannot manage to obtain the benefits all by themselves. It, therefore, is a minor and supplemental assistance with a characteristic of subsidiarity. The principle set a boundary to the scope of the service provided by the government: the administrative organs should stay away from the matters which can be handled by the citizens, legal persons or other organizations, adjusted by market mechanism, and solved by the administrative organizations or agencies, except for those provided by law.[17] To stress the principle of the state subsidiarity in the provision of government benefits aims at positioning the function of the Chinese government. China is currently in the process of transformation from the omnipotent government to a limited government. The provision of government benefits may put the government in a dilemma: on one hand, the excessive stress on the feature of limitation on the government may hinder the government from performing it duties and, consequently, affect the provision of the public service; on the other hand, too much stress on the governmental obligation of supply may cause retrogression of the times with the omnipotent government. The principle that government-provided benefits are supplemental only, therefore, actually defines the scope of governmental functions.

(2) Principle of law reservation. The principle of law reservation provides that the administrative acts should be in compliance with law, that is, the administrative organs should be found liable when they act unless expressly empowered by law. Under the administrative legal system with intervention administration as a core, the government act should be strictly reserved by law, while, in the field of the provision of government benefits, the adoption of the principle of law reservation has been challenged for the beneficial attribute of the provision of government benefits. In fact, the provision of government benefits may be also detrimental to the rights and interests of the citizens. On one hand, it may cause detriment to fairness since a particular group of people have advantage over their competitors because of the special supply or service they receive from the government and, hence, become privileged, threatening the legal rights and interests of their competitors; on the other hand, the government's refusal to supply may cause direct detriment to the citizens' positive rights, since refusal of supply may cause bankruptcy of enterprises. Refusal to supply scholarship may cause a student to quit his schooling, which has the identical detrimental effect to fairness and property right (requiring a proprietor to install a certain kind of protective devices to their facilities, or requiring a student to follow an order.[18] Therefore, even though beneficial, the provision of government benefits may be detrimental to the basic rights of the concerned person, so it should be subject to the principle of law reservation. However, since the provision of government benefits aims at providing benefits and material assistance to the concerned person, the government need and should be given more room for discretion than intervention

[17]Luo Wenyan, Service-Oriented Government and the Transformation of the Administrative Law: from the Perspective of the Idea of "Good Governance" in the Administrative Law, *Studies in Law and Business,* 2009, issue 2.

[18]Jin Chendong, On the Principle of the Administrative Law Reservation, *Zhe Jiang Social Science*, 2002, issue 1.

administration. Therefore, a breakthrough should be made in the original principle of law reservation. The theory of material matter reservation is applied nowadays in Taiwan, China, where the Interpretation of the Grand Justice of the Judicial Yuan No. 443 states that the provision of government benefits is less regulated by law than limitation of the rights of private party. In case the material matter of public interests is involved, it is natural that control should be made over it by law. The author believes that, in addition to law, the provision of government benefits may be carried out in accordance to the regulatory instruments including the administrative regulations, local governmental regulations, and administrative rules. Meantime, the above administrative regulations, local governmental regulations, and administrative rules should not conflict with the Constitution and law so as to ensure the realization of the governmental functions and satisfaction to the people's needs and avoid detriment to the principle of rule of law.

(3) Principle of proportionality. The principle of proportionality requires the administrative goals objectively match the administrative measures. It forbids the state organs taking excessive measures and ensures that, with the prerequisite of realizing the statutory goals, the state activities should be as little detrimental to the citizens as possible.[19] Due to the limited national resources, the inappropriate or excessive supply to people will cause detriment to the national resource and the public interest, so the principle of proportionality should be applied to the provision of government benefits so as to ensure the relief measures taken is proportionate to the relief goals. Firstly, the relief measures should be helpful to achieve the administrative goals. Secondly, the administrative goals should be achieved in a way that minimum detriment is caused to the public interest or the national resources. Thirdly, the adverse impacts caused by the relief measures should not be obviously disproportionate to the targeted benefits. The provision of government benefits is beneficiary to the concerned person. Special attention, therefore, should be paid to whether the goals can be achieved in the end so as to prevent excessive and insufficient relief. Meanwhile, relief level should match the level of the national economic development.

(4) Principle of equal right protection. This principle means that in the process of enforcement of the administrative power, substantive or procedural, same incidents should be treated in the same way except with rational justification. The supply of administration should not violate the principle of equality. The equal right protection applied in the provision of government benefits means that the state should treat all eligible the relief receiver equally when supplying the relief. No difference should be made in the treatment. All the eligible receivers should have equal right to the relief in both substance and procedures including measures. Meanwhile, the government should take various subjects and the circumstances into consideration and reasonably treat different people and incidents differently so as to achieve genuine and substantial equality.

(5) Principle of trust protection. The principle of trust protection aims at realizing social justice, establishing social security system, constructing the social order of

[19]Chen Xinmin, *Principles of the Administrative Law of China*, China University of Political Science and Law Press, 2002, p. 43.

fairness and justice, protecting the reliance of the poor and those who need special protection on the provision of government benefits and sharing the social risk with them, assisting the private parties in crisis and emergency situation through fairly allocating resources according to law, so as to grant special protection to the disadvantaged people in the society.[20] The principle of trust protection is established on the legal basis that law should protect the reasonable reliance developed by the individuals on the enforcement of public power and the benefits derived from the reliance. It is of particular significance to apply the principle of legitimate expectations to the provision of government benefits, esp. in the aspects of cancellation or rescission of beneficial administrative behavior. Since the provision of government benefits is realized mainly by beneficial administrative behavior, the cancellation and rescission of the beneficial administrative behavior will create direct influence on the public service which the provision of government benefits aims at. Therefore, the effective and legal beneficial administrative behavior generally should not be cancelled, rescinded, or modified for no reason. Where the circumstance has changed and the behavior becomes no longer legitimate, the administrative organ should modify the behavior according to law, but it should compensate the concerned person for any detriment he or she incurs to the benefits derived from his or her reliance on the continuity of the administrative behavior, which is required by both the principle of administration according to law and the principle of trust protection. However, in terms of illegal beneficial behavior, where the administrative organ believes that the concerned person's reliance benefits from the behavior outweighs the protection of the public interest, the administrative organ should not cancel the beneficial administrative behavior and let it continue to exist; where the public interests outweighs the private interest, the administrative organ may cancel the behavior, but it should compensate the concerned person for the detriment incurred to the reliance benefits.

3. The scope of government benefits

The provision of government benefits is essentially the deliverance of benefits to some recipients. It, therefore, necessarily should have definite scope and clearly identifiable beneficiaries. Ever since the concept of the provision of government benefits came into being, its scope of application and the eligibility requirements have been expanding with the social development. According to Ernst Forsthoff, the government benefits that are designed to provide living care should cover the following three areas: (a) public utility, including water, electricity, and gas; (b) domestic transportation; (c) the basic facilities people need to sustain a normal life. Thereafter, of all of the government's administrative duties and tasks, the deliverance of tangible benefits to the citizens has been increasing in proportion. It has also become a research topic for those who study administrative law. Further studies of the theories of administration have been carried out in various countries, and the scope of government benefits and the eligibility criteria have been expanding. At present, in Germany, government

[20] Cheng Zhongmo, *Genera Principles of the Administrative Law (II)*, San Min Book Co., Ltd., 1997, p. 207.

benefits cover such areas as infrastructure, guaranteed provision, social care promotion, information and so forth. In Japan, the provision of government benefits is a public administrative act aimed at improving welfare for citizens. It mainly includes: (a) social administration (social security administration), which generally includes public assistance, social insurance, fully-subsidized pension, social allowance, social welfare, and public sanitation; (b) the administration of government-provided funds and services necessary for sustaining a normal life. These are provided either by public infrastructure facilities or, as in the case of power, gas, water, transportation, postal service, and broadcasting, by state-owned enterprises; (c) the financial aid administration. The administration of financial aid refers to the provision of subsidies, funds, financing services, debt-guaranteeing, and so forth,[21] carried out by administrative subjects by providing particular financial aid to the concerned person performing a particular public service. In China's Taiwan province, the provision of government benefits refers to the function of providing citizens with relief, services, or other benefits,[22] specifically including social insurance, public assistance, supply of basic necessities, occupational training, financial aid, and cultural services.

Today, most Chinese legislations regarding the provision of government benefits pertain to basic necessities, and labor and social security. Such legislations include the Law of the People's Republic of China on the Protection of Disabled Persons, Elderly Rights Law, Education Law, Law of the People's Republic of China on Promotion of Privately-run Schools, Regulation on Pensions and Preferential Treatments for Servicemen, the Regulations on Guaranteeing Urban Residents' Minimum Living Standard, Measures on Administration of Public Relief for Vagrants and Beggars without Any Assured Living Source in Cities, the Interim Measures on Placement of the Chinese People's Liberation Army (PLA) Volunteers Released from Active Service, Measures on Placement of the Soldiers Released from the Military Service, Regulations on the Rural Five-Guarantee Work, and so forth. In terms of legislation, the provision of government benefits in China nowadays mainly focuses on the projects of disaster salvation and poverty alleviation. The concerned person is mainly the poor and special groups of people. The scope of the benefits is too narrow to meet the needs of the development of the provision of government benefits in modern times or what are required to promote economic and social development in contemporary China. Since the beginning of reform and opening-up in China, a socialist market economy has gradually been taking shape. The economic system reform requires the transformation of governmental functions. On one hand, the government should loosen the control over the enterprises, strengthen macroscopic regulation and control, and bring the market into full play. On the other hand, the government should promote social justice by social policies and undertake the responsibility of assisting citizens, and reduce the burden of the enterprises. Therefore, the economic system reform requires the government to stress the function of service, advocate the socialization of service, increase the diversity of service, expand the counterpart of relief,

[21]Murakami Takenori, *Issues on Provision of Government Benefits*; Ogawa Ichiro (ed.) *the Great Modern Administrative Legal System, vol. I*, Yuhikaku Publishing Co., Ltd., 1983, p. 103.

[22]Wong Yuesheng, *The Administrative Law*, China Legal Publish House, 2002, p. 29.

and develop the relief targeted at special disadvantaged group of people into one that serves the whole society. In terms of the relief scope, the expansion should be made from the original "livelihood attention" to "development attention" and even further to "enjoyment attention". The relief should include the paid supply of public facilities and services for people free of any trouble in life as well as the unilateral supply for the people in need of financial assistance in daily life. In terms of the concerned person, the provision of government benefits should be divided into a particular type of relief provided to individuals and the relief provided to the whole social members by building the public facilities, and so forth. In another word, both individuals and the society can be recipients of the provision of government benefits. We should be aware that the provision of government benefits is a general term of various administrative activities carried out by the administrative subject to achieve its fixed goals. It covers the most majority of fields in which the modern welfare state administration can function other than a specific administrative behavior.

4.3 Provision of Government Benefits and the Development of China's Administrative Law

Provision of government benefits emerged when the idea of welfare state was proposed. Covering a broad range whose exact boundaries are constantly changing, it has included not only forms of social security such as social insurance, public assistance, social welfare, but also the provision and management of public service facilities, and supportive measures such as interest-free loans, and budgetary funding. Different types of government benefits can differ considerably in terms of foundational values, legal doctrine rule, and behavior model. This book intends to analyze the challenges faced by and the development outlook of the Chinese traditional administrative law specifically from the perspective of provision of those government benefits that pertain to social security.

1. The development of the rationales for administrative law

The contemporary study of Chinese administrative law began at the end of 1980s on the basis of administrative litigation. Since order administration aimed at maintaining order inevitably cause detrimental effect on the citizens, prevention of abuse of administrative power becomes the primary function of administrative law. The purpose of government benefits is to redress market failure and protect basic human rights by applying means available to the state and the greater society to execute the distribution and redistribution of wealth. As such, social justice is the basic requirement of social security. Under the planned economic system, the bifurcation of the Chinese population into the urban and rural defined people's identity on the basis of their place of residence and in the national economy. Following profound changes to the economic foundation of the society, failure of the government to fill in the gaps led the social security in the rural area to fall into neglect and out of the scope of the government's responsibility. An integrated social security system should be based on the legal identity of citizens, and safeguarding citizens' equal rights to social welfare should be the theoretical basis of social welfare administration. Fairness means equality in the opportunity to receive benefits and equity in benefits received. The government, in providing various kinds of services, should treat all eligible benefits recipients with impartiality in both substance but also procedure and measures taken. Finally, fairness should also manifest itself in efforts to mitigate inequality.

2. The Clarification and differentiation of governmental functions

The right to social welfare, as a right that requires active function of the state, is dependent on the development of the social economy. The development of the provision of government benefits may put the government in a dilemma: unilaterally stressing the limitation on the government may hinder the government from actively performing its duties and, hence, the supply of public service may be adversely affected which cause difficulty for the citizens in livelihood crisis; but excessively stressing the governmental relief responsibility may cause the state fiscal unsustainable and high dependence of the public on the government, and consequently weaken the independence capability of the people and retreat to the times of omnipotent government.

To avoid the crisis of the welfare state, some scholars propose that government benefits must essentially be a form of supplement should. In other words, these benefits must only be provided if and when the recipient is unable for some reason to obtain the same goods and benefits through their own labor and efforts. This principle demarcates the scope of government-provided services: administrative organs should not intervene in those matters that private citizens, legal persons and other organizations can adequately handle by relying on either market mechanism, or the involvement of administrative bodies or intermediary agencies. The only exception will be those for which direct government involvement is provided by law. Under the planned economy, the relationship between the government and the market is distorted, which directly affected the way the governmental functions. The excessively tight control of the government may stifle the enterprises' and individuals' initiative, and hinder the functioning of other social subjects. For instance, in the endowment life insurance, the level of the basic endowment life insurance provided by the state is so high that less space is left for other insurances so that it is difficult to establish a multi-tiered endowment security system. In such a system there would be base endowment provided by the state, supplemental endowment insurance provided by the enterprises, and saving endowment insurance by individuals. In the process of transformation of the omnipotent government under the planned-economic system to the limited government under the market economy, the principle of the state subsidiarity can help clarify the scopes of functions between the government and the market and reduce the strong reliance of the society to the government.

Meanwhile, the obstacles to the execution of the principle the state subsidiarity only should also be taken seriously. On one hand, there is the possibility of inadequate government investment, underfunding of welfare programs, and tension between supply and demand. Over-emphasis of the principle could be used by the government as an excuse to shirk its responsibilities. On the other hand, the tension between the growing diversity of beneficiaries and underdevelopment of social organizations has been escalating. Since a society compatible with the market economy is still some way off, there are some things that the government should get out of and other things that it should get into. Rather than the market incubating a democratic state, it should fall on a powerful government to support and nurture the growth of the society and market.[23] The author believes that, to mitigate such conflict under the principle of the state subsidiarity, only the system of provision should treat people with different needs differentially. Protecting people's right to livelihood, as a basic human right, calls for government leadership. However for protection of the right to development, a higher-level right, both the individuals and the society should play a primary role, while the government a minor and supplementary one.

3. The deepening of the basic principles of the administrative law

The principle of the administration according to law is the basic principle of the Administrative Law of the People's Republic of China. This principle is specified into the principle of law reservation, principle of proportionality and the principle of reliance protection. While all three principles apply to both order administration and benefit administration, they functions somewhat differently in these two areas. For order administration, compliance with the law requires legal basis for all government conduct, that is, the administrative organs should not engage itself in administrative activities unless mandated by law to do so. Under the administrative law system with order maintenance as its core, the government should strictly adhere to the principle of law reservation. Since most of benefit administration are meant to deliver benefits to their recipients, it is given a certain degree of laxity in the application of the principle of law reservation. Any activity which is carried out within the scope of mandate authority provided by the Administrative Organization Law, and in accordance with the budget with the approval of the People's Congress constitutes government-provided benefits even though it lacks the grounds in the Administrative Law."[24] Leniency toward the provision of government benefits in the traditional theory of the administrative law has been corrected. An increasing number of scholars believe that at a time when the objectives of the government and its administrative model have undergone tremendous change, the provision of government benefit should be subject to the principle of law reservation and be allowed to be exempt only in exceptional cases.[25] There are three types of circumstances under which the provision of government benefits may result in "harm". First, recipients

[23]Luo Wenyan, A Service-Oriented Government and the Transformation of the Administrative Law, *Law and Business Studies,* issue 2, 2009.

[24]Weng Yuesheng (Taiwan), *The Administrative Law (I)*, China Legal Publishing House, 2002, p. 670.

[25]Liu Yantao, *Studies on the Provision of Government Benefits*, Shandong People's Publishing House, p. 349; Huang Xuexian, Studies on the Issues Regarding Applying the Principle of Law Reservation to the Provision of Government Benefits, *Jianghai Journal*, 2005, Issue 6; Hartmut Maurer (Germany), *The General Theories of the Administrative Law*, translated by Gao Jiawei, Law Press China, 2000, p. 113.

can be harmed directly when benefits have been cancelled; their terms changed or annulled altogether. Second, fairness in industry competition may be compromised as a result of preferential treatments in taxation by the government toward certain entities. Third, the provision of government benefits might give rise to tension between guarantee for the interests of the individual and the fair sharing of the public interest. For instance, the controversial recent decision by the Ministry of Housing and Urban-Rural Development in permitting to use money in the housing provident fund toward constructing affordable housing for low-income urban residents has been challenged by some scholars, who contend that this is a misuse of the housing provident fund which should be used to benefit only those who contributed towards the fund. The government, according to these scholars, should finance the building of affordable housing by means of regular budgetary funding.[26] The provision of welfare benefits could also lead to violation of right and should be subject to the principle of law reservation. The fact that the provision of government benefits is inherently more changeable than the maintenance of order in terms of both substance of process helps explain the lack of legal rigor of this area of administrative activities. As a country undergoing transformative changes, China is caught in the conflict between legislative and institutional underdevelopment of the provision of government benefit on the one hand and the acute and growing needs of the public for social services on the other. In the absence of relevant laws to guide the provision of benefits, the government has had to resort to policies instead. This necessarily calls for breakthroughs in welfare legislation, and full compliance with the principles of administrative law.

Given the finitude of government resources, both deficiency and excess of benefits amount to wastage of the state resources that harms the public interests. The principle of proportionality, therefore, should be applied, so that means and ends form a rough fit. First, the means of provision should be effective; second, the means chosen should make the most efficient use of the country's resources so as to keep waste to a minimum; third and finally, the adverse effect of the provision of government benefits should not obviously outweigh its beneficial effects, so that just the right amount is delivered that is appropriate given the developmental stage the country is now in.

The jurisprudential basis of the principle of legitimate expectations is that law should protect the trust citizens have in government administration and associated expected benefits insofar as they are rational. The significance of the principle is particularly pronounced in the provision of government benefits, especially in cases involving the cancellation and annulment of benefits. Since the provision of government benefits is executed by means of administrative actions, the cancellation and annulment of these benefits has direct impact on the purpose of public services. Benefits that have already been delivered cannot in principle be cancelled, annulled or modified without reasonable grounds. If changes in circumstances constitute ground for declaring illegitimate any administrative activities retroactively and lead to corresponding adjustments in these activities, individuals whose legitimate expectations

[26]Li Chunhui, *Why Is It Wrong to Construct Security Houses on the Expenses of the Housing Provident Fund?*, http://money.163.com/special/focus479/, latest access on March 3, 2012.

have thereby been frustrated should be compensated for their loss. This is demanded by both the general requirement that administrative activities comply with the law and the particular principle of legitimate expectations. However, in cases of administrative actions that are themselves unlawful that are aimed at providing benefits, if the administrative organ believes that the interests of the affected individuals trump the public interest, then it must not discontinue the actions; But if the public interest is deemed to outweigh the interests of individuals, then the administrative organ may order the cessation of the action, but must also compensate individuals affected.

4. Provision of government benefits promotes the legislation of people's livelihood.

The establishment of the socialist legal system with Chinese characteristics symbolized the establishment of the socialist legal framework consisting of seven bodies of law, including social legislation.[27] An important component of the socialist legal system with the Chinese characteristics is social legislation, which is aimed at protecting the public, especially those who are vulnerable. However, compared with economic legislation, social legislation is underdeveloped in both quantity and quality. All basic institutions are not yet in place. Existing legislations and the other regulatory instruments do little more than defining in broad terms the government's responsibilities and obligations to provide benefits, and tend to lack specifics on issues such as eligibility requirements, scope, standard, enforcement procedure, and delivering measures. In addition, a large number of government benefits have their theoretical basis in policies. Meanwhile, as economic development continues, social conflicts have become more numerous and acute. Governmental legislation no longer focuses exclusively on economic development but is now just as concerned about improving people's livelihood. The need is urgent for government legislation to improve so it can provide guidance on such issues as reform of medical and health care system, the rural endowment life insurance, employment, and the rights and interests of migrant workers. In the State Council's legislative plan for 2012, legislation related to people's livelihood would continue to be the dominant issue. More specifically, work would be ramped up on enacting rules and regulations on such areas as endowment life insurance, medical insurance, new-type rural cooperative medical insurance, national social security funds, basic housing security, among others. In the following several years, legislation related to people's livelihood will continue to be the lawmakers' primary area of focus. The government should expand the scope of such legislation and improve the social security system so as to provide institutionalized legal protection for those groups that need it.

---

[27] *The White Paper on The Socialist Legal System with the Chinese Characteristics* issued by the State Council on Oct. 27, 2011, states that by the end of August, 2011, China has passed and released the current Constitution and 240 laws, which are in effect, 706 administrative laws and regulations, and 8600 local regulations. Different bodies of law which cover all kinds of life in the society have been established, each containing the its basic and principal laws and correspondingly administrative regulations and local regulations. A scientific and harmonious uniformity has been achieved within the legal system. And the socialist legal system with Chinese characteristics has been established.

5. Provision of government benefits augments the diversity of administrative conduct.

Chinese theories on administrative acts are heavily informed by judicial thinking. Distinctions among administrative acts that are specific, abstract, internal and external are made by reference to the relevant type of judicial review and their scope. The traditional theories of administrative law show obvious path-dependency in their approach to the classification of administrative acts. They tend to subsume new types of administrative acts under existing categories to make them easily manageable in judicial practice. This approach obviously constitutes a source of constraints for the provision of government benefits. Compared with the order administration, the provision of benefits is less rigid in that it can be carried out in a variety of ways. For example, the government may do this by itself, or engage other entities in public-private partnerships. Either public law or civil law may be used as the government's basis for discharging its obligations to provide benefits. Compared to having to rely on the government alone, the availability of a range of mechanisms for providing benefits has obvious advantages. Public-private partnerships promote consultation and the commitment to contracts, but it also makes it more difficult to define the essential properties of contracts according to public law or contracts according to civil law. Since the scope of government-provided benefits grows as the magnitude of state welfare expands, it has become increasingly difficult for all types of administrative acts to be covered exhaustively by microscopically-focused classifications. The only solution to this problem is to replace this with a classification method that focuses more on the more macroscopic and what is at a higher level of abstraction.

The provision of government benefits has engendered the shift from a highly centralized model of governance with the government at the center to a model featuring multiple centers. Instead of being solely and fully responsible for providing benefits directly, the government is now also responsible for guaranteeing the delivery of benefits. This role change from the entity that provides benefits to the entity that oversees and guarantees the provision of benefits has not only helped to reduce its fiscal burden, but also placed increased demands on the government to provide oversight and guarantee. Meeting these demands has presented a challenge to the government. On one hand, lax oversight has resulted in inadequate protection for the interests of a third party and weakening force of the law. In addition, the government's shirking its responsibilities, lowered efficiency, increases in costs, and public-private collusion for purpose of making illegal gains are all known to have happened. On the other hand, traditional thinking about administrative law has long become outdated given the diversity of delivery methods for government benefits,[28] making government oversight system reform increasingly necessary. Such reform will no doubt give rise to debates about the legitimacy and efficacy of different ways in which the government discharges its duty of oversight. For instance, at the center of the case involving social security that took place in Shenzhen in 2009 was a dispute about whether it should be considered an instance of administrative law enforcement or execution

[28]Cheng Mingxiu (Taiwan), *The Administrative Act and the Theories of Legal Relations*, New Sharing Culture Enterprise Co. LTD., p. 139.

of a contract.[29] Genuine progress in oversight can only be achieved by improving the government's own capacity, increasing public participation, promoting public-private cooperation and collaboration.

6. The provision of government benefits enhances administrative procedure rigor.

With a government which had limited aims and was equipped with weak means transforming into a modern administrative state, the elaboration of the concept of due process has become the main way to reposition constitutionalism.[30] Risk management and welfare improvement are the two functions of provision of government benefits. Given the considerable room for discretionary judgment in providing government benefits, citizens rely more on due process in the field of social laws. Compared with the maintenance of order administration, the provision of government benefits has a tighter organic connection with due process, which plays an especially important role in safeguarding citizens' welfare rights in practice and preventing abuse of power. The diversity of delivery mechanisms cannot easily be accommodated by a single set of procedural requirements.

There are generally two ways for government benefits to reach those who are eligible to receive it: with or without an application from them. In practice, due to information asymmetry, insufficiency or inaccuracy on their part, many of the eligible failed either to file an application at all or to submit it on time. Rigid adherence to rules of application procedure could, therefore, be detrimental to eligible beneficiaries. Currently the law contains no relevant provisions pertinent to this. We believe the author suggests the government should not only be obligated to provide comprehensive and accurate information in a timely manner but also be held accountable should eligible applicants fail to submit their applications on time because of dereliction of duty in this area on the part of the government and held liable for any such application delay or failure due to lack of information or insufficiency of information service provided.

---

[29]The workers of Shenzhen Social Security Bureau repeatedly pretended to be patients in the health centers in Shenzhen including the Second Health Center located to the north of Lian Hua, producing the medical insurance certificates bearing photos of the certificate holders who look extremely like the pretending patients. Then the Bureau punished the health centers for the doctors' failure to check the medical insurance certificates. The event caused a stir in the country and was deemed by some media as "entrapment". The Shenzheng Social Security Bureau responded that the Social Security Bureau is authorized to supervise and administrate the hospitals. Hospitals provide medical service and the insured accept it. The Social Security Bureau, which is entrusted by the insured, supervises and checks, pursuant to the agreements with the medical insurance companies, whether the designated medical institutions provide medical service pursuant to the agreement or whether the social security funds are abused. The Social Security Bureau dealt with the designated medical institutions pursuant to the stipulations of the two parties. The punishment imposed by the Social Security Bureau on the designated medical institutions for the breach of contract is not law enforcement but a contractual act. Shenzhen Social Security Bureau Charged of Entrapment for Committing Inspection by Its Workers Pretending to be Patients, *Yangcheng Evening*, http://news.sohu.com/20091118/n268304235.shtml, Last visit March 3, 2012.

[30]Jerry L. Mashaw, *Due Process in the Administrative State*, translated by Shen Kui,Higher Education Press, 2005, p.1.

The procedural due process is also critical in the provision of government benefits. In terms of beneficiaries, it would be a case of tort if the government disqualifies somebody for receiving government benefits thereof without due process. In accordance with the Chinese administrative law, hearing is applied in deciding cases involving administrative sanction, administrative permit, and so forth. However,in the laws regarding provision of government benefits, such as the Social Insurance Law and the Regulations on Guaranteeing Urban Residents' Minimum Living Standard, no similar provisions are available according to which that the relevant parties affected have the right to hearing before decisions are made on the termination of the such things as enjoyment of insurance or the provision of money or property needed to maintain the payment of minimum living allowance. Rejection of the application for beneficial relief or the cancel of the beneficiaries' qualification are disadvantageous to those affected, who should be given the opportunity to so that the relevant parties' statement and argument can be heard in a hearing.

Questions such as whether decisions to cancel or rescind benefits apply retroactively, and whether beneficiaries should return what they have already received concerns legitimate expectation. Most current laws provide that in cases in which government benefits, in cash or kind, have been claimed through misrepresentation or any kind, the government should recover the benefits, and in addition, impose fines and other forms of penalty. In other circumstances, it is at the discretion of the administrative organs whether the benefits that have already been dispensed would be recovered. In some countries, compared with other kinds of general-purpose benefits, government benefits to the needy and vulnerable are subject to more stringent requirements when it comes to decisions to cancel or to rescind. Among those countries, some no long require recipients to return the benefits even after the pertinent administrative order has been cancelled.[31] For instance, in the German Social Administrative Procedure Act legitimate expectation is subsumed under the principle of sozialstaat. On one hand, such principle takes full consideration of the special condition of the needy and vulnerable and the raison d'être of administrative law, and give them the benefit of the doubt whenever possible; but on the other hand, the same principle also imposes strict requirement on those who try to obtain benefits by gaming the system. In sum, the aim is to make sure that legislations in the area of government benefits reflect two fundamental principles: personal responsibility and mutual assistance.[32] We suggests that in China's administrative law, decisions about whether to recover benefits that have been de facto dispensed should aim at a proper balance between the interest of the public and legitimate expectation of the beneficiaries, who are, after all, from disadvantaged groups.

[31] Jiang Bixin and Shao Changmao, The Reform of Sharing Right, the Provision Procedure of Government Benefits and the Administrative Reform, *Administrative Law Review*, issue 4, 2009.

[32] Sun Naiyi (Taiwan), The Protection of the Reliance benefits of the Beneficiaries in the Social Welfare Administration: Lessons learned from the German Social Administrative Procedure Act, *Fu Ren Legal Science*, issue 37, June, 2009.

7. Provision of government benefits adds to the types of administrative litigation

Within China's the current legal system, dispute resolution in the provision of government benefits is settled through such measures as administrative review and administrative litigation. The main purpose of the Administrative Litigation Law of the People's Republic of China, promulgated at the end of 1980s, is to protect the rights of concerned individuals from being infringed upon as a result of the abusive exercise of administrative power. So far as the provision of government benefits is concerned, while some articles, such as No. 11 on benefits for the disabled and death gratuity and No. 68 on compensation in administrative disputes, do provide legal basis for administrative litigation, this is still a distinctly difficult area for legal practitioners in particular. Issues of contention include who have the "standing" to file a lawsuit, which public or civil laws are applicable in any particular case, the burden of proof in a case involving government benefits, and sentencing decisions. For a long time, litigation involving administrative contract has been in a kind of legal limb. While its use continues to increase, litigations in this area face both theoretical and practical difficulties, leaving a large number of disputes resolved unsatisfactorily, and the interests of concerned parties without proper protection. In addition to demands for dispensation of benefits, there are now also litigation cases in which the litigants demand the defendant to cease or abstain from a particular course of action. These all pose challenges to the traditional understanding of administrative litigation as a means for defending people's rights. The emergence of administrative actions in the area of provision of government benefits and the alternate use of a variety of administrative activities facilitate the maturation of the classification of administrative litigations. The Law of Administrative Procedures should be modified to clarify who can sue, the scope of acceptable cases, rules about burden of proof, applicable laws, sentencing guidelines, and other important questions.

Chapter 5
Legislation of Due Process and Administrative Procedure

5.1 Formation of the Concept of Due Process: Imported Practice of Public Hearing

1. Institutionalization of Public Hearing System.

The traditional Chinese way of administrative management was to "value substance over procedure". This began to change after the adoption of the Law of Administrative Procedure in 1989. Article 54 of this Law provides: "The People's Court may annul a specific administrative act entirely or partially if the act was undertaken in violation of legitimate procedure." Since then, procedure issues of administrative acts have gradually drawn more attention. The Administrative Penalty Law enacted in 1996 was the very first statute in China that regulated operation of administrative acts. It incorporated both substantive and procedural rules and the concept of procedures of administrative act began to be understood and accepted by the public. Public hearing procedure was first established by the Administrative Penalty Law to protect the object of an administrative act, which drew broad public attention and its application gradually expanded in various aspects of administrative practice. The author's research of current laws and regulations in force[1] showed that from 1996 when the Administrative Penalty Law was enacted to 2012, provisions regarding public hearings were found in 8 statutes,[2] 25 administrative regulations[3] and 50 other forms of

[1] The data in this Chapter are mainly from the database of China Laws and Regulations of Chinalawinfo (of the Peking University?).

[2] These include *Price Law* (1997), *Legislation Law* (2000), *Law on Appraising of Environment Impacts* (2002), *Administrative Permission Law* (2003), *Foreign Trade Law* (2004), *Public Security Administration Punishments Law* (2005), Urban and Rural Planning Law (2007).

[3] These include the *Telecommunications Regulations* (Sept. 25, 2000), *Regulations on Public Cultural and Sports Facilities* (June 26, 2003), *Anti-Dumping Regulations and Safeguard Measures*, *Anti-Subsidy Regulations* (March 31, 2004), *Regulations on Grievance Petitions* (Jan. 10, 2005) etc.

© Social Sciences Academic Press and Springer Nature Singapore Pte Ltd. 2018
H. Ma and J. Wang, *Building a Government Based on the Rule of Law*,
Research Series on the Chinese Dream and China's Development Path,
https://doi.org/10.1007/978-981-13-0999-1_5

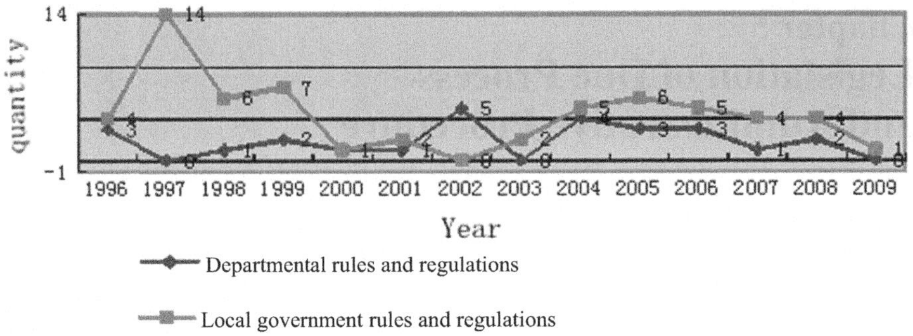

Fig. 5.1 Comparison of numbers of rules and regulations released by government agencies vs. local governments, 1996–2009

directive documents. In addition, public hearing procedure was mentioned in 228 departmental regulations, of which 55 regulations involved administrative penalties, 33 on administrative permits, 19 on administrative legislation and rule-making, 5 on administrative review, and 116 on other issues. Among the 26 departmental regulations with subject title of "public hearing", 6 were regarding general rules of public hearings and the rest 20 regulations were regarding hearings of specific administrative acts (8 on administrative penalty public hearing; 6 on administrative permit public hearing, 5 on investigative public hearing; and one on price adjustment public hearing). The author also found 738 local legislative statutes containing public hearing provisions. Among the 11 local legislations that had the term "public hearing" in the subject-title, 9 were concerned about public hearing for legislative process and 2 for administrative penalty matters.[4] And for rules and regulations of the local government, 554 rules and regulations mentioned public hearing, among which 61 had the term "public hearing" in the title (with 28 on public hearing for administrative penalty; 9 on administrative permit; 8 on decision- making process; 4 on administrative review; 4 on price adjustments; 3 on rule- making; 2 on commercial site establishment; and 2 on general provisions of public hearings.)[5] This book involves 6755 pieces of local rules and regulations that mention "public hearing" in their texts, among which 195 documents bearing "public hearing" in the title (28 on administrative penalties; 39 on administrative permits; 33 on price adjustments; 37 on major decision making; 22 on grievance petitions; 9 on administrative review; 6 on planning; 4 on general provisions of public hearing,[6] and 17 on others).

Figure 5.1 illustrates a comparison of departmental rules and rules and regulations made by the local governments within certain period of time.

The figure indicates that administrative public hearing in China was first provided in law in 1996.

[4]Jiangsu Province and Shanghai Municipality.

[5]Shenzhen City and Ningxia Hui Autonomous Region.

[6]The cities of Xinyu, Wenzhou, Huaian, and Jiangmen.

It is also shown that the earliest legislation of public hearing in China began in 1996. Thereafter the local governments were more active in making public hearing rules, which reached its peak in 1997. By that time 14 local governments had enacted and promulgated special regulations regarding public hearing procedure, whereas the public hearing regulations of central government agencies under the State Council did not reach its peak until 2002.

In terms of the subject-matter of public hearing rules, from 1996 to 1997, the majority of the rules were regarding public hearings on administrative penalties. After 1998, public hearings were made mainly on administrative penalties and price adjustments. After 2004, more and more rules regarding hearings on administrative permits and decision-making process have been formulated. The principal public-hearing regulations contained in the Administrative Penalty Law, the Pricing Law and the Administrative Permits Law provided important guidance. There was a common characteristic of the public-hearing rules made by the departments under the State Council and the local governments, i.e. there were few general provisions regarding public hearings, but there were more rules on hearings for specific administrative acts. How come? The reason being more legal basis was available for specific administrative acts such as penalties, permits, and pricing policies. Therefore among public hearing rules most were about administrative penalties, followed by hearings for administrative permits.

According to the author's statistics, 29 provincial-level governments (including provinces, autonomous regions and municipalities directly under the central government) have adopted laws, regulations or directives regarding public hearings, which account for 94% of all the provincial-level governments in China. Among the 29 provinces, only Yunnan provincial government used directive document; all the rest had public-hearing laws or regulations. At the provincial level, only Henan and Fujian do not have uniform public hearing regulations, but some of the agencies under these two local governments have public hearing procedures for specific matters. Among larger cities, 22 have made rules or directives for public hearings, accounting for 45% of the total; of which 14 only have rules, accounting for 29%. Also 5 local governments empowered agencies to make directives regarding public hearings on particular matters. Thus, on the whole, the imported practice of "public hearing" has been popularized in China, reflected in administrative decision-making, penalties, permits, administrative review, and handling of grievance petitions.

Nevertheless, despite the fact that public hearing procedure has been institutionalized in China, there are still problems, such as selection of public-hearing representatives, disconnection between public hearing and decision-making, and "hearing but no actual listening". These could cast doubts on the value of public hearings. Here the author would use the example of public hearing on pricing policies in the U.S. to shed some lights.

2. Price public hearing in the United States and lessons learned from it.

Public hearing first appeared in the US in 1946. It was first written in the Administrative Procedure Act, in which public hearing as a procedure was clearly defined and public hearing became necessary whenever the relative party's interests are concerned. Nowadays, public hearing can be normally seen in legislative, administrative and judicial procedures. Public hearing is playing a significant role in ensuring the public's right to know and to participate. In the US, public hearing is divided into formal public hearing and informal public hearing. As for the informal public hearing, there is no strict form and procedure, which enhances the flexibility of public hearing in practice. But some of the core principles are still firmly followed.

(1) Diversifying participants and emphasizing participation.

Utility pricing is subject to administrative decision, of which specific procedures are mainly provided in the state law. Mostly price public hearings use informal public hearing procedures, aiming to get most of the public to respond. Price public hearings are characterized with the widest public notice and participation, the clearest suggestions and the simplest procedure. There are various types of participants to public hearing, including applicants for price adjustment and representatives thereof, interested people, and representatives of environment, commerce, labor, and trade associations of which interests could possibly be affected. As for pricing public hearing, consumers' participation is critical. The law authorizes the public advocate to attend the hearing on behalf of the consumers. Individuals are also encouraged to attend the hearing as long as they can prove their interests would be damaged by the price increase of water, electric, gas and telephone. Consumers may attend a public hearing individually or with consumer or other associations. Where a consumer intends to attend a public hearing but knows little of the facts, he or she may apply to attend a meeting, where the situation is introduced, held by the Office of Public Counsel in the region affected by the price increase. Under the American public hearing system, there is no representative required, so an interested person who files an application for participation in accordance with the provisions is permitted in. The hearing usually lasts a few days and sometimes even dozens of days due to the large number of participants. As to some important proposals, public hearings will be held in several areas to ensure the presentation of maximum public comment. For example, before releasing the Clean Water Act in 1972, public hearings, which lasted 44 days, were held in several areas of America and in the afternoon or evening for the convenience of consumer. Although hearings cost much time and expense, they, as procedures of facilitating full exchange of views and information gathering, greatly reduce the resistance of the related policy.

(2) Influential and professional social associations.

In a price public hearing of public utilities, many social associations representing consumer interests not only attend the hearing but also actively encourage consumers' participation to show that the issues in question are related to larger public interests. Social associations can provide the customers, who are willing to attend the hearing, with professional advice, including how to file a public hearing application, how to put forward proposals or give suggestions, how to answer questions and so forth. The existence of a large number of social associations makes possible the participation of people with different interests. In a price public hearing in America, consumer associations are a principal power to safeguard consumer interests. With professional staff and sufficient funds, these associations usually can produce highly technical, logical, and informative suggestions, which may make greater impact on administrative decision-making.

(3) High degree of openness in public hearing.

Public hearings must be held publicly unless the state secrets and security, personal privacy, business secrets and other matters protected by law are involved. When a hearing is to be held, the government organs concerned are required to publish the notice by various means of publication, including newspaper, broadcasting, television and other public media so as to ensure the voice of the interested individuals and organizations are heard to the greatest extent. The organizers will also post the notice of public hearing on the official billboard in the regions affected by the proposed price fluctuation, or send the notice to particular associations and groups by mail or other means. The notice of public hearing includes reference to the date and time, location, agenda of the public hearing and the brief of matters to be heard. In addition, the hearing, which is governed by the state law of open meetings and proceedings, should also follow the provisions regarding the notice of meeting. Some cities and counties also choose the unprovided ways for notification. Subject to the provisions otherwise, the best way is to notify the interested people and regions and allow sufficient time for preparations for the hearing. Generally, the notice of public hearing should be given a week or ten days in advance. The public hearing examiners are usually conducted by the administrative judges or the members of the public utilities commission on a relatively independent and highly authoritative basis. At the beginning of a hearing, the specific procedures and disciplines of public hearing are announced. In case the large number of witnesses willing to testify is anticipated, each witness will be limited in terms of the time for his testimony and required to be consolidated and direct. The whole process of public hearing should be recorded and noted down, ensuring it accessible to the public for consultation and duplication. Principle of Openness should be implemented through the whole process. The hearing should be live televised and broadcasted and afterwards accessible to the public. To ensure that witnesses take the testimony serious in the hearing, the public hearing examiners would ask the witness, regardless of their willingness, whether he will take an oath before stating his views, which is called sworn statement. Generally, the sworn statements gain more attention from the decision-makers, which would make the witnesses responsible for their opinions as well as reduce malicious interference and inefficiency of hearing.

(4) Lessons learned from the United States in pricing hearing.

Public hearing has become an indispensable process to American administrative procedures. In spite of the absence of specific statutory requirements for public hearing, public hearing process is applied to nearly all bills submitted. Especially, the significant administrative legislations and decisions are rarely passed and released without public hearing.

Firstly, experts' participation in the public hearing can improve the scientific level of legislation and decision-making. In the highly specialized and technical fields, experts of the field in question can provide legislators and decision-makers with scientific advice before legislation is made.

Secondly, a wide range of participants and deep involvement thereof in the public hearing may make it possible to collect more opinions from the public and improve the democracy of decision making. In America, there is no requirement of public hearing representatives in the public hearing of legislation or decision-making. Whoever can prove that his or her interests will be affected by the price increase is entitled to apply for attending the hearing. The representatives of different interests can fully express their opinions, which can make the administrative agencies better informed. Due to the wide range of participants, challenges are not usually made to the qualification of representatives and alike in China's public hearings of pricing. Besides, in America, many public hearings are attended by the representatives of well-developed social associations. These representatives are comparatively professional, which can effectively solve the problem of information asymmetry.

Thirdly, high-degree of transparency in hearings makes it possible for the public to exercise effective all-round oversight of decision-making process, which can better protect the interests of the people concerned, and also make it easier for all parties involved to accept the results of the public hearing. In America the laws especially emphasize the necessity of openness of the decision-making process. The Freedom of Information Act protects the confidentiality of internal information exchange within an agency and among different agencies during the process of discussion, but once a decision is made, the documents on which the decision is based must be immediately made accessible to the public for its effective oversight of the process and the basis of the decision made. In addition, state laws regarding freedom of information, open meetings, public records also provide that all meetings of important decision-making must be held publicly unless involving state secrets, trade secrets, privacy and other matters provided by law. The public, therefore, can be well informed of the process and background information of government decision-making, which is critical for the public to understand government decisions, and to reduce resistance of policy implementation due to misunderstanding caused by information imbalance held by one side.

5.2 A Breakthrough Measure of Uniform Administrative Procedure Legislation: The Rules of Hunan Province on Administrative Procedures

It is well-known that since the passage of the Administrative Litigation Law the demand for enacting an administrative procedural law has not ceased. In recent years, many representatives at the National People's Congress (NPC) and the Chinese People's Political Consultative Conference (CPPCC) kept submitting bills and proposals, demanding for enacting the administrative procedural law. In 2003, enactment of this law was included in the five-year legislation plan of the Standing Committee of the 10th National People's Congress, but it has not been materialized due to various reasons, one of which is that the academia and the functionaries' circle have different opinions on whether China is ready for making such a legislation. A breakthrough was made in Hunan province by adopting the Rules of Hunan Province on Administrative Procedures (hereinafter as the Hunan Rules), which filled in the blank and undoubtedly has boosted the administrative procedure legislation at the provincial and the national level. However, under the current Chinese legal system, the administrative procedure legislation still lacks empirical analysis. This paper aims to draw an overview sketch of administrative procedure legislation through searching, sorting out and analyzing all current laws, regulations, and provisions in this regard.

The authors used the Hunan Rules as a model version and, selected keywords of important procedures contained in the Human Rules for a comprehensive search to find out current laws and regulations on administrative procedures and the developing trend of administrative procedure legislation. Compared with other laws and regulations regarding administrative procedures, the Hunan Rules was the first statute whose title expressly bore the term "administrative procedure", constituting a landmark in the area of administrative procedure legislation. It's a relatively comprehensive statute, covering the procedures of administrative decision-making, regulatory rule-making, administrative law enforcement, special administrative acts and emergency response, public hearings, administrative information disclosure, oversight of administration, and accountability. Others were less comprehensive, covering only either part of the administrative acts or a particular administrative procedure. The Hunan Rules contained nine chapters with 178 articles: Chapter I regarding general principles; Chapter II regarding subjects of administrative procedures; and Chapters III–IX regarding specific provisions of administrative procedures. This paper selected 11 keywords from the text of Hunan Rules for analysis, which were the procedure of administrative decision-making; regulatory instruments; administrative law enforcement procedure; administrative contracts, administrative guidance, administrative ruling, administrative mediation of special administrative acts; administrative public hearing, administrative information disclosure; oversight of administration; and accountability mechanism.[7]

This paper used "Chinalawinfo: The Retrieval System of China Law" developed by the Peking University as the search repository, which contained more than 150,000 legal documents since 1949. The search repository was divided into 21 sub-databases, including 11 major databases, 10 reference databases, covering almost all aspects of law and legal text resources. It was regarded as one of the most comprehensive database of law in terms of its contents. This paper primarily relied on two sub-databases. One was the Database of China's Laws, Regulations, Departmental Rules, and Judicial Interpretations, totaling 16,211 documents passed and released

[7]Given the characteristics of terms in the administrative legislations, the paper, in analysis of some of the administrative procedures, also searches the words which are related to the keywords for information retrieval.

by the (Standing Committee of) National People's Congress, the State Council and its departments, the Supreme People's Court and the Supreme People's Procuratorate. The other was the Database of China's Local Statutes, Regulations, and Other Regulatory Instruments, totaling 295,069 documents adopted and promulgated by the standing committees of the local people's congresses and governments of provinces, autonomous regions, municipalities directly under the Central Government, provincial capital cities or the larger cities approved by the State Council and some county-level cities. Two retrieval methods were applied in the study, searching the keywords in titles and searching the keywords in full texts. The objects of the study were valid China's laws and regulations. Thus, "current and valid" were the criteria. Unless otherwise noted, the issuance time of the referred legal documents in this paper, is consistent with the date of issuance marked in the database. The regulatory instruments retrieved for the study were issued prior to or on July 31, 2009.

1. Administrative Decision-Making.

Section One of Chapter III of the Hunan Rules provides procedures of administrative decision-making on significant issues. The authors, used keywords of "procedure of administrative decision-making" and "administrative decision-making on significant issues" for full-text searching and found no current laws available.[8] However there were two regulations on procedure of administrative decision-making: one was the Decision of the State Council on Strengthening Administration according to Law in the Municipal and County Governments (May 12, 2008), which aimed to improve the administrative decision-making mechanism of municipal and county governments; the other was Notice of the State Council on Distributing the Outline Regarding Comprehensive Promotion of (effective on March 22, 2004), which advocated to improve administrative decision-making procedure. Two departmental rules provided that public hearings should be held before an administrative decision was made when major public interests were involved and provided procedures of public hearing.[9] Seventy-four department-level directives required establishing and improving administrative decision-making procedure and mechanism. Some had specific provisions regarding expert advisory opinion in public hearing. These government agencies included 15 agencies under the State Council, which were: Ministry of Land and Resources, Ministry of Information Industry, Ministry of Finance and Ministry of Agriculture, General Administration of Quality, Inspection and Quarantine, State

[8]There is a law prescribing decision-making procedure. Article 71 of the Law of the People's Republic of China on the State-Owned Assets of Enterprises provides that where a director, supervisor or senior manager of a state-invested enterprise commits any of the following acts, which has caused losses of state-owned assets, he shall be liable for compensation according to law; if he is a state functionary, he shall be subject to a sanction according to law: 6) making a decision on a major matter of the enterprise in violation of the procedures for decision-making as prescribed by laws, administrative regulations and enterprise bylaws.

[9]*The Public Hearing Rules of Commission of Science, Technology and Industry for National Defense* (Dec. 25, 2006) and the *Public Hearing Rules of China Food and Drug Administration* (for Trial Implementation) (Dec. 30, 2005).

Administration of Taxation and State Forestry Administration, State Administration of Grain, and the State Oceanic Administration.[10]

There were two local government regulations which explicitly provided procedure for administrative decision-making. One was the Rules of Shenzhen City on Prevention of Professional Crimes (effective April 1, 2005), of which Article 9 provided that the government and its agencies shall abide by the law in administration; establish and improve procedures of administrative decision-making and permit examination; standardize work process; make government affairs public; and enhance transparency of administrative actions. The other was the Rules of Datong City on Administrative Law Enforcement Responsibility (effective July 1, 2004), of which Article 13 provided that administrative law enforcement agencies shall establish public hearing system of administrative decision-making and that significant decisions involving public interests shall be subject to public hearing. The said public hearing shall abide by the principles of openness and freedom of attendance by the public, etc.

In recent years, the local governments had been attaching more and more importance to procedure of administrative decision-making on significant issues. Seven governments at the provincial level and three governments at the level of larger city had enacted rules exclusively regarding the procedure of decision-making on significant issues.[11] Many local governments have provided administrative decision-making procedure with directive documents, totaling 190 according to the study. Among them, 42 directives clearly used the term of "important decision-making" or "administrative decisions on significant issues" in their titles, and specifically provided for expert consultancy, notice publication, hearing, and evaluation. Among the 42 directives, 3 were adopted by the provincial governments, namely Yunnan, Heilongjiang and Sichuan provinces[12]; 6 by departments under the provincial govern-

[10]The Author searched the key word of "administrative decision" on a text basis for information retrieval and makes analysis of the contents of each instruments.

[11]By keyword searching, the terms of "administrative decision-making procedure on significant issues" and "decisions on significant issues", the author finds that, in addition to the *Administrative Procedural Rules of Hunan Province*, there are also the *Provisions of Qinghai Province on the Procedures of Administrative Decision-Making on Significant Issues by the People's Governments* (Oct. 2, 2009), the *Provisions of Jiangxi Province* on the Procedures of Administrative Decision-Making on Significant Issues by the People's Governments at and above the County Level (Aug. 20, 2008), *Provisions of Tianjin Municipality on the Procedures of Administrative Decision-Making on Significant Issues by the People's Governments* (May, 23, 2008), *Interim Provisions of Guangxi Zhuang Autonomous Region on the Procedures of Administrative Decision-Making on Significant Issues by Administrative Organs* (Nov. 26, 2007), *Interim Provisions of Gansu Province on the Procedures of Administrative Decision-Making on Significant Issues by the People's Governments* (March, 19, 2007), *Provisions of Chongqing Municipality on the Procedures of Administrative Decision-Making on Significant Issues by the People's Governments* (Nov. 1, 2005, and the provisions issued by larger cities, including *Provisions of Shantou City on the Scrutiny of Administrative Decisions by the People's Governments* (Aug. 28, 2008), *Provisions of Anshan City on the Legitimacy of Demonstration Procedure of Administrative Decision-Making on Significant Issues by the People's Government, Provisions of Kunming City on the Procedures of Administrative Decision-Making on Significant Issues by the People's Governments* (Nov. 23, 2004).

[12]*Decisions of the People's Government of Yun Nan Province on the Implementation at the County Level within the Province of the Four Systems Including Public Hearing on Decision-Making on the*

ment; 32 by municipal governments; and one by the department under the municipal government.[13] The Provisions of Shantou Municipal People's Government on Basic Procedures of Administrative Decision-Making on Significant Issues of April 18, 2002, was one of the earliest relevant directives. Since 2005, more similar directives had been adopted. According to the authors' statistics, 10 provinces, autonomous regions and municipalities directly under the central government and 13 larger cities made specific provisions for procedures of administrative decision-making on significant issues, accounting for 32% of the provinces, autonomous regions and municipalities,[14] and 27% of larger cities.[15]

2. The Regulatory Instruments and Administrative Law Enforcement.

Section Two of Chapter III of the Hunan Rules provided procedures for making regulatory instruments. The authors keyword-searched "regulatory instrument" for information retrieval and found one regulation Notice of the State Council on Further Regulating Rules and Regulatory Instruments Involving Foreigners (Nov. 29, 2006). There are three agencies under the State Council, which had rules or regulations regarding the procedures of making or "file for record" of regulatory instruments,

Signification Issues, Publication of Important Matters, Notification of Work Priorities, and Consultation of Government Affairs (Feb. 25, 2009), *Notice of the People's Governments of Heilongjiang Province on Provisions of Heilongjiang Province on Issuance of the Regulations on Administrative Decisions Making on Significant Issues by the People's Governments* (June 26, 2006), *Notice of the People's Governments of Sichuan Province on the Implementation Measures of Sichuan Province for Expert Consultancy and Demonstration of Administrative Decision Making on Significant Issues by the People's Governments (for Trial Implementation)* (Dec. 27, 2004).

[13]For instance, *Provisions of Xi'an City on the Procedures of Administrative Decision-Making on Significant Issues by the People's Governments* (Feb. 20, 2009), *Provisions of Yinchuan City on the Expert Consultancy and Demonstration, Disclosure and Hearing for the Procedures of Administrative Decision-Making on Significant Issues by the People's Governments* (Nov. 3, 2008), *Interim Provisions of Huizhou City on for the Procedures of Administrative Decision-Making on Significant Issues (Sept. 8, 2008), Provisions of Xinyu City on for the Procedures of Administrative Decision-Making on Significant Issues by the People's Governments* (2008.08.28), *Notice of Hangzhou Municipal Governments on Further Improving the Principles and the Procedures of Administrative Decision-Making on Significant Issues Concerning the Economic and Social Development* (April. 16, 2007), *Implementation Measures of Chaoyang City for the Procedures of Administrative Decision-Making on Significant Issues by the People's Governments* (Jan. 31, 2007), *Provisions of Benxi City on for the Procedures of Administrative Decision-Making on Significant Issues by the People's Governments* (May 24, 2006).

[14]The ratio shown in this paper is calculated on the basis of the number of provisions with title bearing the selected keywords for searching, that is, the special administrative procedure legislations with the keywords in the title rather in the text.

[15]Currently, in China, there are thirty one provincial governments (for the convenience of calculation, Taiwan province will not be counted in), forty nine "comparatively large cities", which include 27 provincial capital cities, 4 Special Economic Zones, and 18 other cities approved by the State Council. The State Council has approved 19 cities as the "comparatively large city" for four times (Chongqing was upgraded to the municipality in March, 1997.), including 13 cities including Tangshan, Datong, Baotou, Dalian, Anshan, Fushun, Jilin, Qiqihar, Qingdao, Wuxi, Huainan, Luoyang and Chongqing approved in October, 1984; Ningbo in March, 1988; Zibo, Handan and Benxi in July, 1992; and Suzhou and Xuzhou in April, 1993.

including Provisions Regarding Procedures of Making Regulatory Instruments by Operational Departments of the General Administration of Civil Aviation of China (Sept. 10, 2007); Measures for Review of Legality of Regulatory Instruments Regarding Land Resources Management (Nov. 27, 2006); and Measures for Filing Regulatory Instruments for the Record by the Ministry of Energy (Oct. 5, 1990), and five ministry-level regulatory instruments issued by the Ministry of Railroad, Ministry of Foreign Trade and Economic Corporation, Ministry of Justice, Ministry of Communications, and the State Administration of Foreign Exchange.[16] Some other agencies also formulated departmental rules regarding procedures for adopting, publishing and "file for record" of regulations and other regulatory instruments, which was not discussed in this paper due to irrelevance.

There were 15 local regulations which had the term "regulatory instrument" in the title, of which 14 were made by provincial governments and one by a larger city government.[17] These local statutes mainly regulated "file for record" procedures of regulatory instruments. In addition, 69 local government regulations had the term "regulatory instrument" in the title, of which 14 were regarding both "the making and 'file for record' procedures of regulatory instruments"; 17 regarding "management of regulatory instruments"; 8 regarding "the formulating procedure of regulatory instruments"; 21 specially for "filing for rerecord of regulatory instruments"; and 9 for other procedures including "supervision, sorting out, interpretation, confirmation and notification; and objection review". In terms of administrative level, 38 regulatory instruments were adopted by provincial governments,[18] and 31 by larger city governments. Among the rules and regulations made by the local governments, the earlier ones were the Rules of Ningbo City on "File for Record" of Regulatory Instruments released on April 1, 1990, and Rules of Tangshan City on the "File for Record" of Regulatory Instruments of Administrative Agencies released on Dec. 1, 1990. Among the local regulatory instruments, 159 were regarding the "procedure of the rule-making", and 129 regarding the procedure of "file for record"; and 18 regarding procedures of both the rule-making and "file for record". According to the author's statistics, all of the provincial governments and governments of 43 larger

[16]*Notice of Ministry of Railways on Further Regulating the Formulation of Rules and Regulations and Other Regulatory Instruments by Ministry of Railways* (Sept. 07, 2003), *Measures of the Ministry of Foreign Trade and Economic Cooperation for the Drafting of Laws and Administrative Regulations and the Formulation of Ministerial Rules and Regulatory Instruments* (Aug. 1, 2002), *Notice of the State Administration of Foreign Exchange on Relevant Issues Concerning the Formulation of Regulatory Instruments by the Branch at Various Levels on Foreign Exchange Administration* (June 3, 1999), *Provisions on the Filing and Review of the Regulatory Instruments Concerning Transportation* (Sept. 9, 1996), *Reply of the Ministry of Justice on the Issuance of Regulatory Instruments by the Head of Provincial Bureau of Justice* (May 1, 1991).

[17]They are Hubei, Shandong, Qinghai, Fujian, Hunan, Zhejiang, Jiangsu, Guangdong, Sichuan, Anhui, Henan, and Jinan provinces, Guangxi Zhuang Autonomous Region, Tianjin municipality, and Jinan city.

[18]All provincial governments have formulated local regulations and rules regarding the formulation of *regulatory* instruments, among which Gansu, Anhui, Jilin, Shanxi, Xinjiang, and Jiangxi provinces and Tianjin municipality have formulated two local rules, respectively providing the procedure of enactment or the procedure of filing and examination.

cities (88% of the total number of larger cities) had regulated procedures for formulating and/or "file for record" of regulatory instruments through the forms of local regulations, rules or other regulatory instruments.[19]

Chapter IV of the *Human Rules* provided procedures of administrative law enforcement. The Administrative Penalty Law and the Administrative Permission Law of China, as well as the Decision of the State Council on Strengthening Administration by Law in Municipal and County Governments provided detailed procedures of administrative penalty and administrative permit. Among the departmental regulations released by the ministries of the State Council, there are 14 regulations prescribing procedures of administrative law enforcement, covering the aspects of quality control and inspection, surveying and mapping, agriculture, press and publication, transportation, coal, forestry, culture, patent, earthquake, commodity inspection, electric power, and salt industry management. More central departments specifically provided for administrative law enforcement, including warrant for administrative law enforcement, certificates for enforcement, and certificates for investigation and evidence collection. The 153 such departmental regulatory instruments covered the fields of industrial and commercial administration, marine industry, business operation, safe manufacture, certification of products, intellectual property, health, telecommunication, environment, industry and information, air raid defense, etc.

As for the local governments, among 31 local government rules and regulations bearing "administrative law enforcement" in the title, 7 were issued by provincial governments, and the earlier ones included the Provisions of Fujian Province on the Procedure of Administrative Law Enforcement of Aug. 3, 1992, and the Rules of Hunan Province on Administrative Law Enforcement of Sept. 28, 1996.[20] The government of Guangdong province adopted the Regulations of Guangdong Province on Management of Administrative Law Enforcement Team (Sept. 22, 1997); the Standing Committee of the People's Congress of two large cities also passed regulations on administrative law enforcement, namely, the Amendment to the Regulations of Shijiazhuang City on Administrative Law Enforcement (1994) and the Regulations of Urumqi City on Administrative Law Enforcement (Revised in 1996).

In addition to the Human Rules, 153 local government rules and regulations had the term "administrative law enforcement" in the title. Among them, 8 governments including Chongqing, Sichuan, Guangxi, Hebei, Hainan, Beijing, Heilongjiang, and Tianjin made general provisions for administrative law enforcement.[21] And the earli-

---

[19]The comparatively large cities which have no special instruments regulating the "formulation of *regulatory* instruments", are Zhuhai, Changchun, Lhasa, Xining, Guiyang, and Kunming.

[20]Included are *Regulations of Hubei Province on Administrative Law Enforcement (Revised 2006)* (Dec. 1, 2006), *Regulations of Liaoning Province on Administrative Law Enforcement* (Jan. 8, 2005), *Regulations of Shanxi Province on Administrative Law Enforcement* (July 29, 2001), *Regulations of Heilongjiang Province on Administrative Law Enforcement* (Dec. 14, 2000), *Regulations of Hunan Province on Administrative Law Enforcement* (Sept. 28, 1996), *Provisions of Fujian Province on the Procedure of Administrative Law Enforcement* (Aug. 31, 1992), *Regulations of Jilin Province on Administrative Law Enforcement* (Revised 1997) (Sept, 26, 1997).

[21]*The Basic Norms of Chongqing Municipality for Administrative Law Enforcement (for Trial Implementation)* (July, 22, 2008), *Provisions of Hebei Province on Administrative Law Enforce-*

est was the Interim Provisions of Sichuan Province on Procedures of Administrative Law Enforcement released on Oct. 13, 1989. The government of Yunnan and Hainan provinces also adopted rules on administrative law enforcement for certain matters.[22] The government of Hubei province passed Measures of Coordinated Dispute Settlement in Administrative Law Enforcement (April 13, 2006). Additionally 20 provincial governments made rules on special administrative law enforcement,[23] Among the 7 larger cities that made general rules on administrative law enforcement, the earliest was the Interim Rules of Jinan City on Administrative Law Enforcement issued on Oct. 14, 1991.[24] Also 4 larger cities adopted rules specifically for mechanism of dispute settlement regarding administrative law enforcement[25]; 6 large city governments adopted administrative law enforcement warrant certificate rules[26]; and 3 large cities adopted the procedure of agent administrative law enforcement.[27] Dalian city adopted the Methods of Case File Management in Administrative Law Enforcement

ment and Administrative Law Enforcement Supervision (Nov. 28, 2003), *Provisions of Hainan Province on Administrative Law Enforcement and Administrative Law Enforcement Supervision* (Dec. 8, 1999), *Provisions of Guangxi Zhuang Autonomous Region on the Procedure of Administrative Law Enforcement* (Dec. 3, 1997), *Notice of the* Legislative *Affairs Office of Tianjin Municipal Government on the Implementation of Six Working Rules for Administrative Law Enforcement and Administrative Law Enforcement Supervision* (March 3, 1992), *the Interim Provisions of Beijing Municipality on Administrative Law Enforcement and Administrative Law Enforcement Supervision* (Sept. 24, 1990), *the Interim Provisions of Heilongjiang Province on Administrative Law Enforcement and the Supervision and Inspection of Administrative Law Enforcement* (June 26, 1990), *the Interim Provisions of Sichuan Province on the Procedure of Administrative Law Enforcement* (Oct. 13, 1989).

[22]*Provisions of Yunnan Province on Administrative Law Enforcement Regarding Patent* (May 10, 2005), *the Interim Implementation Measures of Hainan Province for Administrative Law Enforcement and Administrative Law Enforcement Supervision over Pig Slaughter* (March 16, 1999).

[23]Included are Huainan, Changchun, Zhengzhou, Shantou, Wuxi, Nanchang, Hefei, Zibo, Jinan, Suzhou, Nanning, Chengdu, Benxi, Ningbo, Wuhan, Hangzhou, Shenyang.

[24]*Provisions of Qingdao City on Administrative Law Enforcement and Administrative Law Enforcement Supervision (Revised 2007)* (Dec. 29, 2007), *Several Provisions of Development Zone in Nanchang City on Administrative Law Enforcement* (Nov. 20, 2000), *Measures of Nanchang City for Administrative Law Enforcement* (Dec. 6, 2001), *Measures of Guiyang City for the Separation of Investigation and Evidence-Taking from Review and Decision in Administrative Law Enforcement (For Trial Implementation)* (July 13, 1999), *Measures of Xuzhou City for Administrative Law Enforcement and Administrative Law Enforcement Supervision* (Jan. 17, 1998), *Decision of Nanjing Municipal People's Government on Amending the Interim Provisions of Nanjing City on Administrative Law Enforcement and Administrative Law Enforcement Supervision* (1997 Edition) (June, 25, 1997), *Notice of Jinan Municipal People's Government on Issuing the Interim Provisions of Jinan City on Administrative Law Enforcement* (Oct. 14, 1991).

[25]*Provisions of Guangzhou Municipality on Administrative Law Enforcement Coordination* (Dec. 29, 2005), *Measures of Yinchuan Municipal People's Government for Administrative Law Enforcement Coordination* (April 16, 2005), *Measures of Shenzhen Municipal People's Government for Administrative Law Enforcement Coordination* (June 14, 2004), *Measures of Anshan City for the Settlement of Administrative Law Enforcement Disputes* (May 5, 1994)

[26]Xiamen, Zhengzhou, Shenzheng, Qingdao, Xi'an, Chengdu.

[27]*Provisions of Benxi Municipal People's Government on Entrusting Local Tax Invoice Management Agency with Matters of Administrative Law Enforcement* (May, 1, 2009), *Provisions of Shenzhen Municipal People's Government on Authorization of Administrative Law Enforcement against Ille-*

(Jan. 28 2008). Shenzhen City adopted the Provisions on the Management of Subject Notification of Administrative Law Enforcement (May 31, 2003).

Many of the regulations and rules provided procedures regarding partially consolidated power of administrative penalty and procedure of comprehensive administrative law enforcement.[28] Some regulated procedures of urban management such as Zhejiang province and Xi'an, Qingdao, Zhuhai and Xiamen cities.[29] The government of Zhejiang province and Shanghai municipality introduced Measures for Comprehensive Administrative Law Enforcement in Cultural Markets.[30] In addition, governments of Beijing, Tianjin, and Shanghai municipalities and Anhui province introduced rules on partially consolidated power of administrative penalty in urban management.[31] And 21 governments of lager cities like Fushun, Anshan, Guiyang and Harbin, formulated local rules and regulations on the partially consolidated power of administrative penalty or comprehensive urban management enforcement.[32]

Studies by the authors found that 14 provinces, autonomous regions and municipalities directly under the central government, had adopted statutes or regulations on procedures of administrative law enforcement (accounting for 45% of all such regions in China); 20 provincial governments, accounting for 65%, had introduced special rules on administrative law enforcement; 15 larger cities, accounting for 31%, adopted administrative law enforcement rules; 5 provinces (including municipalities directly under the Central Government) and 25 larger cities (accounting for

---

gal Transportation Business (Sept. 26, 2008), Several Provisions of Zhengzhou Municipal People's Government on Entrusting the Matters of Administrative Law Enforcement (Oct. 16, 2007).

[28] The author searched the keyword "comprehensive administrative law enforcement" on a text basis for information retrieval, and then the keywords of "comprehensive administrative law enforcement", "partially consolidated administrative penalty" and "relative centralization" on a title basis among the instruments he had retrieved and made an analysis on the instruments retrieved.

[29] *Regulations of Xi'an City on Comprehensive Law Enforcement on Urban Administration* (Jan. 7, 2009), *Regulations of Zhejiang Province on Partially consolidated Power of Administrative Penalty in Urban Administration* (Sept. 19, 2008), *Regulations of Qingdao City on Partially consolidated Power of Administrative Penalty in Urban Administration* (July 28, 2006), *Regulations of Zhuhai City on Partially consolidated Power of Administrative Penalty in Urban Administration* (Aug. 17, 2005), *Regulations of Xiamen Special Economic Zone on Partially consolidated Power of Administrative Penalty in Urban Administration* (Dec. 2, 2004).

[30] *Measures of Beijing Municipality for the Relative Consolidation of the Power to Impose Administrative Punishment in Urban Management* (Nov. 18, 2007), *Provisions of Tianjin Municipality on Partially consolidated Power of Administrative Penalty in Urban Management* (Jan. 23, 2007), *Measures of Anhui Province for Partially consolidated Power of Administrative Penalty in Urban Management Sector* (June 28, 2006), *Interim Measures of Shanghai Municipality for Partially consolidated Power of Administrative Penalty in Urban Management (Revised 2005)* (June 27, 2005).

[31] *Measures of Beijing Municipality for the Relative Consolidation of the Power to Impose Administrative Punishment in Urban Management* (Nov. 18, 2007), *Provisions of Tianjin Municipality on Partially consolidated Power of Administrative Penalty in Urban Management* (Jan. 23, 2007), *Measures of Anhui Province for Partially consolidated Power of Administrative Penalty in Urban Management Sector* (June 28, 2006), *Interim Measures of Shanghai Municipality for Partially consolidated Power of Administrative Penalty in Urban Management (Revised 2005)* (June 27, 2005).

[32] Included are Huainan, Changchun, Zhengzhou, Shantou, Wuxi, Nanchang, Hefei, Zibo, Jinan, Suzhou, Nanning, Chengdu, Benxi, Ningbo, Wuhan, Hangzhou, Shenyang.

16% of all the provincial regions and 51% of all larger cities respectively), provided comprehensive enforcement measures on cultural markets or urban management. Some regulations and rules were created regarding administrative law enforcement oversight and accountability mechanism, which would be discussed in the part of administration oversight of the book.

In addition to the uniform provisions on administration enforcement, 9 local regulations and 30 local government rules specifically provided discretion in administrative penalty. Among them, 6 local government regulations had the term "discretion" in the title, including rules by Xiamen, Jilin, Shenzhen, Fuzhou, Ningbo and Zibo, explicitly prescribing discretion. In addition, 175 local regulatory instruments had the term "discretion" in the title, which were all directed at the issue of administrative penalty discretion.

3. Special administrative acts.

Chapter five of the Human Rules provided procedures for particular administrative acts, such as administrative contracts, administrative guidance, administrative ruling, and administrative mediation.

As for administrative contracts, there had been no regulatory instruments made yet with the title of "administrative contract". The authors, by text keyword searching, found that the Notice of the State Council on Issuing the Program for Comprehensively Promoting Administration according to Law was the most authoritative pertinent regulatory instrument. In addition, 9 ministry-level agencies had regulatory instruments regarding administrative contracts.[33] At the local level, only the Rules of Zibo City on the Management of Passenger Bus Transport (Jan. 24, 2002) mentioned administrative contracts. Six local governments had regulations regarding administrative contracts, including 2 at provincial level and 4 at lager city's level,[34] also 130 local regulatory instruments involved administrative contracts. Among all

---

[33]*Notice of the Ministry of Land and Resources on Implementing Property Law of the People's Republic of China* (May 8, 2007), *Notice of the General Office of the National Population and Family Planning Commission on Issuing the "Eleventh Five-Year Plan" for Administration According to Law in Population and Family Planning System* (March 21, 2007), *Opinions of the State Bureau of Surveying and Mapping "on Implementation of Five-Year Plan (2006–2010) for Promotion of Administration According to Law in National Surveying and Mapping System"* (April 30, 2006), *Notice of Ministry of Labor and Social Security on Issuing the Program for Implementing "Five-Year Plan" of State Council for Comprehensively Promoting "Administration According to Law"* (Jan. 16, 2006), *Guiding Opinions on Pushing Forward the Responsibility System of Administrative Law Enforcement in the National System of Civil Administration, Notice of the Ministry of Finance "on Issuing the Opinion on Comprehensively Promoting Administration According to Law and Financial Transactions by Law in National Financial Departments* (May 17, 2005).

[34]In addition to *the Administrative Procedure Rules of Hunan Province*, also included are: *Measures of Dalian City for Administration according to law in Management of Archives* (Jan. 28, 2008), *Measures of Taiyuan City for the Administrative Nonfeasance of State Administrative Organ and its Working Staff (for Trial Implementation)* (Sept. 24, 2005), *Measures of Nanjing City for the Administration of Toll Roads and its Ancillary Facilities* (June 21, 2005), *Interim Provisions of Tangshan City on the Preliminary Examination of the Legality of Important Administrative Acts by Administrative Organs* (Feb. 27, 2004), *Measures of Shanxi Province for the Measures of Administration of Breeding Stock and Poultry* (July 24, 1998).

the above-mentioned instruments the Human Rules contained the most specific provisions for administrative contracts[35] while the others only generally mentioned that "administrative contracts should be signed or play its role".

Administrative guidance had been mentioned in the Notice of the General Office of the State Council on Reiterating the Promulgation of National Regulations and Policies on Foreign Economic Relations and Trade on Sep. 23, 1993, before the Notice of the State Council on Issuing the Program of Comprehensively Promoting Administration according to Law. At present, 2 ministry-level departments under the State Council have formulated rules involving administrative guidance in the process of administrative review: Rules on Administrative Review of Work Safety Disputes (Oct. 8, 2007) and Measures of China Securities Regulatory Commission for Administrative Review. (Nov. 25, 2002). In addition, there are 44 departmental regulatory instruments regarding administrative guidance, of which 23 were issued by the State Administration of Industry and Commerce, accounting for 52%, and 21 by other departments, accounting for 48%.[36]

Three local regulations touched upon administrative guidance, including Rules of Hefei City on Optimizing Investment Environment (Jan. 5, 2007), Rules of Fushun City on Optimizing Economic Development Environment (July 29, 2005), and Rules of Sichuan Province on Donations by Overseas Chinese (Sep. 26, 2002). Additionally, 6 local government rules involved provisions of administrative guidance, which besides the Human Rules, also included Measures of Beijing Municipality for the Relative Consolidation of the Power to Impose Administrative Punishment in Urban Management (Nov. 18, 2007); Measures of Shanghai Municipality on Supervision and Management over Delivery of Group Meals (July 11, 2005); 2 mentioning administrative guidance in provisions concerning administrative review, namely Measures of Hainan Province on Implementing Administrative Review Law (Jan. 17, 2005) and Rules of Guangzhou City on Administrative Review (May 2, 2004); and 1 regulation with respect to the optimizing investment environment, named Measures of Huainan City on Optimizing Investment Environment (Nov. 19, 2008). Among the above 9 local regulations and rules addressing administrative guidance, 3 were related to investment environment (accounting for one third), which emphasized the significance of administrative guidance on building a harmonious society and optimizing local investment environment. There were 267 local regulatory instruments involving administrative guidance, including 7 bearing the term of "administrative guidance" in the title. Among the 7 instruments, 5 were issued by agencies of industry and

---

[35] Articles 93 to 98 of the *Administrative Procedural Rules of Hunan Province*.

[36] The instruments include 1 by Accreditation Administration, Maritime Safety Administration, 1 by Ministry of Agriculture, 1 by Ministry of Land and Resources, 1 by National Population and Family Planning Commission, Ministry of Commerce, 1 by Ministry of Information Industry, 1 by Ministry of Public Security, Commission of Science Technology and Industry for National Defense, 1 by State Tobacco Monopoly Administration, 1 by State Development Planning Commission, 1 by Ministry of Foreign Economic Relations and Trade, 1 by Ministry of Education, 1 by Ministry of Civil Affairs, 1 by State Bureau of Surveying and Mapping, 2 by Ministry of Health, 2 by Ministry of Labor and Social Security, and *the Outline of the Plan for the Reform and Development of the Pearl River Delta*.

commerce (4 by Fujian Administration of Industry and Commerce and 1 by Anhui Administration of Industry and Commerce, entitled Opinion of the Anhui Administration of Industry and Commerce on Promoting Administrative Guidance within the Provincial Agencies for Industry and Commerce (for Trial Implementation) (May 19, 2009). The other two were Notice of Key Points in Administrative Guidance and Enforcement Supervision by Law issued by the Office of Legislative Affairs under the People's Government of Jilin (Mar. 24, 2008); and the Opinion of Promoting Administrative Guidance in Urban Management issued by Beijing Bureau of City Management and General Administrative Law Enforcement (April 20, 2007).

The studies found that administrative guidance was mostly applied in the field of industry and commerce administration. Different agencies had difference views; therefore, the provisions were rather general without specific procedures. At the local level, administrative guidance was more emphasized in its role in mitigating social conflicts, easing antagonistic law enforcement, and optimizing investment environment. Relatively speaking, the Human Rules[37] and rules by administrative authorities for industry and commerce had more detailed provisions on administrative guidance, are with the former focusing on basic principles and the latter on concrete work measures.

Administrative ruling refers to the activities by administrative agencies in handling, pursuant to authorization of laws and regulations, civil disputes among citizens, legal persons and organizations that are closely related to their administrative function. It is mainly applied to administrative matters such as ownership of natural resources, compensation for housing demolition and relocation, and so forth. There were two laws and two national regulations involving administrative ruling: Water Law of the People's Republic of China (2009 Revision) and Audit Law of the People's Republic of China; Regulations on Urban Housing Demolition (Jun. 13, 2001) and Regulations on Implementation of Land Management Law of the People's Republic of China (Dec. 27, 1998). The three regulatory instruments involving administrative ruling included: the Notice of the General Office of the State Council on Forwarding the Opinion of the Ministry of Supervision and the Office of the State Council for Correcting Unhealthy Work Styles (Mar. 22, 2006); the Notice of the General Office of the State Council on Control over the Scale of Urban Housing Demolition and Tightening the Management (Jun. 6, 2004); and the Notice of the General Office of the State Council on Forwarding the Opinion of the Ministry of Land and Resources and the Ministry of Agriculture on Protecting State-Owned Farms' Legitimate l Rights and Interests According to Law (Feb. 2, 2001).

Among the departmental rules, 6 involved provisions of administrative ruling, of which 2 related to legal services, namely, Management Measures for Grassroots Legal Service Workers (Mar. 31, 2000) and Detailed Rules for Legal Service Practices in Villages and Towns (Sep. 20, 1991). The other four were: Detailed Implementation Rules regarding Regulation on National Awards for Science and Technology (2008 Revision); Implementation Measures for Administrative Review of Quality and Technical Control (Apr. 24, 2000); Rules of the National Bureau of State Assets

[37] Articles 99 to 108 of *the Administrative Procedural Rules of Hunan Province.*

Management for Mediation and Settlement over Property Disputes and Notice of Circulating Beijing Municipality Procedures of Mediation and Settlement of Property Disputes (Aug. 15, 1997); and Measures for Announcement of Land Acquisition (Oct. 22, 2001). Additionally, 23 departmental regulatory instruments were issued by 15 department agencies, including 9 instruments issued by the Ministry of Housing and Urban-Rural Development, accounting for 39% of the total and all related to housing demolition and relocation of houses.[38]

Among the 87 valid local statutes involving administrative ruling, most focused on natural resources management and housing demolition, of which 34 were regarding housing demolition and relocation, accounting for 39% of the total, and 31 on natural resources management, accounting for 36%. Among the 31 local rules, 10 were regarding land resource management, 8 on utilization of water resources, 7 on of mineral resource management and mine safety, 4 on grassland and pasture management, and 1 on forestry and fishery management. Those were subject matters of earlier local regulations regarding administrative ruling. In recent years, such local regulations regarding audit, labor protection and alternative dispute resolutions began to involve administrative ruling. In addition, 85 local government rules provided the administrative ruling, 27 directly on housing demolition, accounting for 32%; 6 on land resource, accounting for 7%; 7 on water or forestry resource, accounting for 8%; and 16 on labor protection, bidding or environment pollution, and accounting for 19%. Also 28 local government rules involving accountability for administrative law enforcement provided that misconduct in administrative ruling would be held accountable.

The Human Rules laid down general principle of administrative ruling,[39] while the above-mentioned rules provided for specific procedures of administrative ruling on issues like housing demolition and natural resources management.

Administrative mediation refers to the mechanism in which an administrative agency, as an impartial party, mediate and resolve civil disputes closely related to the agency's administrative function. One departmental regulation regarding administrative mediation was the Measures of Administrative Mediation for Contract Disputes (Nov. 3, 1997) issued by the State Administration for Industry and Commerce. Additionally, 32 central-government department regulatory instruments mentioned administrative mediation, of which 15 were issued by the State Administration for Industry and Commerce, accounting for 47%. Among the rest, 3 were issued by the Ministry of Labor and Social Security, such as Notice on Further Strengthening Settlement of Labor Disputes; 4 issued by the Ministry of Health including Opinions on

[38]E.g.: *the Guiding Opinions of the State Administration of Work Safety and the State Administration of Coal Mine Safety on Further Regulating the Law Enforcement of Work Safety* (Sept. 21, 2007), *Notice of the State Forestry Administration on Pushing Forward the Administrative Law Enforcement Responsibility System in Forestry Departments* (March 14, 2006), *Notice of the Ministry of Information Industry on Issuing the Opinions of Ministry of Information Industry on Comprehensively Promoting "Administration According to Law"* (July 8, 2005), *Notice of the National State Assets Management Bureau on Policies Concerning the Work of Settling Disputes Arising from Property Rights of State Assets* (Feb. 9, 1998).

[39]Articles 109 to 114 of *Administrative Procedural Rules of Hunan Province*.

Further Strengthening the Work of Grievance Complaints Visits (March 26, 2009), and Opinions on Comprehensive Practice of Mitigating and Resolving Conflicts and Disputes in the Medical System (Feb. 15, 2007). Some others included Notice on Strengthening Settlement of Fishery and Maritime Disputes by the General Office of the Ministry of Agriculture (Feb. 7, 2007) and Notice on Strengthening Mediation of Marine Fishery Disputes by the Bureau of Fishery and Fishing Port Management (Feb. 24, 2006). There were 10 local regulations[40] and 3 local government rules provided administrative mediation, aside from the Human Rules, there were also Interim Measures of Anshan City for Contract Supervision and Administration (Feb. 25, 2003), and Measures of Jiangsu Province on Administrative Assessment According to Law (Dec. 3, 2008). Additionally, 364 local regulatory instruments involved the said issue.

Similar to the situation of administrative contract, the Human Rules was the first and the most comprehensive regulatory instrument on administrative mediation.[41] The rest only mentioned administrative mediation or provided procedures for specific issues and lacking general principle provisions.

Administrative emergency response refers to emergency response measures authorized by the Emergency Response Law of China and implemented by relevant agencies in situations such as natural disasters, accident disasters, public health or social safety incidents. It has been widely applied to emergency situations but rarely explicitly provided in regulatory instruments due to its lower degree in legal context compared with other administrative acts. For example, laws, such as Food Safety Law, Water Pollution Prevention and Control Law and Flood Control Law, authorized relevant agencies to adopt emergency response measures, but none explicitly used the term "administrative emergency response". It was the same case with 24 administrative regulations such as Regulations on the Post-Wenchuan Earthquake Reconstruction and Regulations on Prevention and Control of Schistosomiasis. And, among 127 regulatory instruments with respect to emergency response, only one explicitly mentioned the term of administrative emergency response, which was the. Notice on Appropriate Handling of Conflicts and Disputes Arising from Prevention and Treatment of SARS issued by the General Office of the State Council. Also, none of the 88 governmental regulations dealing with emergency incidents used the term "administrative emergency response". And only 2 of the 29 departmental regulatory rules with "emergency incidents" in the title employed the term "administrative emergency response", namely Basic Responsibilities of Diseases Prevention and Control

[40]E.g.: *Decision of the Standing Committee of Xiamen People's Congress on Improving the Diversified Dispute Resolution Mechanism* (Oct. 26, 2005), *Regulations of Urumqi City on Administrative Law Enforcement* (Dec. 24, 1996), *Regulations of Gansu Province on the Administration of Construction Project Costs* (July 27, 2007), *Regulations of Yunnan Province on the Administration of Construction Project Costs* (Nov. 26, 2004), *Regulations of the Shenzhen Special Economic Zone on the Promotion of the Harmonious Labor Relationship* (Oct. 6, 2008), *Regulations of Ningxia Hui Autonomous Region on Patent Protection* (Nov. 7, 2002), *Regulations of Jilin Province on the Protection of the Lawful Rights and Interests of Collectively-Owned Enterprises in Cities and Towns* (July 23, 1989).

[41]Articles 115 to 121 of *Administrative Procedural Rules of Hunan Province*.

Agencies at All Levels and the Performance Evaluation Standards of Disease Prevention and Control Work, both issued by the Ministry of Health. At the local level, all of the 7 local regulations involved emergency incidents and response measures, but none used the term "administrative emergency response". Among 15 local government rules regarding emergency incidents, only the Hunan Regulation explicitly used the term "administrative emergency response". And among 874 local regulatory instruments regarding emergency incidents, only 4 mentioned "administrative emergency response".[42] Although the actual term was rarely used, the prototype or similar principles, measures and procedures of administrative emergency response provided in Articles 122 to 129 of the Hunan Rules could be found in the above-mentioned legal instruments.

4. Administrative Supervision and Accountability.

Chapter Eight of the Human Rules provided administrative supervision, over the administrative agencies. The authors, by keyword title searching of "administrative supervision", found out that in many departmental regulations and local government rules, administrative supervision referred to supervision of administrative agencies over certain industry or field of trade, such as Notice of the Ministry of Finance on Further Strengthening Administrative Supervision on Accounting Firms with Security Trade Qualifications (Feb. 3, 2009); Opinions of the Ministry of Housing and Urban-Rural Development on Strengthening Administrative Supervision on Bidding and Tendering of Housing, Building and Municipal Infrastructure Construction (Oct. 10, 2005): and Detailed Rules of Qinghai Province for Implementation of Administrative Supervision on the Social Security Funds (Feb. 25, 2004). The connotation of the term "administrative supervision" in these documents differed from that in the Hunan Regulation except for one, namely the Measures of Shaanxi Province on Administrative Supervision by Law (Sep. 29, 2007). Therefore the authors expanded title keyword searching with the term "administrating by law" and found out that most of the departments under the State Council drafted their programs of administrating according to law in accordance with the State Council's directive, that is, "Effectively Implementing the Guidelines of Administrating by Law. Among local government rules apart from the one of Shaanxi Province mentioned above, three other regional regulations also mentioned administrating by law. They were the Measures on Administrative Assessment According to Law of Guangxi Province, Jiangsu

[42]*Guiding Opinions of General Office of Sichuan Provincial People's Government on Preventing and Handling the Administrative Disputes in Post-Earthquake Recovery and Reconstruction* (Sept. 26, 2008), *Notice of General Office of Zhaoqing Municipal People's Government on Issuing the Medical Emergency Response Plan of Zhaoqing City* (Jan. 9, 2008), *Notice of General Office of Wenzhou Municipal People's Government on Further Improving the Predetermined Scheme System and the Emergence Response Mechanism for the Emergency and Public Crisis* (2005.05.13), *Notice of General Office of Zhejiang Provincial People's Government on Issuing the Plan for the Important Survey Project of "Accelerating the Construction of Administrative Emergence Response Mechanism of Zhenjiang Province, Improving the Capability of Government to Respond the Emergency and Public Crisis"* (May 13, 2004).

Province and Dalian City.[43] Additionally Tianjin Municipality, Gansu Province, and Shenzhen, Hefei, Nanning, Hangzhou, Shijiazhuang and Nanjing cities also adopted regulatory measures regarding administrative evaluation according to law.

Chapter Nine of the Human Rules was regarding administrative accountability mechanism against illegal misconducts of administrative agencies and the staff. The authors, by title keyword searching of "accountability" found out that on the central government level the State Council issued the Provisions on Administrative Accountability for Extraordinarily Serious Safety Accidents (Apr. 21, 2001). Thereafter two other statutory regulations were issued, namely the Notice of Issuing the Interim Measures of Accountability for Causing Incidents Regarding Farmers Burdens (Aug. 9, 2002) issued by the General Office of the CPC Central Committee and the General Office of the State Council, and the Instruction of the State Council on Approval of Establishing Inter-Ministerial Joint Coordination System Regarding Accountability for Extraordinary and Serious Work Safety Accidents (Sep. 14, 2007). Additionally 7 State Council departments had rules regarding accountability, including Measures of Accountability for Asset Losses of State-Owned Enterprises; Accountability for Violation of Follow-up Fund Use for Relocating People of Large- and Mid-Size Reservoirs; Provisions on Accountability of Traffic Administrative Permit Supervision Inspection; Provisions of the Ministry of Agriculture on Implementation of Accountability Mechanism for Administrative Permits; Accountability Mechanism for Supervision on Administrative Law Enforcement and Misconducts in Quality Control Inspection and Quarantine; Accountability Mechanism for Misconducts in Law Enforcement by Policemen of Public Security Agencies; and Accountability Mechanism for Misconducts in Law Enforcement by Policemen Working in Prison or Reform-through-labor Facilities. More departments provided accountability by issuing rules and regulations which involved more than 10 fields of work, such as railways, transportations, forestry, fire prevention, land and resources, education, finance, taxation, health, industry and commerce, cultural relics, insurance, construction, quality supervision and inspection and people's bank.

At the local government level, the authors conducted title search with the keyword "accountability" and found that 4 provinces and 3 lager cites had local regulations regarding accountability mechanism,[44] of which 3 provinces and 1 lager city mainly addressed accountability of judicial personnel, and 1 province and 2 lager cities

[43] *Measures of Guangxi Zhuang Autonomous Region on Assessment of the Administration according to Law* (Feb. 6, 2009), *Measures of Jiangsu Province on Assessment of the Administration according to Law* (Dec. 3, 2008), *Measures of Dalian City on Assessment of the Administration according to Law* (June 23, 2008).

[44] *Regulations of Jiangxi Province on Investigation of Liabilities for the Cases Wrongly Decided by the Judiciary (Revised 2007)* (March 29, 2007), *Regulations of Shandong Province on Investigation of Liabilities for the Misconducts of the Judicial Officials in Handling Cases* (June 18, 1999), *Regulations of Inner Mongolia Autonomous Region on Investigation of Liabilities for the Misconducts of the Judicial Officials in Handling Cases* (Sept, 28, 1998), *Measures of Hangzhou City for the Supervision of Investigating the Cases Wrongly Decided* (Dec. 30, 1997), *Measures of the Standing Committee of Changchun People's Congress for the Supervision of Investigating Wrongly-decided Cases in Administrative Law Enforcement* (Dec. 1, 1997), *Regulations of Hebei Province on Investigation of Liabilities for the Wrongly-decided Case and Faults in Law Enforcement* (Sept. 3, 1997),

focused on accountability for administrative law enforcement. Among local government rules 59 directly concerned accountability for administrative law enforcement, covering 24 provincial regions (including provinces, autonomous regions or municipalities directly under the central government) and 12 larger cities.

The authors also title searched with the keyword of "law enforcement accountability" and one statutory regulation issued by the General Office of State Council, namely, Opinions on Promoting Accountability Mechanism for Administrative Law Enforcement (July 9, 2005). Also 13 departments of the State Council issued regulatory instruments regarding accountability mechanism of administrative law enforcement within their respective agencies.

At the local level, 2 provinces and 7 lager cities established accountability mechanism for administrative law enforcement with local statutes while 14 provinces and 9 larger cities with local government rules.

In short, the above statistics showed that all provincial regions (including provinces, autonomous regions or municipalities directly under the central government)[45] had rules and regulations on accountability mechanism for administrative law enforcement, of which 28 provincial regions regulated it in forms of rules or regulations, accounting for 90%. And among 43 larger cities, 24 regulated it in forms of rules or regulations, accounting for 86%, the other 19 larger cities adopted regulatory instruments in this regard.[46]

5.3 The Development Trend of Administrative Procedure in China: A Uniform Law of Administrative Procedures

In China, administrative power is very strong which dominates all aspects in society. Therefore, how to regulate administrative power has been a topic of great concern among the administrative law scholars since the era of reform and opening-up. In 1990s, they began to pay great attention to legislation of administrative procedures. Most scholars held that a uniform law of administrative procedures should be enacted and put forward detailed plans for it. However, this view was challenged by practical government agency representatives, who contended that the nature and function of the agencies differ greatly, thus a uniform law of administrative procedures is impractical in current situation. The Chinese legislature, the National People's Congress and its legislation plans were also in favor of the decentralized legislative approach. The authors believe that the lack of a law of administrative procedures makes it hard for

Measures of Jinan City for Investigation of Accountability for Misconducts in Law Enforcement (Dec. 16, 1999).

[45] *Regulatory* instruments are formulated to regulate it in Xinjiang autonomous region, and Zhejiang and Jiangsu provinces.

[46] The larger cities, including Lhasa, Xining, Tangshan, Baotou, Anshan and Handan, have no special rules and regulations regarding the responsibility for wrongly-decided cases in law enforcement or the administrative law enforcement responsibility system.

administrative officers to establish the concept of due process, and the uniform law is a necessity measure to raise their awareness of due process. Moreover, the law of administrative procedures aiming at openness, fairness and efficiency in administrative activities will lay down the fundamental basis for a modern country to regulate its administrative power. With the current situation in China where government administration has unprecedented power, without a comprehensive law of administrative procedures, the goal of the realization of rule of Law would be unreachable and the lawful rights of the citizens could not be protected. Therefore, an urgent task for China now is to launch the drafting of a uniform administrative procedures code as soon as possible, to accomplish a well-rounded modern administrative procedure system.

1. The practice of administrative procedure legislation in China.

The study indicates that there are numerous statutes and regulations regarding administrative procedures in China today, especially in the forms of governmental rules and other regulatory instruments, and local government rules and regulations and other regulatory instruments. The authors analyzed 8 administrative procedures, namely, administrative decision-making, regulatory rule-making, administrative law enforcement, special administrative acts, administrative public hearing, administrative information disclosure, administration oversight, and accountability. The results showed all provincial regions in China had made special regulations on 4 of the 8 above-mentioned procedures, namely, rule-making or "file for record"; administrative public hearing; administrative information disclosure (on government affairs or administrative information), and accountability in administrative law enforcement (or administrative law enforcement responsibility system). Regulations on other administrative procedures were rather common too: 32% of the provincial regions adopted special regulations on the procedure of administrative decision-making; 45% adopted general provisions on procedures of administrative law enforcement; and 65% adopted special rules on certificate mechanism of administrative law enforcement. The situation of larger cities was similar to that of the provincial regions in terms of administrative procedures legislation. All the larger cities had special regulations on administrative information disclosure; 27% had rules on procedures of administrative decision-making; 88% had rules on formulating or recording of regulatory instruments; 31% had rules on administrative law enforcement and specific measures; 45% had rules on the administrative public hearing; and 86% had rules on accountability in administrative law enforcement or administrative law enforcement responsibility system. Due to on-going institutional reform of the State Council, which resulted in frequent change of department set-up, it's hard to calculate the percentage of administrative procedures of each department in its entire rule-making. Yet on the whole, it appeared that, compared to the departments under the State Council, local governments were more active in making relevant regulations on administrative procedures.

Through comparison of the retrieved documents, the authors also noticed a high degree of similarity among the regulations on the same procedure; especially if the central government had issued regulations on certain procedures, regulatory rules adopted by departments of the State Council or local governments would clearly follow suit. For example, after the General Office of the State Council issued the Opinions on Promoting the Administrative Law Enforcement Responsibility System, the central government departments and local regions made similar regulations on the same issue. Regulations on administrative public hearing of various local regions were also more or less the same.

The authors further compared the model version of the Hunan Rules with other retrieved documents and also found a high degree of similarity. In the authors' view, innovative idea of the Hunan Rules did not lie in the specific procedures of administrative acts, but in the legislative pattern or model. Most of the administrative procedures provided in the Hunan Rules could be found in other earlier documents in terms of administrative decision-making, regulatory rule- making, administrative law enforcement, administrative public hearing, administrative information disclosure, administration oversight and accountability. As He Anjie, head of the Legislative Affairs Office of Hunan Provincial Government, explained that this statute is a uniform legislation of administrative acts, covering many aspects of government's work, including administrative decision-making, administrative law enforcement, administrative contracts, administrative ruling, and administrative mediation.

Regarding specific administrative procedures, the innovative measures of the Hunan Rules mostly expressed in procedures of special administrative acts, in particular it provided definitions of special administrative acts such as administrative contract, administrative guidance, administrative ruling, administrative mediation and administrative emergency response. It also provided the general principles governing these administrative acts, which were absent in other regulatory rules and improvements urgently needed in practice.

In terms of specific legislation of administrative procedures, besides the Hunan Rules, 4 more local governments had adopted special rules by the end of 2014.[47] Among them, the Regulations of Administrative Procedures of Shandong Province was the second administrative procedure rule in China (herein after as the Shandong Regulations). For the purpose of building a government based on the rule of law, the Shandong Regulations clearly provided the fundamental principles of administrative procedures, the subject of administrative procedures, procedures of administrative decision-making on significant issues, procedures of regulatory rule-making, procedures of law enforcement, procedures of special administrative acts, and procedures administration oversight and accountability. Thus, it became a significant regulation which regulated and protected administrative acts, thus promoting administration according to law and building a government based on the rule of law. Among the other municipal government rules, the Rules of Shantou City of Administrative Procedures (hereinafter as the Shantou Rules) was the first at the municipal/prefecture and special economic zone level. The Shantou Rules contained 10 chapters with

---

[47]The four rules refer to *the Administrative Procedural Rules of Haikou City* (effective in Aug. 1, 2013), *the Administrative Procedure Rules of Xi'an City* (effective in May 1, 2013), *the Administrative Procedure Rules of Shandong Province* (effective in Jan. 1, 2012) and the Administrative Procedure Rules of Shantou City (effective in May 1, 2011).

182 articles, which amended, and incorporated single administrative procedures into a comprehensive regulation suitable the social and economic development. It covered almost every aspect of government administrative procedures, including general principles, subject of administration acts, the procedure of administrative decision-making on significant issues, the procedure of law enforcement, the examination and approval procedure of non-administrative permits, the procedure of administrative contracts, administrative guidance, administrative ruling, administrative mediation, special procedures of administrative planning, procedures of administrative public hearing, administrative information disclosure, oversight of administration and accountability, thus, establishing a system of administrative procedures. Additionally, in 2013 Xi'an City and Haikou City also adopted its own respective Administrative Procedural Rules. The Xi'an City Administrative Procedural Rules consisted of 6 chapters with 142 articles, covering the general principles, procedures of administrative processing, procedures of special administrative acts, procedures of significant administrative decision-making, and appendixes. The official of the Legislative Affairs Office of the Xi'an City, who participated in the drafting of the Rules, explained that administrative procedural legislation in most cities in China was incomprehensive, lacking uniform code, which gradually became a bottleneck of the advancement of administration according to law. The uniform regulation of Xi'an City, as the first one in 15 semi-provincial regions, filled the gap and made a breakthrough. According to the survey, two provisions were especially popular with the public: one being that if the law enforcement officer failed to show an ID, the party concerned shall have the right to refuse to comply; and the other one being sneaking photos shall be regarded as illegally collected evidence thus inadmissible in adjudicating. Similarly, the Rules of Haikou City for Administrative Procedures also covered concentrates on subject of administrative procedures, procedure of decision-making on significant, procedure of law enforcement, procedure of special administrative acts, and accountability, which contributed to sound decision-making of administrative agencies and enhanced efficiency of work in Haikou city.

As for the degree of institutionalization in the country as a whole, among various administrative acts listed in the Hunan Rules, the procedures for regulatory rule-making and/or "file for record" ranked the number one. As previously mentioned, all provincial regions and 88% of larger cities in China had local regulations on this issue. Besides, the procedure of administrative law enforcement also had comparatively high degree of institutionalization. Fourteen (14) provincial regions (including provinces, autonomous regions and Municipalities directly under the Central Government) had general provisions on this issue, accounting for 45%; 20 provincial governments adopted special rules in this regard, accounting for 65%; 15 lager cities had regulatory instruments regarding administrative law enforcement and specific measures, accounting for 31%; 5 provinces (including Municipalities directly under the Central Government) and 25 larger cities provided comprehensive enforcement rules in cultural events or urban management (accounting for 16% of all provincial regions and 51% of all larger cities respectively). In contrast, the procedure of administrative decision-making was less institutionalized, with 37% of the departments of the State Council, 32% of the provincial regions and 27% of the larger cities had specific regulations on this issue.

Compared to administrative acts of administrative decision-making, procedures of regulatory rule-making, administrative law enforcement, administrative public hearing, administrative information disclosure and administration oversight, procedures for special administrative acts were less institutionalized on the whole. Take administrative contracts for example, no current laws or regulations had the term "administrative contract" in its title. Procedures of administrative guidance were obviously uneven among the departments of the State Council. Of the 44 departmental regulations on administrative guidance, 23 were issued by the State Administration of Industry and Commerce, accounting for 52%; and 21 issued by other departments, accounting for 48%. And, among 267 local regulatory instruments on administrative guidance, 7 had the term "administrative guidance" in its title and 5 were issued by the administrative agencies for industry and commerce.

The above analysis also indicates that China is shifting its focus from substantive law to procedural law. With over a decade's efforts and development, statutory administrative procedures regarding regulatory rule-making, administrative public hearing, administrative information disclosure and accountability are quite common now has laid a relatively sufficient foundation for national uniform administrative procedure legislation on these issues. As for the less common procedures of special administrative acts, although there are difficulties and challenges, on the other hand, a national uniform legislation is even more urgently needed. In conclusion, the time of paying attention to procedures has come in today's China. As pointed out by the 17th National Congress of the CPC, administration by law means that administrative agencies must "exercise powers and perform duties in accordance with the statutory authority and procedures", therefore, "the legal structures and procedure rules must be improved." Perfecting procedure rules constitutes one of the two cornerstones of building a government based on the rule of law. Now the subjective and objective conditions are ready for making uniform administrative procedure legislation. Especially since 2004, all central government departments and local authorities have positively responded to the three procedure regulations issued by the State Council, namely, the Implementation Program of the State Council for Promoting Administration According to Law; Opinions of the General Office of State Council on Promoting Administrative Law Enforcement Accountability Mechanism; and the Decision of the State Council on Strengthening Administration According to Law by Municipal and County-level Governments. This proves that, to some extent, the authorities have made considerable progress in accepting procedure legislation is necessary. Rule of law also means rule of procedures. Time is calling for accelerating the process of administrative procedure legislation.

2. Choices of approach of uniform law of administrative procedures in China.

The Law of Administrative Litigation Law of 1990 provided "according with statutory procedures" as one of the three elements defining a lawful administrative act and thus established the necessity of institutionalizing administrative procedures in applying the rule of law in administrative matters. In the following 20 years, Chinese scholars of administrative law, including jurists and law practitioners, have made unremitting efforts for improving China's administrative procedural legislation. The efforts have resulted in great progress in terms of the concept of due process, theoretical research and rule-making of practical procedures. The conditions are becoming more and riper for enacting a uniform administrative procedural code at the national level. Scholars and functionaries have the following recommendations regarding the future legislation of administrative procedure.[48]

(1) Objectives of the administrative procedural law. Most people believe that the direct legislative objective of China's administrative procedural law is to create a uniform administrative procedure law system that will ensure the minimum fairness and justice. The criteria of such minimum standard justice of administrative procedure include the following elements: (a) the principle of due process, i.e. procedures of administrative acts should be fair and just; (b) the principle of transparency, i.e. administrative procedures should be operated in an open manner; (c) the principle of participation, i.e. the parties that will be negatively affected by the procedure should have the opportunity to fully and meaningfully participate in the process; (d) the principle of efficiency, i.e. administrative agencies should act in a timely and efficient manner. Most scholars and functionaries also believe that the future China's administrative procedural law should adopt a model that gives equal weight on rights and efficiency for the following reasons: (a) both fairness and efficiency are the goals of administrative procedure legislation, and overemphasizing either of the two aspects would make it one-sided. Overemphasizing protection of citizens' rights would make administrative procedure more like judiciary proceedings, which will reduce efficiency and ultimately negatively affect people's rights. Similarly, overemphasizing administrative efficiency is likely to result in administrative disputes and neglecting citizens' rights, and ultimately reduce administrative efficiency. Therefore, equal weight should be given to protecting rights while improving efficiency; (b) the equal weight approach is the developing trend worldwide. The countries that have adopted the rights approach or the efficiency approach are moving to the direction of valuing and balancing both.

(2) Relations between the administrative procedure code (the Code) and other relevant special laws. There are two kinds of views: (a) the Code should serve as the fundamental and basic law of administrative procedures and, therefore, the principle of conflict should apply, i.e. the basic law is superior to the non-basic law in conflicts between the Code and other relevant laws. This is to prevent from putting the Code in a supplementary status and function; (b) the Code is a general law while other administrative acts are special laws, so principle of general law and special law should apply. The majority opinion is that the Code must first be recognized as the basic law of administrative procedures, and under this premise the relations of the Code and other special laws should be determined. This view reflects the idea of abandoning existing laws and regulations and enacting an all-round uniform administrative procedure code. In contrast, the minority view of supplementary status

[48]Ying Songnian, The Prospect of Chinese Administrative Procedure Legislation, *China Legal Science*, vol. 2, 2010.

holds that the existing procedure laws and regulations should be maintained, and uniform legislation should be made only in areas where there are no clear rules for certain administrative acts. The latter view reflects the idea of filling the blanks in legislation, which has been fiercely opposed by the advocators of the former opinion.

(3) The content selection of China's administrative procedural law. Four issues regarding the contents have been: (a) whether the Code should include substantive rules in addition to procedure rules? (b) whether the Code should also regulate internal procedures of the agencies in addition to external procedures? (c) whether the Code should also regulate ex-post relief procedures in addition to procedures during administrative acts? (d) what types of administrative acts should the Code cover? The authors agrees with the majority of scholars and experts on that, firstly, China's administrative procedural law should include the contents of both procedure and substantive rules, with the substantive rules containing fundamental principles of administrative law, the formation and validity of administrative decisions, administrative contract and administrative guidance; secondly, China's future Code should include rules of both internal and external procedures, which not only suits the status quo of administrative procedure legislation but is also conducive to realizing legislative objective of making the Code; thirdly, the current Administrative Review Law and Administrative Litigation Law already established ex post relief mechanism, therefore there is no need to include this in the Code, and the Code should focus on beforehand procedures; Finally, the future Code should include provisions on administrative decision-making, regulatory rule-making, administrative contracts and administrative guidance, but provisions on administrative planning should be excluded.

(4) The framework of China's administrative procedural law. Since it is necessary to include substantive provisions in the Code, the framework of the Code needs to resolve two important issues: one is the balance of the substantive rules and the procedure rules; the other is the primary content—the structure of procedure rules. For the first issue, the authors suggest that the Code be formulated in the order of subjects, operation procedures and consequences. Specifically, it should include fundamental principles, administrative subjects, and establishing and validity administrative acts. For the second issue, the authors suggest that first, the chapters be arranged on the category of administrative acts, and each chapter addresses one type of administrative action, covering a complete systematic procedures regulating the certain category of administrative acts. Secondly, each chapter be arranged in the order of the process of procedure from the beginning, during and ending of each procedure. Furthermore, separate chapters are devoted to administrative information disclosure and public hearing respectively. Last, internal administrative procedures should be incorporated in the part of subjects of administrative procedures.

In recent years, with the advance in the rule of law, the State Council has been attaching greater importance to administrative procedure legislation. The Legislative Affairs Office of the State Council made great efforts of survey and research for the preparation of the adoption of the Regulations on Procedures of Administrative Decision-Making on Significant Issues. The Office held discussion forums in March of 2014 to listen to the ideas and recommendations from the heads of the legislative affairs office of 7 provincial governments (including Shanghai, Jiangsu, Zhejiang, Anhui, Fujian, Jiangxi and Shandong), and 10 municipal and county governments in 4 provinces (including Shanghai, Jiangsu, Zhejiang and Anhui). Information was also collected regarding grassroots public affairs service and legal advice facilities. The above-referenced Regulations was drafted on the basis of local experience and comprehensive consideration of various complex factors throughout the country. This made it possible for administrative agencies of the central and local governments to act according to law, as well as enhanced the quality administrative decision-making. In addition, many provinces and cities also adopted regulations to regulate administrative law enforcement and to promote administrating according to law.[49] In order to coordinate and resolve conflicts and contradictions in making administrative law enforcement procedures by various regions all over the country, the State Council deemed it necessary to adopt a national regulation on administrative law enforcement procedures. For this purpose, the State Council conducted extensive onsite studies by experts and will soon issue the Regulations on Administrative Law Enforcement Procedures applicable to the whole country. In the meantime, regulations on specific administrative acts have been put on the legislative agenda, such as the Regulations on Food and Drug Administrative Penalty Procedures.

In conclusion, in a country like China, where "substance is valued more than procedures" and where citizens' rights awareness is rather weak, there is a still a long way to go and many obstacles to be overcome before a modern administrative procedural system is fully in place. Nevertheless, on the one hand, a national uniform administrative procedural law is absolutely needed for building China as a country based on the rule of law, for protecting the lawful rights of citizens, as well as for developing the socialist legal system with Chinese characteristics. And on the other hand, the 30 years reform efforts not only make adopting such legislation urgent but also possible. Time is ripe to enact a national uniform administrative procedural law, and the legislative work should be launched as soon as possible.

[49] Such as Fujian province, Liaoning province, Guangxi Zhuang Autonomous Region.

Chapter 6
Information Disclosure and Government Transparency

6.1 Government Information and Its Composing Elements

The notion of "government information" has two parts: government and information. In modern societies, information covers a fairly wide range. It is reflective of political, economic, scientific development and cultural conditions of the time, and therefore constantly changing. Due to its complexity, a fixed definition of the notion of "information" may not be possible. From a philosophical point of view, information is the common and essential attribute of everything. The characteristics of things are sensed by other things through a certain medium or transmission mode, such as sound wave, electromagnetic wave, image, text, symbol, and so forth. What embodies the characteristics of a thing and could be sensed by other things is the information that the thing communicates to others. Things have different natures, characteristics and law of motion. Through the information communicated by a thing, people could identify that thing and distinguish it from others.[1]

The process of social development is accompanied by increases in personal, economic and national security value of information. Human beings are developing, planning for, controlling, integrating and making use of information resources with growing intensity and precision. Information has fallen into public domain, and has gradually displayed its public nature therefore it falls on the government to regulate it by means of the law. Regulation over government information began with Sweden's Freedom of the Press Act of 1766. Since then, law-making activities have increasingly focused on information disclosure, so as to promote transparency of government operation. Information disclosure legislations worldwide could be put in two categories: broadly defined or narrowly defined. Broadly defined information disclosure covers information held by all public institutions, including not only government agencies, but also legislatures, judiciaries, enforcement agencies, as well

[1] Wang Zhirong, *the Fundamentals of Information Law*, China Legal Publishing House, 2003, p 1.

© Social Sciences Academic Press and Springer Nature Singapore Pte Ltd. 2018

H. Ma and J. Wang, *Building a Government Based on the Rule of Law*,
Research Series on the Chinese Dream and China's Development Path,
https://doi.org/10.1007/978-981-13-0999-1_6

as other public organizations. Narrowly defined disclosure is limited to government agencies and administrative information. Government information defined in Article 2 of the Regulation on Government Information Disclosure (hereinafter the Regulation) refers to information generated or acquired in the process of administrative agencies' performance of their duties and the information is recorded and retained in certain ways. Correct understanding of the definition of government information is crucial to implementation of government information disclosure practice.

Defining government information involves four key elements. First, the holder of the information. Government information refers to those held by government administrative agencies. In a broad sense they include not only governments at all levels and their divisions, but also organizations authorized by laws and regulations to handle public affairs, such as China Securities Regulatory Commission (CSRC), China Banking Regulatory Commission (CBRC), and China Insurance Regulatory Commission (CIRC). According to the British legal scholar William Wade, government is not an end in itself, but a means to an end. A government does not have its own interest besides the interest of its people. From the perspective that "there is no private matter in a government", all information held by the government is public information and public products owned by all the people. However, it does not mean that all government information should be disclosed to the general public. Article 37 of the Regulation provides that the following information need to be disclosed in reference to this Regulation, i.e. information generated and acquired in the process of providing public service by entities in the fields of education, health and medical care, family planning, utilities (water, electricity and gas), environmental protection, and public transportation. Here "in reference" means that information held by public entities and information held by the government is similar in some ways yet different in others. Both are public information but to a different extent. Compared with government information, the information of public-service entities is not entirely public. Only the information generated and acquired in the process of performing public-service related duties could be regarded as public information, and the rest is non-public information. For example, college financial information could be divided into several parts, and only the information involving government-funded budget and final accounting of education expenses are public information which is subject to disclosure to the general public. Funds and assets from social contributions are non-public information, and whether the information is subject to disclosure should be decided by donors. Profits and dividends gained by colleges as shareholders of companies belong to the category of corporate information and internal information of colleges. This kind of information could be disclosed within the college, but not necessarily to the general public.

The second element concerns duties, which is also the key element in defining government information. Government information is generated when administrative agencies perform their duties. The contents of duties could be seen at three levels. On the macroscopic level, government duties cover economic development, market oversight, social management and public service. On the medium-scopic level, the duties of central and local governments are regulated by the Organic Law of the State Council and Organic Law of the Local People's Congresses and Local People's

Governments. On the microscopic level, the three regulations, namely, Regulations on Major Duties, Institutions' Internal Regulations, and Regulations on Personnel Arrangement are the foundation for determining specific duties of administrative agencies at various levels. Which kind of information should be generated or obtained by which agency is closely related to the duties of the agency.

The actions of duty performance of government agencies could also be categorized in three ways. First, according to the object to which a duty is performed, the action could be defined as external management or internal operation. Second, depending on how closely the action is related to duties, it could be direct duty performance or related duty performance. Third, according to the attribute of the action, the performance could be of administrative nature or a civil activity.

As for the difference between internal and external information, some hold the opinion that duties referred to in the Regulations are limited to external duty performing, and only external duty performing could constitute government information. Otherwise it is not government information. Some others hold that government information is divided into internal information and external information, and the Regulations only regulates external information. For example, some courts have decided that, "such information as government accounting books, vouchers, files, and staff subsidies could not be regarded as government information, because such information is not directly related to economic and social management and public services, and therefore could be defined as government information."[2] Whether the view that internal information could not be regarded as government information, or the view that internal information is government information but not subject to disclosure, both are based on the fact that government actions are divided into internal and external functions, thus internal functions generate internal information and external functions generate external information.

To decide whether internal information is government information, it is necessary to look at it more specifically. The content of internal information, could be categorized in three kinds: first, instruction requests, reports, responses and opinions between the superior and subordinate agencies; second, correspondence, opinions and notifications among agencies of the same-level; and three, internal working documents and human resource management information within an agency. In the reality of administrative management internal information could be very complex in its forms. The effect of an internal information could be clear, for instance, the instruction response of the superior agency, or the effect could be uncertain, for instance, the request for instruction of the lower-level agency. Internal information could be factual information, such as the investigation report of a safety accident, or an opinion, such as instruction from the higher-level agency. It could be directive, such as the discretion benchmark of law enforcement agencies, or it could be an administrative decision that has not been delivered. The subject of internal information could be limited to within the administrative system, such as among agencies

[2]Shanghai High People's Court, *A Study on Legal Issues concerning Government Information Disclosure, Administrative Law Enforcement and Administrative Adjudication* (vol. 1, 2008), by the administrative division of the Supreme People's Court, People's Court Press, 2008.

of different levels, agencies of the same level, or within an agency. It could also involve citizens, legal persons and other organizations outside of an agency, such as the instruction of a higher-level agency over the initial decision on an administrative permit of a lower-level agency. Document exchanges among agencies, instruction requests and responses between agencies at different levels, and internal rules and discussions over cases within an agency are all preparation for or foundation of performing duties externally, therefore should be regarded as part of the duty performing process. The Regulation uses the term "in the process of duty performing", which indicates that duty performing is a process, covering a period of time, not just a point of time. Thus the three above-mentioned internal agency actions are all related to performing government duties and an integral part of duty performance.

Under the premise of recognizing internal information as government information, then we can further discuss which should be and which should not be subject to disclosure. The Opinions of the General Office of the State Council on Better Handling of Government Information Disclosure Requests (2010) provided that "Internal operational information generated and acquired by administrative agencies in their routine work, and processing information in the course of internal study, discussion and review, generally do not belong to the government information category that should be disclosed within the meaning of the Regulation." This provision has raised controversies in practice,[3]especially regarding what's the criteria of "in general" and "in special cases"; what's the relationship between internal operational information and in-process information; and whether non-disclosure of these two kinds of information is justifiable.

As discussed above, since internal information is very complex, therefore it seems inappropriate to exclude all internal operational information from disclosure by the sweeping argument that it is not government information.[4] Internal information could be characterized as directly or indirectly related to performing external administrative duties depending on the degree of relevancy of the information and duty per-

[3]In March, 2011, Friends of Nature, a NGO, applied to the Ministry of Agriculture for the disclosure of *the Application for Adjusting the Scope of the National Natural Reserve of Rare and Endemic Fishes in the Upper Reaches of Yangtze River* and *the Comprehensive Inspection Report on the Adjusted Parts of the National Natural Reserve of Rare and Endemic Fishes in the Upper Reaches of Yangtze River*. The Ministry of Agriculture turned down the request on the grounds that the requested documents are in-process information. Then Friends of Nature appealed for administrative review.

[4]In the cases of *Sun Rongfa v. Hangzhou Municipal Bureau of Real Estate Property Management* and *Luo Juxian v. Hangzhou Municipal Bureau of Real Estate Property Management*, the court restrictively interpreted the government information in Clause 2 of the *Regulations* as: "government information involved in administrative disputes of government information disclosure refers to the government information that is generated when administrative agencies with the function of administrative management externally perform their administrative management duties." The court held that information on the examiners of administrative permit applications was the information of internal administrative management; the examination opinions and evidence, grounds and reasons supporting the opinions were proposed opinions coming from the decision-making process and relevant factors that shaped those opinions; information about the discussions of the leadership group on written decisions were discussion records within the agency and factors shaping those records; all the information above did not belong to the government information defined in Clause 2 of the *Regulation*.

formance, and this relevancy should be the significant factor in determining whether the information should be disclosed. For example, an administrative agency usually has three kinds of staff: full-time civil servants, assistant staff on contract, and logistical workers. Obviously, they have different relevance with administrative duty performing: civil servants are directly involved in duty-performing; assistant staff assist in duty-performing, and logistical workers are unrelated to duty-performing. In fact, some information is indeed only concerning internal management and logistical support. For example, cultural, entertainment, and sport activities organized by the Labor Union of an agency and matters like residential housing allotment are not closely related to the agency's external administrative management function, and thus there is no need for disclosure. But it's worth mentioning that not all such information should be exempted from disclosure. For instance, the expenses of such activities funded by the agency fall into the disclosure scope according to the Regulations. Therefore, internal information should not be simply excluded from disclosure scope as a whole. Factors like the content and effect of internal information should be considered to measure the relevancy between the information and the governmental function, which could be directly relevant, considerably relevant or indirectly relevant. I suggest that "considerably relevant" should be the criterion to determine whether the internal information needs to be disclosed.

The division between internal and external information is determined by whether the information is derived from or used for an agency's internal operation or external management function; whereas in-process information is determined by the time period and effect of information. Due to different criteria, these two types of information could overlap with each other, i.e. some internal information could be in-process information at the same time. The common practice worldwide is to restrict disclosure of in-process information. There are generally two ways of doing it: in countries like Sweden and Finland, in-process information is not regarded as official documents, therefore no need for disclosure. Yet in the U.S., Japan, Australia, Thailand, and some other countries, internal information is regarded as government information, and the laws clearly define the scope and reasons for non-disclosure. The non-disclosures are primarily for the following reasons. First, the principle of candidacy, to avoid impediment of free exchange of ideas and to allow candid internal discussion in policy-making; Second, the principle of fairness, to avoid impediment of fair and efficient investigations; Third, to avoid obtaining unjust interests or social chaos caused by disclosure, and misunderstanding caused by early disclosure of immature policies; and to prevent certain people from gaining illegitimate interests or suffering undeserved damages. Selective disclosure of in-process information could help governments hear different opinions and make informed decisions. The Civil Servant Law of PRC also has confidentiality provisions based on similar reasoning mentioned above for non-disclosure of in-process information. It's worth noting that certain in-process information could be disclosed, especially factual and statistical information, such as investigation report of accidents and disasters. Public opinions collected for administrative rule-making should also be disclosed, as well as certain information regarding administrative permits review and issuance.[5]

Does the term "duty performing" in the Regulations only apply to administrative actions? In other words, can government information only be information derived from administrative actions? For example, Article 2 of the Regulations of Hangzhou City on Government Information Disclosure provides that "Government information in this Regulations refers to information generated or acquired, and recorded and retained in certain ways by the government at various levels in the process of performing their administrative management duties or providing public services." Compared with the Regulations mentioned earlier, this Regulations adds "administrative management" before "duties", which seems to emphasize the nature of administrative actions. Yet government actions are not necessarily always administrative actions. For example, administrative agency renting office space, purchasing office supplies, and hiring assistant personnel are all civil but not administrative acts. This type of acts is not direct performing of administrative management duties but is closely related to it. Thus information derived from such acts also should be regarded as government information. Whether information of such civil activities is subject to disclosure should comply with not only the Regulations, but also other relevant laws and regulations such as the Government Procurement Law and Labor Law.

The third element, in terms of the source of information, government information includes not only information generated by administrative agencies when performing duties, such as laws, regulations, and directive documents, but also information acquired from other government agencies, social organizations and citizens in the process of performing duties. For example, administrative agencies may ask citizens, legal persons and other social organizations to provide information regarding their company registration, real estate property ownership registration, and so forth, or they could collect such information themselves in accordance with certain regulations. In this way such information will go through a conversion process, from personal information to government information, and vice versa.

Fourth, as the form of carrier of information, government information is recorded and retained "in certain ways", which could be paper copies, electronic media or other carrier as long as it could be recognized by humans.

Information disclosure constitutes a government revolution of its own initiative. It has also made important contribution to social progress as a whole. In order to meet the growing awareness of citizens' rights and social demand for more information, the government needs to further promote information disclosure in the following aspects.

First, enhancing the understanding of information disclosure. The government should not treat it as another chore, but should realize its great value in increasing productivity. The 21st century is a new era of information. Along with social evolution information becomes more valuable in personal life, economic development, and national security situations. As people are developing, planning, controlling, inte-

[5]Zhou Chong, Increasingly Transparent Examination and CSRC's Advocacy of "the Disclosure of In-Process Information", *Shanghai Securities News*, March 28, 2012. p. 02.

grating and making use of information resources, the public nature of information becomes more prevalent. The government has an unraveled advantage than any other entities, in terms of access to information, quantity of data collected, and the capability of analyzing information. Government information is highly regarded because of its objectivity, comprehensiveness and authority. It is a tremendous resource and wealth that should be put into good use in promoting economic development, serving public needs, and advancing technological and social progress.

Second, the government needs to expand disclosure scope and intensify their efforts in information disclosure by making breakthroughs in the fields that concern people's life the most, such as environmental protection, livelihood protection, and food safety. The usefulness and effectiveness of information disclosed need to be improved.

Third, the government should also enhance its capability of integrating and publicizing information so as to better serve the public's needs and tap into the great potential of information in accelerating technological and economic development.

Fourth, it is necessary for the government to provide more channels of disclosure and make it more accessible, so as to help ensure people's rights to be informed, and their rights to free expression, participation and oversight.

Fifth, the government needs to strengthen supervision over information disclosure disputes and provide remedies to safeguard citizens' legitimate rights and interests. Mechanism such as administrative accountability and social commentary can be used to ensure that the government's duty of disclosure is fulfilled.

6.2 Administrative Information Disclosure and Government Transparency

1. The principle of administrative information disclosure.

Disclosure as a basic principle of administrative procedure began to be implemented in China in 1980s with the introduction of government transparency practice, and it has gone through the following development stages.

(1) From 1988 to 1996, the initial form of public affairs disclosure began to emerge and the principle of disclosure began to be incorporated into laws.

In March 1988, the Communist Party of China (CPC) held the second plenary session of CPC Central Committee, and made public affairs disclosure an important measure of strengthening oversight on power and fostering integrity within the Party. It was emphasized that Party and administrative agencies at all levels must do their best to make the procedures transparent for the people to exercise oversight. To implement this policy, the central government launched pilot program of public affairs disclosure in Dongcheng District of Beijing, Huangpu District of Shanghai, Yantai city of Shandong Province and some other areas, which marked the very beginning of public affair disclosure in China. In January 1996, the 14th session of the Discipline

Inspection Commission of CPC Central Committee held its sixth plenary meeting and decided to establish the public disclosure mechanism. The meeting directed that "all counties (cities), villages, townships, administrative villages and grassroots administrative units must disclose to the public as much as possible the contents, procedures, results of administrative affairs to the public for supervision, especially those matters that concern immediate interests of the people, such as finance. This was the first time that "public affairs disclosure" had appeared in the document of CPC Central Committee, and with the primary focus on public supervision and clean government. In the same year, Administrative Penalty Law of the PRC, the first law in China to regulate a particular administrative act, was promulgated, which also confirmed disclosure as a basic principle. Article 4 of the Law provides that "Administrative penalties shall be based on fairness and transparency…; regulations of administrative penalties on certain illegal acts must be publicized. Otherwise such regulations shall not be used as basis of administrative penalties." Article 31 of this law provides that "Before issuing an administrative penalty, relevant, administrative agency shall inform the parties of the facts, reasoning, and legal basis of the decision, as well as the legal rights the parties are provided by law."

(2) From 1997 to 2000, public disclosure expanded from selected pilot areas to covering all villages and townships and began to be explored at county and municipal levels. More administrative statutes adopted the principle of disclosure.

In 1997, the Report of the 15 National Congress of the CPC stated that "Democratic election system in grassroots organs of political power and grassroots people's self-governing organizations should be improved, and disclosure of administrative and financial matters should be implemented." In the same year, as required by the central government, pilot program of public disclosure was launched and gradually extended to villages and townships. On December 6, 2000, General Office of the CPC Central Committee and General Office of the State Council jointly issued the Notice on Implementing Public Affairs Disclosure in All Village-and-Township-Level Organs of Power in China (General Office of the CPC Central Office [2005] No. 25), indicating a major progress in implementing administrative information disclosure level by level from the bottom up. The Notice laid out the principles and requirements, namely, disclosure according to law, being truthful and fair, paying attention to effectiveness and efficiency, easier oversight by the public, and promotion of democratic practice. The Notice also specified matters that should be disclosed, and in particular, required that budget and final accounting of governments at village or township level should be disclosed after approval by the People's Congress of the same level. And for important matters disclosure should be made for collecting public opinions before final decision is made. The Notice instructed that this practice is to be followed by urban sub-district administration offices; government agencies at and above the county-level should implement it gradually; and agencies at the provincial and national level should formulate specific disclosure regulations.

Clause 2, Article 23, the Administrative Review Law (1999) provides that "the applicant and the third party may have access to the written reply, the evidence, basis and other relevant materials supporting the specific administrative act submitted by the defending party, and the administrative review agency may not refuse to disclose unless the relevant materials involve State secrets, commercial secrets or personal privacy." Clause 2, Article 52, the Legislation Law provides that "once a law is promulgated upon signing, it should be immediately published in the Bulletin of the Standing Committee of the National People's Congress and in the newspapers with a nationwide distribution." Also, in the Legislation Law, Article 62 provides that "once an administrative regulation is promulgated upon signing, it should immediately be published in the Bulletin of the State Council and in newspapers with a nationwide distribution. The text of administrative regulations published in the Bulletin of the State Council shall be the standard text." Article 70 provides that "once local ordinance and specific regulations of local governments and autonomous regions are promulgated, they should be published in the gazette of the standing committee of the local people's congress and in newspapers distributed within the administrative region. The text of local governments or autonomous regions regulations and specific rules published in the gazette of the Standing Committee of the local People's Congress shall be the standard text."

(3) From 2001 to 2007, government affairs disclosure was implemented at all levels. Local governments began to legislate on government information disclosure.

In 2001, China joined the World Trade Organization (WTO). Almost all WTO statutes incorporate the principle of transparency, which require that laws, regulations, policy measures related to trade should be fair and transparent. This greatly contributed to the popularization of public disclosure and launching of legislation on government information disclosure in China. In 2002, the Central Government stated to establish an administrative management system featuring legitimate actions, coordinated operation, justice and transparency, with integrity and high efficiency. Hence, disclosure practice became an important part of China's administrative reform, and the principle of governance of the new administration at that time. In 2003, the outbreak of SARS accelerated the progress in setting up and improving the press spokesman mechanism of central and local governments and their departments. By the end of 2004, the three-level news release system was basically established. On March 24, 2005, the General Office of the CPC Central Committee and the General Office of the State Council jointly issued the Directive on Further Promoting Administrative Disclosure (General Office of the CPC Central Committee, [2005] No. 12), which marked the strategic advancement of administrative information disclosure at all levels throughout the country. The Directive extended administrative information disclosure from village-and-township level to provincial and national level, requiring that administrative agencies at county and municipal levels to practice administrative information disclosure in an all-around way under enhanced planning and guidance of the provincial and national government. In terms of practical implementation the Directive called for the following: active exploration of various means of disclosing the policy-making process, such as public notice, expert consultation, and meeting observation; accelerating legislation of administrative information disclosure by enacting Regulations on the Government Information Disclosure in a timely manner; adopting relevant local rules in areas where conditions allow; and practicing the two major approaches of disclosure: pro-active disclosure and disclosure by request. This Directive laid the foundation for the Regulation on Disclosure of Government Information of 2008, and served as the most important guiding document for China's administrative disclosing.

In March 2003, to strengthen its leadership of administrative information disclosure, the State Council set up the National Leading Group for Disclosure of Administrative Affairs, an advisory and coordinating unit under the State Council. Later, in September 2007, the Leading Group Office was transferred from the General Office of the Commission for Discipline Inspection of the CPC Central Committee to the National Bureau of Corruption Prevention. Thus, government information disclosure was under the charge of both the General Office of the State Council and the National Leading Group. The Leading Group regarded government information disclosure as part of public affairs disclosure.

In the mean time, some local governments also began to adopt regulations on government information disclosure. On January 1, 2003, the Regulations of Guangzhou City on Disclosure of Government Information took effect officially, becoming the first city in China to have legislations on government information disclosure. In February 2004, Measures of Shenzhen on Online Disclosure of Government Information began to be implemented, and it became the first city in China to disclose government information on the Internet. In April 2004, Foshan city of Guangdong Province launched its online searching center of current valid government documents, being the first such website in China. On May 1, 2004, the Regulations of Shanghai on Disclosure of Government Information became effective. In September 2004, the Legislative Affairs Office of Beijing released the Opinions on Further Advancing Administrative Information Disclosure According to Law. In addition, before the national legislation, i.e. the Regulations of PRC on Disclosure of Government Information was enacted, the following local government rules or regulations of government information disclosure had been adopted[6] (see Table 6.1).

(4) From 2008 to the present, the Regulations of PRC on Disclosure of Government Information (the Regulations) marked the completion of the initial stage of lawmaking for information disclosure, and the next step would be comprehensive implementation. People's awareness of procedural rights was greatly enhanced.

On May 1, 2008, the official implementation of the Regulations began, which meant that now the government information disclosure was regulated under a nationwide uniform set of rules. This had two major impacts: first, it's a breakthrough in itself; also it brought a wide-range boosting effects. The Regulations adopted by the State Council served as the highest level of legal basis in the field of government information disclosure, which showed the will of the State and the authority of laws.

---

[6]This table is an excerpt from *Public Participation and Administrative Process—A Framework for Theoretical and Institutional Analysis* by Wang Xixin, China Democracy and Law Press, December 2007, pp. 134–135.

Table 6.1 Local government rules or regulations of government information disclosure condition

	Region	Name of statutes	Effective date
1	Fujian	Provisional Measures of Fujian Province on Disclosure of Administrative Affairs	September 11th, 2001
2	Hunan	Proposed Measures of Hunan Province on Implementing the Mechanism of Disclosure of Administrative Affairs (Trial)	August 1, 2002
3	Shantou	Regulations of Shantou Municipality on Information Disclosure of Administrative Affairs	June 1, 2003
4	Taiyuan	Regulations of Taiyuan Municipality on Disclosure of Administrative Affairs	July 2, 2003
5	Harbin	Regulations of Harbin Municipality on Disclosure of Administrative Affairs	February 1, 2004
6	Chengdu	Regulations of Chengdu Municipality on Disclosure of Government Information	May 1, 2004
7	Hubei	Regulations of Hubei Province on Disclosure of Government Information	July 1, 2004
8	Wuhan	Provisional Regulations of Wuhan Municipality on Disclosure of Government Information	July 1, 2004
9	Chongqing	Provisional Regulations of Chongqing Municipality on Disclosure of Administrative Information	July 1, 2004
10	Datong	Rules of Datong Municipality on Disclosure of Government Information	August 1, 2004
11	Jilin	Measures of Jilin Province on Disclosure of Administrative Information	September 5, 2004
12	Hangzhou	Regulations of Hangzhou Municipality on Disclosure of Government Information	October 1, 2004
13	Jinan	Provisional Regulations of Jinan Municipality on Disclosure of Administrative Information	October 1, 2004
14	Ningbo	Regulations of Ningbo Municipality on Disclosure of Government Information	November 1, 2004
15	Hebei	Regulations of Hebei Province on Disclosure of Government Information	July 1, 2005
16	Zhengzhou	Regulations of Zhengzhou Municipality on the Disclosure of Government Information	October 1, 2005
17	Hainan	Measures of Hainan Province on Disclosure of Government Information	October 1, 2005
18	Shaanxi	Regulations of Shaanxi Province on Disclosure of Government Information	January 1, 2006
19	Liaoning	Regulations of Liaoning Province on Disclosure of Government Information	February 1, 2006
20	Heilongjiang	Regulations of Heilongjiang Province on Disclosure of Government Information	April 1, 2006

The Regulations prescribed that government agencies should: prepare a catalog and a guidebook of government information; designate specialized personnel for information disclosure; provide physical conditions at government offices for the pubic to access government information; respond to disclosure requests within the time limit; and establish accountability system against illegal acts. It laid down comprehensive requirements for the management of government information resources, and prompted government agencies to improve their overall management system. A diverse yet strict disclosure procedures were prescribed in the Regulation. They included pro-active disclosing and disclosing by request; and statutory and non-statutory disclosing. In particular, the provision of disclosure by request effectively safeguarded citizens' right to be informed. The Regulation also provided various legal remedies, such as complaint reporting, administrative review, and administrative litigation, to promote effective dispute resolution and oversight of information disclosure of government agencies.

Second, using administrative regulations to promote government information disclosure, on the one hand it is conducive to providing guidance from the higher level; on the other hand, and more importantly, it gives more means for the public's oversight of the government. The Regulations clearly specified the duties, powers, operation procedures, related results, and supervision methods of administrative agencies, which is helpful for proper exercise of administrative powers. It also emphasized the public's right to administrative litigation, and provided more means for public's participation and supervision. Meanwhile the Regulations incorporated the following important matters into the disclosure scope: policies and implementation concerning poverty alleviation, education, medical care, social security, employment enhancement; supervision inspection over environmental protection, public health, safe production, food and pharmaceutical product quality control; and urban/rural construction and management issues. Thus the Regulations provided an institutional platform to prevent and eradicate corruption from its source, as well as institutional guarantee for establishing and improving an anti-corruption system that incorporates education, punishment and supervision.[7]

To analyze China's legislation on administrative information disclosure, research was done for statutes with "administrative information disclosure" as the key words. By 2009, 96 laws, 88 administrative regulations, 609 directive documents, 2259 local government regulations, 2194 local rules and 41,123 other local regulatory instruments had been made on disclosure. Among them, the Regulation on Disclosure of Government Information was the highest-level statutory document that specialized in regulating government information disclosure. Thirteen other national level regulations included the Notice on Comprehensive Implementation of Village Affairs Disclosure and Democratic Management in Rural Areas (April 18, 1998), the Notice on Comprehensive Implementation of Administrative Affairs Disclosure in all Rural Village-Township Administration (December 6, 2000), and the Notice on Implementing Factory Affairs Disclosure (June 3, 2002). All the three Notices regulating

[7]Chen Zhuo, *Studies on China's Legal System on Government Information Disclosure* (D), Dissertation of Fudan University, 2008, pp. 27–28.

village affairs disclosure, administrative affairs disclosure, and factory affairs disclosure were issued by the General Office of the CPC Central Committee and the General Office of the State Council. Twelve governmental rules had provisions regarding government information disclosure, among which the earlier one was the Provisional Regulations on the Financial Affairs Disclosure of Rural Collective-Economic Organizations (December 16, 1997). Also 60 ministry-level rules regulated information disclosure, and 50 regulated administrative affairs disclosure.

Among local government legislations, 20 had "disclosure" in its title [6 on village affairs disclosure, 11 on factory (or enterprise) affairs disclosure, and 3 on administrative affairs disclosure]. Twenty-one local government rules had "government information disclosure" in its title, among which 10 were adopted by provincial governments and 11 by governments of big cities. Also 10 local government rules had "administrative affairs disclosure in the title (5 by provincial governments and 5 by governments of big cities). In addition, 1264 local ordinances had "administrative affairs disclosure" or "government information disclosure" in the title. According to the research, so far all provincial governments and governments of big cities have adopted laws, regulations, and rules regarding government information disclosure, public affairs disclosure or administrative information disclosure, among which 15 were by provincial governments[8] and 14 by governments of big cities[9] accounting for 45% of provincial governments and 29% of governments of big cities.

6.3 Current Situation of China's Government Information Disclosure

So far, there has been no official study on the overall situation of China's government information disclosure. Only two civil research institutes have conducted such studies, i.e., the Center for Public Participation Studies and Support (CPPSS) at Peking University, and Chinese Academy of Social Sciences (CASS). These two institutes selected targets of evaluation (TOEs) and evaluation methods, and established observation indicators in accordance with the Regulations on Disclosure of Government Information. As the output document they published the Annual Report on China's Administrative Transparency and Government Transparency respectively and their latest were the 2011–2012 Reports. For accuracy our analysis of China's government information disclosure is based on latest reports of these two research institutes.

1. Report on China's Administrative Transparency (2011–2012).

(1) TOEs, indicators and methods.

---

[8]Liaoning, Hebei, Shaanxi, Tianjin, Shanghai, Gansu, Xinjiang, Heilongjiang, Hubei, Hainan, Guangdong, Sichuan, Fujian, and Zhejiang.

[9]Hangzhou, Chengdu, Ningbo, Nanjing, Shenzhen, Benxi, Suzhou, Zhengzhou, Guiyang, Wuhan, Gaungzhou, Handan, Taiyuan and Harbin.

From November 2011 to August 2012, the CPPSS at Peking University, conducted an in-depth observation and evaluation on government information disclosure in cooperation with seven other universities (China University of Political Science and Law,[10] Nankai University, Jillin University, Northwest University of Political Science and Law, Zhejiang University, Sichuan University and Guangdong University of Foreign Studies). Using the System of Evaluation Indicators on China's Government Information Disclosure that they developed, the TOEs selected by the eight teams covered 43 departments under the State Council, 30 provincial-level administrative agencies, all prefecture-level administrative agencies under the six provincial governments (Heilongjiang, Henan, Jiangsu, Gansu, Hunan, and Yunnan), and 38 county-level administrative agencies under some of the provincial agencies.

The evaluation was conducted with the above-mentioned indicator system. To make it more practical, depending on TOEs and the purposes three versions of the evaluation system were developed: the State Council version for evaluation of ministries, commissions, and bureaus, under the State Council; the provincial government version for administrative agencies at the provincial and prefectural level, and the county-level government version for county-level administrative agencies. Each version consisted of five parts, namely organizational structure, institutional support, proactive disclosure, disclosure by request, and supervision and remedies. The aggregate score of each version was 100 points.

Two methods were utilized for evaluation: online searching and onsite inspection. For the provincial government version, in all the 41 evaluation indicators 33 items of information needed could be obtained through online searching, reviewing government bulletins and annual reports on information disclosure, and directly requesting information from the government. The remaining 8 indicators required onsite evaluation. For the State Council version, 30 items were obtainable through the searching method and 8 required onsite visit. And for county-level government version, among all 45 three-level indicators 37 could be obtained through the searching method, 6 through case-testing, and 2 required both methods. For case testing, volunteer testers could be recruited to make evaluation through their personal experience, or evaluation team members could make disclosure requests for test cases.

(2) Findings.

According to the evaluation results, agencies under the State Council generally performed well, although some agencies were slow in making progress. Over 50% provincial-level agencies got acceptable scores. The result at the provincial level showed that performance in information disclosure did not necessarily correspond to the level of economic development of the locality. For instance, developed area like Guangdong province did not score very high. On the whole as far as government information disclosure was concerned, provincial agencies did better than agencies

[10]The author was the group leader of CUPL (China University of Political Science and Law). CUPL group evaluated the information disclosure of 41 agencies under the State Council and completed the research report. The contents and data in this section mainly came from *the Report on China's Administrative Transparency* (2011–2012).

under the State Council. Even though the central government agencies had made remarkable progress in recent years, they still lagged behind provincial agencies. However, the progress should be recognized since it showed the efforts for improvement.

The provincial agencies also scored higher than lower-level agencies in terms of organizational structure, system support, and proactive disclosure. Although different evaluation indicators were applied, the data result confirmed that at grassroots levels the lower the level was, the more improvement was desired.

In general, the improvement of scoring of the provincial agencies and those under the State Council proved that as the central government is paying more attention to information disclosure, continuous progress has been made at both the central and local government levels.

2. Annual Report on China's Government Transparency (2012).

(1) TOEs, indicators and methods.

In 2012, the study group of Chinese Academy of Social Sciences selected 59 agencies under the State Council, 26 provincial governments and 43 governments of large cities for the study on the implementation of government information disclosure rules.

Since notable progress had been made in information disclosure, and some disclosure mechanism had been well-developed, the study group made adjustments for evaluation indicators in 2012 to make it more realistic. The adjustments were primarily to reduce assessment on formalities. The number of indicators related to formalities and the weight that they carried were cut down. The number of test-case indicators and their weight were increased. The study also put more emphasis on disclosure of important information.

In the evaluation of 2012, the guidebook of information disclosure was taken out as an evaluation indicator. For the agencies under the State Council, the study and evaluation on disclosure of work information were added. For provincial governments, the study and evaluation on government bulletin, directive documents, and disclosure of administrative approval or denial were added. For governments of big cities, the study and evaluation on directive documents, and the disclosure of environmental information were added.

Evaluation indicators used were as follows: (1) five for agencies under the State Council: lists of government information that could be disclosed, work information, directive documents, disclosure in response to application, and annual reports on information disclosure, with a score totaling 100 points; (2) seven evaluation indicators for provincial governments: lists of government information that could be disclosed, directive documents, approval or denial of administrative permits, environmental protection, disclosure in response to application, and annual reports, totaling 100 points; (3) seven evaluation indicators for governments of big cities: lists of government information disclosure, directive documents, administrative approval/denial, food safety, environmental protection, disclosure in response to application, and annual reports, totaling 100 points.

The study began on March 5, 2012, and ended on December 15 the same year, of which the study of annual reports was from March 5, 2012 to April 1. In the evaluation on disclosure in response to application, government agencies were given longer time than the statutory time limit. The study group not only went through the contents and information on the government websites, but also tested the validity of information links, retrieval system, and the platform of disclosure requests. To avoid mistakes, if a researcher could not find any information or open a webpage, other researchers would try again. They would try different search engines, different computers, and different ways of Internet access at different times, to check the validity. For disclosure by request, if an online submission platform (including e-mail) was provided, the researchers would submit an application personally for verification. If disclosure by request was allowed but no online platform was available, researchers would send written applications by mail (via EMS).

(2) Findings.

The results suggested that, in 2012, the situation of government transparency was improving in general. Both central and local governments had made some progress in information disclosure.

First, governments attached great importance to information disclosure. The General Office of the State Council issued the Major Work Arrangements for Disclosure of Government Information in 2012, which pointed out the weakness in the work of the previous year, specified focuses for 2012 in key fields of disclosure according to public demand, and set out major tasks for various agencies. Following this guideline many local governments also formulated their major work arrangements. Some strengthened legislation for information disclosure. For example, Zhejiang Provincial Government adopted Provisional Measures of Zhejiang Province for Government Information Disclosure.

Second, the implementation of the Regulation on Disclosure of Government Information was improved, which best reflected on the issuance of annual reports. Statistics showed that in 2011 only a very small number of government agencies did not release their annual reports on information disclosure on time. The effectiveness of online links for proactive disclosure and its consistency both improved greatly. Governments also made obvious progress in providing information by disclosure application responses. Several agencies also responded and provided information to the study group's requests.

Third, the data in annual reports showed that administrative agencies received more applications for information disclosure. In 2011 very few agencies did not receive any disclosure requests and more agencies received increased amount of applications. This situation indicated that more and more people were using the system of government information disclosure to meet their needs, which certainly put greater pressure on governments and urged them to enhance their management capability and efforts of executing administrative power by law.

The study also exposed some problems in government information disclosure, which need attention and improvement. First, the awareness of government information disclosure needs to be strengthened. According to the study, quite a few government staff still regarded information disclosure as a burden, and were not willing to comply. Some even showed unwillingness and resentment in their communication with applicants. Second, organizational structure was not satisfactory. The Regulations on Disclosure of Government Information had been implemented for over five years, but some administrative agencies still had not set up specialized units or designated specialized personnel for this job, which adversely affected information disclosure. Third, online disclosure devises were problematic. Some agencies did not have websites, or the website did not function, or website information was rarely updated. Fourth, a small number of agencies did not fully perform their duty of proactively disclosure. Some did not disclose the information required by law; some disclosure was incomplete, or online disclosure links invalid or inconvenient for access, updating delayed, layout confusing and information disclosed inconsistent under different content columns. For some governments, information disclosure was still a mere formality. Fifth, some agencies still restricted people's access to government information. Sixth, government agencies should guard against "non-action". Quite a few agencies admitted that they had not collected the information on newly-appointed officials (such as, number of these officials, their positions, gender ratio, education background and majors). Also they had no data regarding disciplined officials (such as the number, the reason and the type of discipline imposed), therefore such information was not available for disclosure.

3. Development trend and suggestions.

The Regulations for Disclosure of Government Information had been implemented for more than five years. Practices in recent years and the latest evaluation results suggest that the most remarkable progress shows in the establishment of the basic systems and disclosure of government budgets and final accounting; the most expected improvement lies in information disclosure of social organizations and public entities; and the most sustainable development of government information disclosure depends on positive interactions of the government and the public. Based on my research and the evaluation data of CPPSS and CASS, I believe the following issues need to be addressed to further advance government information disclosure.

First, governments need to take the initiative to disclose budgets and final accounting, and ensure the promptness, effectiveness, and convenience of proactive disclosure, so as to meet people's demand for disclosure. Governments should earn people's trust by proactive disclosure to enhance governments' credibility in the society as a whole.

Second, governments need to strengthen organizational structure for information disclosure. People's growing demand requires information disclosure to be more specialized and timely. This cannot be achieved without specialized units and personnel. These staff must have specialized knowledge in management, in relevant statutes, and information technology.

Third, governments need to raise awareness of information disclosure among their staff. This is a long-term process. The old-fashioned training model of numerous meetings and document reading should be discarded, and instead to adopt engaging, lively and systematic training to incorporate the concept of transparency into the staff's working attitude and style and rid of the slothful mentality and manner.

Fourth, establishing clear standards for information disclosure is urgently needed, such as standards on website design, content column arrangement, disclosure platform, scope of disclosure, information not subject to disclosure, and required components of annual reports. These standards will enhance the effectiveness of information disclosure and also make supervision and evaluation easier.

Fifth, governments should adopt new models to manage their websites and information disclosure. To reduce costs and increase efficiency, scattered management needs to be consolidated. Local governments should separate information disclosure from the websites of their department, and put all disclosed information on the web portals.

Sixth, the Regulation of the Supreme People's Court on Several Issues Regarding Handling Administrative Cases of Government Information Disclosure should be implemented. Judicial supervision and remedies should be promoted. Courts should be encouraged, through accumulated exploration and experience of adjudicating individual cases, to apply the Regulation in adjudication. And provide judicial guidance for cases involving request for government information disclosure.

Seventh, depending on issues of public interest and concern, information disclosure of social organizations and public entities should be fully practiced: One, educating the staff of these organizations so they will disclose information closely related to people's life and interests in a proactive way as a public service and engage in positive interactions with the public. Two, through effective external supervision and providing remedies to, intensify accountability and regulation implementation. Three, introducing the mechanism of external supervision and remedy; under the existing legal framework, academia and the judiciary have not reached a conclusion as for whether and how judicial review should be applied to information disclosure by public organizations and entities. It is advisable to reconstruct the concept of administrative subjects, expand the scope of administrative subjects, and include public organizations into the subject and scope of information disclosure, so as to provide judicial safeguard for people's right to be informed.

Chapter 7
Emergency and Government Response Management

In China various public safety incidents happen every now and then. Although the overall public safety situation is stable and getting better, serious challenges remain in forms of severe natural disasters, safe production accidents, disastrous incidents, and public health crisis, which threaten people's lives and health and affect state security and social stability. Therefore, China's emergency response management faces many new challenges: (a) enormous risks and challenges caused by urbanization and modernization; (b) new and complex risks brought by rapid development of science, technology and the economy; (c) new challenges faced by all countries with diversity and globalization; (d) the unique transitional stage China is going through; (e) people's increased demand for public safety.

We must analyze the new challenges and opportunities based on actual situation of our country, to fully understand the tasks that we face with continued industrialization, technology advancement, urbanization, market development and globalization, to establish and improve government emergency response management, and to effectively handle and mitigate various emergencies in the course of economic and social development.

7.1 The History and Current Situation of China's Emergency Response Management

1. History of China's emergency response management system.

An emergency response and management system as a huge comprehensive systematic undertaking of a modern society began to be built after the founding of People's Republic of China. Since then, the scope of the system has gradually expanded from mainly dealing with natural disasters to covering outbreaks of epidemics, production accidents, and social crises as well as natural disasters. The response management

© Social Sciences Academic Press and Springer Nature Singapore Pte Ltd. 2018

H. Ma and J. Wang, *Building a Government Based on the Rule of Law*,
Research Series on the Chinese Dream and China's Development Path,
https://doi.org/10.1007/978-981-13-0999-1_7

mechanism has also developed from response to a single disaster by a specialized agency to coordinated overall response and management.

(1) Specialized emergency response system.

The specialized emergency response system was created at the beginning of the PRC. At that time preventing and mitigating disasters were part of the responsibilities of the Ministry of Water Resources, the Ministry of Forestry, the Central Meteorological Administration and other agencies. In addition, some central government agencies and their subsidiaries also established their own rescue force, such as: (a) disaster prevention and relief agencies under the Ministry of Water Resources. This Ministry was founded in October 1949 and its name had been changed several times until it was decided in 1988 as the Ministry of Water Resources. Its functions include protecting hydro-electric power facilities on rivers, flood control and drought relief; (b) earthquake prevention and forecasting agencies. In 1971 the State Council decided to abolish the Central Earthquake Task Force Office and set up the State Seismological Bureau to handle earthquake-related work. During the institutional reform of 1983, the State Council decided to change the affiliation of local seismological offices from under the local government to under the dual leadership of the State Seismological Bureau and the local government, with the State Bureau playing the lead role; (c) the Department of Forecast and Disaster Relief under the State Oceanic Administration. In 2008, the State Council approved a new plan for redefining the organizational structure, the responsibilities, and the staffing of its departments. According to this plan, the Department of Forecast and Disaster Relief was established under the State Oceanic Administration, with the mission of ocean observation, forecast, and early warning of marine disasters; (d) fire departments under public security agencies. The firefighting force in China consists of three parts. First, fire brigades under public security agencies, whose staff enjoy the same benefits as members of the Chinese People's Liberation Army and they make up the major force of fire prevention and rescue. Second, professional fire brigades under local governments with members employed on a contractual basis. Third, professional fire brigades under businesses or public service entities. (e) State Administration of Work Safety established in 2001, which marked a major progress in the reform of work safety management, with a new agency and the system up and running.

(2) The formation of a comprehensive emergency response management system.

Emergency response management is a comprehensive undertaking, which incorporates the following factors. (a) Numerous entities are involved and an effective response network should have participation of the general public and combine rescue efforts of self-rescue, mutual-rescue and public-rescue. (b) The targets of emergency response include natural disasters, accidents, public health outbreaks and social safety incidents. It is an all-round risk management. Therefore, the traditional model of certain agencies coping with certain disasters no longer suits the needs of disaster's response of the modern time. To enhance the government's response capability, the Chinese government responded to the United Nation's call and set up China's

National Commission for the International Decade of Natural Disaster Reduction. In 2005, it was renamed as China National Commission for Disaster Reduction. The Commission consisted of 34 members, including relevant ministries and commissions under the State Council, military divisions and research institutes. Its mission was to formulate national guidelines and policies on disaster reduction; coordinate disaster reduction efforts; provide guidance to local disaster reduction work; and promote international exchange and cooperation. Even though only being a consultative and coordinating agency, the Commission represented the early form of China's comprehensive emergency response management system, which has been actively expanded. For instance, in 2006, the State Council Emergency Response Management Office was established to handle the day-to-day operation of emergency response and management. It functioned as a central command post for information collection and coordinated actions round the clock. Since May 2006, local governments at or above the county level also set up their own Emergency Response Management Offices based on the model of the State Council, and by the end of 2006, all such offices were established at or above the county level throughout the country.[1]

2. The development of "One Plan, Three Mechanisms".
(1) Definition.

"One Plan, Three Mechanism" means emergency response and preparedness plan, emergency response system, operation mechanism, and legal framework. "One Plan" refers to the emergency response preparation plan; "Three Mechanisms" refers to emergency response system, operation mechanism, and legal framework. System setup refers to a centralized, strong and efficient command post. Operation mechanism includes monitoring, early warning, reporting, decision-making and coordinating functions. Legal framework refers to administrative actions by law and making the response system better regulated. The system of "One Plan, Three Mechanism" (hereinafter as the "System") is "a top-down design", which provides an overall leadership to emergency response management work.

(2) Background and achievements.

The System was developed based on the experience and lessons learned from fighting the Severe Acute Respiratory Syndrome (SARS), which served as, the direct catalyst of creating the System. In 2006, the 6th Plenary Session of the 16th CPC Central Committee put forward the strategic task of building a socialist harmonious society, and as part of this undertaking, the design of the System was proposed.

(a) Formulation of the emergency preparation master plan.

The emergency preparation plan (hereinafter as the Plan) marked the beginning of the establishment of the System. In 2003, the General Office of the State Council

---

[1] Shan Chunchang, Emergency Response and Management: *Operational Model and Practice with Chinese Characteristics*, Beijing Normal University Press, March, 2011, pp. 19–25.

set up the Plan Task Force and made drafting and revising of the Plan as one of the government's top priorities of 2004. In April 2004, the General Office of the State Council issued the General Guidelines to Relevant Departments and Agencies on Drafting or Revising the Plan for Rapid Response to Public Emergencies. In May of the same year, the General Office released the General Guidelines to People's Governments of Provinces (Autonomous Regions and Municipalities) on Drafting or Revising the Plan for Rapid Response to Public Emergencies.

In January 2005, the State Council held an executive meeting and approved the National Master Preparation Plan for Rapid Response to Public Emergencies (hereafter referred to as the Master Plan). In February 2005, the State Council reported its work on formulation of the Master Plan to the Standing Committee of the National People's Congress and stated that the framework for the national emergency preparation plan had been basically established.[2] In January 2006, the Master Plan was issued by the State Council to guide public emergency response across the country. Depending on the occurrence, nature and handling mechanism, the Master Plan put public emergencies into four categories, namely, natural disasters, catastrophic accidents, public health incidents, and social security incidents. The Master Plan laid out six basic principles for emergency management: (a) put people first and minimize harms; (b) put prevention first and be prepared; (c) consolidate command and clarify responsibilities of governments at each level; (d) abide by laws and strengthen management; (e) respond quickly in a coordinated way; (f) utilize science and technology while emphasizing human capacity. The Master Plan also set forth organization, operation, contingency measures, and supervision of public emergency response. Within a few years, more than 1.3 million emergency plans at all levels were in place across the country, covering all kinds of public emergencies. Thus a national emergency response network was basically established.

(b) Organizational setup.

After the SARS epidemic was contained, China established a new organizational setup for emergency response, featuring the key command of Emergency Response Management Office under the government at each level, with coordination of joint conferences of all departments concerned. In June 2006, the State Council issued the Opinion on Comprehensive Strengthening of Emergency Response Management which emphasized the following: categorized management, responsibility at different levels, territorial management, administrative accountability system under the leadership of the Party Committee, and capacity building of emergency response organizations and rescue teams.[3] In November, 2007, the Emergency Response Law of the People's Republic of China was released. It prescribed that the State shall establish an emergency response management system featuring centralized leadership, integrated coordination, categorized control, responsibility at different levels,

[2]Shen Lutao and Zou Shengwen, *Coping with Disasters Calmly: An Overview of China's Public Incidents Emergency Plan Framework*, Xinhua News Agency, Beijing, Feb. 25, 2005.

[3]Gao Xiaoping, Achievements and Development of the Emergency Response Management System with Chinese Characteristics, *China Administrative Management*, 2008, issue 11, p. 20.

and territorial management. Currently, this setup has been basically in place. Apart from the central government, the departments and local governments also formed their own emergency response management, setup, which further improved the entire network.

In short, the current emergency response management in China is a comprehensive and institutionalized new system. On the basis of the rule of law it provides guaranteed protection in both peacetime and wartime, as well as normal and non-normal situations. In terms of organizational setup, apart from temporary command post and standing operation unit at the central level, local governments at and above the county level also established respective emergency command units, headed by chief officials of the governments, relevant departments, local People's Liberation Army and Armed Police Force. A volunteer system was also established to organize social groups and the general public to participate in emergency response when needed. In terms of functions, the law has made clear that emergency response entities, under normal situations, have the duties of drafting preparation program, coordinating resources and efforts, organizing drills, and checking and eliminating potential risk causes. And in response to emergency situations, government agencies[4] are given the power and authority to take actions as needed.

(c) The operation mechanism.

The operation mechanism for emergency response refers to institutionalized methods and measures in the entire course of emergencies from occurring, unfolding, and changing situations. The Opinions of the State Council on Comprehensive Strengthening Emergency Response Management issued in July 2006 prescribed to build an emergency response mechanism featuring "centralized command, quick response, orderly coordination and high efficiency". Since 2003, a number of documents have been issued concerning establishment of monitoring and early warning mechanism, information report mechanism, decision-making and command mechanism, information release mechanism, and reconstruction mechanism. For instance, in terms of the risk assessment, the General Office of the State Council issued Notice on Inspection and Elimination of Potential Safety Hazards of Major Infrastructure Projects. In terms of information report, in December 2007, the General Office of the State Council issued Notice on Information Report Methods of Public Emergencies (for Trial Implementation). In terms of information release, in February 2004, the State Council approved Opinions on Implementation of Strengthening and Improving Press Release of Domestic Emergency Incidents. In terms of coordination between the military and local governments, in June, 2005, the State Council and the Central Military Commission published Regulations on the Army's Participation in Disaster Rescue. In September, 2006, the State Council and the Central Military Commission jointly issued Notice on Enhancing Information Sharing Mechanisms between the Army and Local Governments Concerning Natural Disasters.[5]

---

[4]Ibid.

[5]Shan Chunchang, *Emergency Management: Operational Model and Practice with Chinese Characteristics*, Beijing Normal University Press, March, 2011, p. 31–32.

After years of efforts, China has established monitoring and early warning mechanism, information report mechanism, emergency response mechanism, emergency handling mechanism, investigation and assessment mechanism, reconstruction mechanism, social mobilization mechanism, emergency resource allocation and requisition mechanism, government-people collaboration mechanism, and international coordination mechanism.

(d) Development of the legal framework.

Law is the fundamental major basis in coping with public emergencies. In recent years, the most salient feature of emergency response management development in China is that "emergency response plans of all kinds and at all levels are formulated based on summarizing people's actual practice experience; then they are, developed into systematic mechanisms which further become a series of laws and regulations, so that there are rules to follow when responding to emergencies."[6]

Before the Emergency Response Law of the People's Republic of China was enacted in 2007, China had already passed 35 laws, 37 administrative regulations, 55 department regulations, and 111 regulatory instruments concerning emergency response. For instance in May, 2003, the State Council issued Regulations on Handling of Public Health Emergencies, which was an important landmark showing that health emergency response began to be codified. The Emergency Response Law became effective in November, 2007, which was the first comprehensive law on coping with all types of emergencies since the founding of the PRC. It provided effective legal basis and safeguards for emergency management and marked that the basic legal framework for emergency response was in place. Since the 16th National Congress of the CPC in 2002, the State Council has issued over 60 more special-purpose statutes and regulations concerning emergency responses, including Regulations on Handling of Public Health Emergencies and Regulations on Handling Major Animal Epidemic Emergencies. The Standing Committee of the National People's Congress organized the amendment of the Law on Prevention and Treatment of Infectious Diseases and the Law on Animal Epidemic Prevention.

In short, China has basically established a comprehensive legal framework for emergency response management, which is based on the Constitution, centered on the Emergency Response Law, and supported by specialized legislations. It is on the right track of being gradually codified and institutionalized.[7]

---

[6]The Address of State Councilor Hua Jianmin at the Conference on Implementation of the Emergency Response Law, Nov. 13, 2007.

[7]Shan Chunchang, *Emergency Management: Operational Model and Practice with Chinese Characteristics*, Beijing Normal University Press, March, 2011, p. 33–35.

7.2 Reform of the Public Emergency Response Mechanism

With the development of urbanization, large cities now face a myriad of urban catastrophes. Natural disasters, urban ecological disasters, urban industrial facilities, severe supply shortage of public goods, and high-tech risks are all potential sources of urban public crises. The impact of urban public crises could be amplified with chain reactions, which not only disrupt the order of the cities, but also harm people's interests, and if not handled properly, might even undermine China's foreign relations and impair its international image. To effectively deal with public crisis events, in recent years some cities have made significant headway in emergency management. They formed public emergency response committees, municipal emergency command centers, citywide emergency command platforms, emergency command offices and command posts for specific types of emergencies. Meanwhile, they drafted or improved emergency plans, including master preparation plans of local governments, disaster response plans, emergency support plans, and comprehensive emergency response plans at the district and county level. Laws and regulations concerning public crises and emergency response management are also being improved. Yet on the whole, there are still deficiencies especially for large city emergency response management: the legal framework needs to be fully established; emergency response laws and regulations are to be better implemented; the organizational setup and operation mechanisms need to be more diverse; coping methods are too simplistic; emergency plans lack operational details; there is little coordination between various departments; and the social mobilization mechanism is not complete. All these issues undermine the effectiveness of the urban emergency response management. Therefore, improving the government's capacity to ensure public safety and cope with public crisis events, preventing and minimizing the damage have become an urgent task for study and solutions.

1. Integrating regular governmental functions with emergency response functions.

Emergency response management has only become a commonly used concept and term in recent years. But emergency response had always been part of the government's public management functions. Traditional Chinese public management only emphasized response in emergency situations, while overlooking prevention and early warning. Under the current system, government management functions are characterized as regular functions and emergency functions depending on the nature of management. Due to the fact that public crises do not happen often, so in practice the government often pays more attention to its regular functions and neglects the emergency functions. Also, in reality, the government of some regions overemphasizes economic development and fails to see the relationship between socio-economic development and crisis, and, therefore, their development plans give no consideration to how to respond in the event of public emergencies. Some projects of high returns also came with high risks, yet they were started in a hurry, bringing potential risks for accidents that might trigger public crises. This is an important cause of frequent occurrence of serious accidents. If these accidents are not properly dealt with, they may completely ruin the fruits of development.[8] Currently, most cities in China are still in the state of passive responding to emergencies, and the significance of prevention is still largely neglected. As a result, the government is at a disadvantaged position. In terms of government administration, their regular functions are closely related to emergency management for they share the same goal of safeguarding public interests. Therefore, the government should raise its crisis awareness and incorporate emergency response management into its regular functions as well as into the socio-economic development plans of the region. In particular, the establishment of prevention and early warning mechanism and the formulation and drills of emergency plans should become part of the government's regular work. It should be a consideration in government's decision-making and also a criterion for performance evaluations of a government's administration capacity.

2. Coordinating different departments and speeding up emergency collaboration.

In terms of organizational structure, emergency response management tends to be handled by separate departments. The vertical management within a department is pretty good but division of labor among different departments is not clearly defined. There are both overlap of responsibilities and absence of management. The inter-department coordination is poor. Some departments only know their own responsibility but have little idea of the responsibility of others. In terms of the management system, there are problems that adversely affect the country's financial resources, such as basic geographical information, communication information, rescue teams and disaster relief equipment are not shared among different departments; instead, each department builds its own capacities, causing enormous waste. Lack of inter-department collaboration not only drains resources, it also undermines effective decision-making in crisis. As a result, the impact of the accidents often aggravates from minor incidents to severe disasters. In reality, the public security, traffic management, firefighting, emergency medical service, flood control, earthquake and other authorities all have their own public emergency information system, but information sharing among them is to be improved.

Take Beijing as an example. According to incomplete statistics, in the past, there were two kinds of emergency aid systems in Beijing. One was the emergency telephone system: 110 for the police, 119 for the fire brigade, 122 for traffic authority, 120 for emergency medical service from hospitals and 999 for emergency medical service from the Beijing Red Cross Society. The other one was public hotlines including the mayor's hotline, emergency or service hotlines of water, power, heat and gas supply, telecommunications, urban management, consumer protection and other departments. These two systems had over 50 telephone numbers belonging to multiple agencies that were not coordinated.[9] In the first half of 2007 the Beijing Non-Emergency Aid Center was opened. It adopted a management model featuring

---

[8]Chen Shuwei, Enhancing the Capacity Building for Urban Emergency Response Management in China, *Journal of Tianjin Administrative College*, May, 2007.

[9]Zhong Kaibin and Peng Zongchao, Emergencies and Establishment of the Capital City Emergency Collaboration System, *Beijing Social Sciences*, issue 4, 2003.

unified platform, categorized response, public supervision and feedback. Under this non-emergency aid system, a call center was set up where residents in Beijing only need to dial the unified emergency service number (12345) if they need urgent assistance. The Center can answer simple inquiries, transfer calls to specialized hotlines, or produce incident reports to its subsidiaries to handle. Thus people can reach many agencies with just one call only. Based on the division of governmental functions, the Center will forward callers' requests to different subsidiaries which will then handle the requests and give feedbacks to the callers. In addition to those transferred from the call Center, the subsidiaries also take phone calls directly from the public. The Beijing Non-Emergency Aid Center coordinates, manages and supervises the non-emergency aid system throughout the city.[10] This mechanism is very helpful in integrating emergency assistance resources of various departments. However, how to effectively connect the emergency response numbers of 110, 119 and 112 with the non-emergency aid system still remains to be resolved. In reality, what starts out to be a non-emergent matter may develop into an emergency as situation changes. If the emergency and non-emergency systems are not effectively coordinated, it may delay the handling of emergencies. Therefore, a citywide or even nationwide emergency collaboration system should be established, and the numerous specialized emergency phone numbers should be replaced by a unified one.

3. Expanding the channels for social participation.

The society, as a community of human existence, is composed of natural environment, population, economy, and culture. The situation and development of these factors play different roles in the operation of a society. Meanwhile, society as a whole is made up of various sub-systems which interact and boost the development of the society. How to harmonize these different systems and factors to ensure smooth operation of the society has always been the goal. Social governance is about providing services and the boundary between the service provider and receiver are blurry and often interchangeable. In a self-governing society, everyone can be a service provider or receiver. It is a co-governance system characterized by everyone providing service for everyone else, i.e. governing together. Co-governing is characterized by diverse subjects of governance, non-confrontational approaches, and adjustable and compatible interests.[11] In a consultative democracy, it is easier for the public to reason and reach consensus; therefore, the decisions taken are easier to be understood and carried out, and thus greatly reduce the cost of implementing public policies.

Public emergencies can cause wide-ranging impacts. The government shoulders the primary but not the solely responsibility of emergency management; it is also the shared responsibility of the whole society. Traditionally, the Chinese society used to emphasize political and administrative mobilization, which was indeed necessary

[10] http://www.ccyl.org.cn/bulletin/qyb_scyqy/200711/t20071112_50568.htm, last retrieved on 2007-11-16.

[11] Tang Yalin and Guolin, From Governed by the Class System to Co-Governance: A Historical Study on the Governance Model of the People's Republic of China, *The Academic Circle*, 2006, issue 4, p. 62.

to cope with public emergencies, and in fact, the capacity to mobilize is an advantage of the Chinese government. However, with the advance of the post-industrial knowledge and information ear, the organizational structure in society has become smaller, looser, and simpler. People tend to adopt diversified, divergent, complex and intertwined ways of thinking. The hierarchical and bureaucratic model is quietly collapsing in every sector and wide public participation in social governance is emerging. Under the traditional system, the government was seen as the only responsible body of crisis management. People expected and relied on the government to tackle crises in every way. The efforts of the government determined the result of crisis management. With this social mentality, the government's burden was too heavy to bear. Therefore, political and administrative mobilization alone is not sufficient to meet the needs of the society today. There is no way that the government can provide every service demanded by the public. Particularly after an emergency breaks out, if the government fails to handle it effectively, it is very likely to cause public panic and proliferation of crises. Wide public participation not only helps improve the efficiency of the government's work, it also cuts the cost of emergency response and reduces losses. If social forces are mobilized and their affinity with the public fully leveraged, it can reduce the people's reliance on the government, ease social panic and stabilize social conditions. This paper suggests efforts in the following key areas to enhance social participation.

(1) Improving the human resource reserve system and establishing profiles of professionals in every community. The handling of public emergencies calls for professionals in many fields. If these professionals intervene immediately after emergencies take place, they can help identify the priorities and provide more targeted response. There are deficiencies in current human resource reserve system at all levels of government, which makes it difficult to meet the demand for instant personnel dispatch in the event of emergencies. In particular, community-based organizations have little information about human resources within their own communities. As a result, they are not able to organize effective self-rescue when crises occur. Therefore, it is necessary to establish a human resource reserve system in each community and enhance the social capacity to respond to crises. Integrating resources of the community helps form grassroots self-rescue organizations and provide the foundation for social relief efforts.

(2) Improving the legal mechanism and promoting the role of insurance in public emergencies. The government should improve relevant laws and incorporate insurance into t accident prevention and rescue system, so that the role of insurance in preventing disasters, mitigating losses and coping with accidents can be fully leveraged. Insurance entities should build their risk management capacities and combine precaution with compensation. They should use insurance rate as an economic lever to incentivize prevention, reduce accidents, promote production safety, and strengthen emergency response management. They can deploy market-based operations, policy guidance, government orders, and law enforcement to provide insurance service products such as safe production liability, construction project liability, product liability, public responsibility, occupational liability, liability of board directors, environmental pollution liability and other types of insurance. The government should have a

pilot project of compulsory liability insurance with the coal mining industry first and then gradually expand the practice to other high-risk industries, crowded public places, and domestic and overseas travels. The safety production risk mortgage measure for high-risk industries need to be improved, which also need to explore to allow professional insurance companies for management and operation.

(3) Enhancing capacity-building of community and business-based rescue teams and specifying their status and code of conduct through legislation. Our current emergency rescue system consists of professional relief agencies and rescue teams under the public security, fire fighting, earthquake, air and maritime authorities, with the government as the major rescue force. The SOS rescue agency under preparation by the government can improve professional rescue capacity to some extent. Now the SOS Call Center is ready to take emergency calls 24 h a day. The Rescue Agency will also build an emergency transport facility with 24 helicopters; other transport and delivery systems are also under development. After the SOS rescue company is established, it may sign agreements with the armed forces, so that military helicopters can be summoned to help in times of emergency.[12] However, the professional rescue teams run by the government cannot meet the increasing demand for handling all public emergencies. The slow response to tourist incidents during the "Golden Travel Week" revealed the deficiencies in the public rescue system. Due to the absence of relevant policies and regulations, the role of non-governmental rescue organizations is not clearly defined. Based on their natures and objectives, the non-governmental rescue organizations can be divided into two categories: non-profit and for-profit. The non-profit rescue organizations are usually founded by volunteers on their own initiative to carry out rescue activities. They are not registered with any government departments. Such organizations include the self-rescue and mutual assistance organizations formed by driving enthusiasts or backpackers. For-profit organizations, such as private fire brigades and salvage teams, are mostly registered with relevant departments and obtained business licenses. Yet in practice, there are still some that are not registered with any authorities. As their social status and scope of power are not clearly defined, the non-governmental rescue teams sometimes run across obstacles when carrying out rescue activities or even have disputes with the people they rescue. In addition, most of these rescue teams are poorly equipped and underfinanced. Currently, except for some for-profit professional organizations in big cities, the non-governmental rescue organizations in rural areas and small towns still use outdated equipment or even refitted homemade equipment. These organizations are mostly funded by private donations. They receive little subsidy from the government. A few rescue organizations are supported by townships and villages but still can hardly make their ends meet. Some organizations charge fees for their rescue service, and their charges are mostly arbitrary and unregulated. In general, due to absence of laws and policy guidance, most of the non-governmental rescue organizations are left to their own means.

---

[12] http://www.ce.cn/xwzx/gnsz/gdxw/200610/21/t20061021_9063268.shtml, last retrieved on 2007-11-17.

In comparison, rescue systems in developed countries are more mature. For example, outdoor emergency rescue is mainly carried out by the government in China, whereas in many developed countries, it is mostly carried out by rescue companies. The person in need of such service can purchase emergency rescue insurance policy and get a card with the basic information of the insured, such as health condition, blood type, medical history, and drug allergies. In emergencies, the person in danger can call the rescue company and report his or her card number. Upon receiving the call, the rescue company will retrieve the caller's information through a computer, locate him or her through the GPS, and dispatch a helicopter or ambulance from the nearest base and the cost is covered by the insurance company. If the person in danger is not insured, the cost will be borne by himself or herself.

Chapter 11 of the California Emergency Services Act prescribes the plan for utilizing volunteer resources in emergency, which includes confirmation, cataloguing, coordination and training of volunteer resources.[13] Article 153 of the Act prescribes that volunteers and persons who join the service are immune from liability during emergency. The New York State Volunteer Firefighters' Benefit Law of 1957 established a benefit system for volunteer firefighters to safeguard their rights and interests and encourage them to serve the public. In France the Act on Modernization of Civil Security (No. 2004-811) promulgated on August 13, 2004, prescribes that volunteers can participate in rescue operations upon approval of the government, and it specifies the benefits they enjoy. For instance, Article 78 of the Act prescribes that if volunteers get injured in emergency response, the State shall cover their medical expenses, treatment cost, transportation cost, accommodation cost, rehabilitation cost, accessory equipment cost, and shall compensate for their income losses and long-term disability. Article 79 prescribes that volunteers shall enjoy the same work time reduction, tax refunds, preferential treatment in employment and other benefits as professional rescue personnel.[14]

In addition to improving government rescue teams, community and business-based rescue teams should also be developed. Public-private partnership should be adopted in emergency rescue operations. The status and rescue charges of private organizations should be regulated by law so as to promote sound development of non-governmental rescue forces. Some regions have already begun to explore the new model of public-private partnership in emergency rescue. For example, the outdoors emergency rescue teams organized by volunteer backpackers[15] in Songshan Scenic Area, Henan Province assisted the police in carrying out several successful rescues.[16]

(4) Giving full play the role of non-governmental organizations in emergency management. The unique nature of non-governmental associations determines that

[13]Wan Pengfei, (edit): *Emergency Response Management Laws in the United States, Canada and the United Kingdom*, Beijing University Press, April, 2006, p. 58.

[14]http://www.legifrance.gouv.fr/WAspad/Ajour?nor=INTX0300211L&num=2004-811&ind=1&laPage=1&demande=ajour, last retrieved on 2007-11-26.

[15]Backpackers (Lv-You in Chinese, a friendly term) refer to outdoor-sport enthusiasts, especially those travel on their own for, mountaineering and hiking adventures.

[16]Ten Backpackers Come to Rescue Five Teachers Trapped on a Cliff at Night, *Beijing Youth Newspaper*, November 28, 2007, B1.

they can play an important role in responding to social risks. Act No. 2004-811 of 13 August 2004 on the Modernization of Civil Security in France defines the status and sets the rules for social organizations' participation in emergency response through a number of provisions. For instance, Article 35 prescribes that, upon government approval, associations with the purpose of ensuring civil safety can take part in crisis rescue and civil support activities; can organize crisis prevention and can participate in first-aid training. Article 38 prescribes that the government can sign agreements with emergency response associations to specify their roles, response actions, and duration, and provide financial support if necessary.[17] The American Rescue Association was founded in 1950 with branches in every state. All its members are volunteers. Its office space is provided by the government; its helicopters provided by the military; and search dogs provided by the police force.[18]

In China, over the past 20 years of reform and opening-up, non-governmental and autonomous social organizations have had few opportunities to operate independently in major public crises. Due to lack of volunteer organizations and community-based mutual aid social groups, people were not effectively mobilized to prevent and cope with crises. Thus the role of the government was greatly inhibited. After a crisis broke out, the government needed time to go through proper procedures before activating response mechanisms. There was little interaction between the government and the public. In some big cities, the population is highly mobile, and there are few religious, cultural, ethics or community connections for the drifting population to be attached to. In crisis situations they feel lonely, frightened without community support. When faced with sudden horror, they have no choice but to run back to hometown, where they have families, clans and neighbors to rely on. Non-governmental organizations can fill up the gap of lacking community support and to some extent satisfy people's needs for human connection.

Many tasks in handling public crises are highly specialized. Non-governmental organizations can also make up for the weakness of the government in this regard. Meanwhile, these organizations can organize self-rescue and mutual aid operations if the government is not yet at the scene. The emergency plans made by governments of all levels should count non-governmental organizations in as public resources and specify their responsibilities and missions so as to bring their role into full play.

(5) Regulating news reports on public emergencies. How to regulate media reports on public emergencies is a sensitive and realistic issue. Timely, accurate and effective media report is essential for saving lives, reducing losses, reassuring the people, and facilitating disaster relief efforts. However, one should also be aware that false or distorted report could cause severe damages. The government emergency response office should set up a specialized unit responsible for media liaison and information release. The government should regulate emergency news reports with more detailed and practical rules. It should define the obligations of reporters, such as obeying orders of the on-site command post, following professional reporting procedures,

[17] http://www.legifrance.gouv.fr/WAspad/Ajour?nor=INTX0300211L&num=2004-811&ind=1&laPage=1&demande=ajour, last time retrieved: 2007-11-26.

[18] http://outdoor.travel.sohu.com/20060522/n243343129.shtml, last time retrieved: 2007-11-17.

keeping sensitive information, protecting the rights of disaster victims (especially privacy of children), taking proper precautions against communicable diseases, and carrying necessary protective equipment. Also, the news agencies should bear the cost for their own reporting activities. The government is obliged to strengthen the training of journalists and improve their abilities of self-protection.

To sum up, it is a global trend to promote centralized command and comprehensive coordination in order to strengthen public emergency management. We should further explore system building and improve the government's capacity to organize concerted actions, so as to form an emergency response management system featuring inter-departmental resource integration, unified coordination and public-private collaboration.

7.3 Improvement of Legal System of Emergency Requisition

With rapid socio-economic development in China, natural disasters, calamitous accidents, public health emergencies and social safety emergencies become more frequent. Emergency response has become a daunting task for the government. Government emergency response is a comprehensive project that calls for a great deal of human, material and financial resources. On the one hand, based on the provisions of the Emergency Response Law of the People's Republic of China and other laws and regulations, governments of all levels have established their emergency supply reserve system. On the other hand, there is an ever-lasting contradiction between emergency demand and reserve. If reserve exceeds practical demand, it will cause waste. If reserve falls short of demand, it will impede emergency response. Since emergencies are urgent and unpredictable, a gap will always exist between reserve and emergency demand. This is the actual ground for emergency requisition. Emergency requisition can make up for the shortage of reserves and improve the efficiency of emergency management. This paper attempts to review the legal framework for emergency requisition, identify its problems and provide suggestions for improvement.

1. An overview of the legal framework.

Requisition system has existed in China for many years. Several versions of the Constitution adopted since the founding of the People's Republic of China all have provisions about requisition.[19] Since the 1990s, laws have been made to allow the government to expropriate, in emergency situations, assets of citizens, legal persons

[19] Article 13 of the 1954 *Constitution*: "The State may, in the public interest, requisition by purchase, take over for use or nationalize both urban and rural land as well as other means of production on the conditions provided by law". Article 6 of the 1975 *Constitution*: "The State may requisition by purchase, take over for use, or nationalize urban and rural land as well as other means of, production under conditions prescribed by law". Article 6 of the 1978 *Constitution*: "The State may requisition by purchase, take over for use, or nationalize land under conditions prescribed by law". Article

and other organizations for public interests. Under the current legal framework, based on the extent of urgency, the term "emergency response" can be used in both broad and narrow sense. Emergency response in its broad sense refers to the response to natural disasters, calamitous accidents, public health incidents, public security incidents and other emergencies specified in the Emergency Response Law. The term in its broad sense also includes the response to martial law and defense mobilization. The two definitions differ in their extent of urgency and government prevention and handling measures. Yet in terms of emergency requisition, the same basic reasoning is applied to both situations, and this paper will discuss emergency requisition system in the broad sense.

While searching the PKU Law Database, we found that some laws and regulations differentiate between "requisition" and "transfer". For instance, in the Law on Prevention and Treatment of Infectious Diseases, requisition refers to the use of social resources by the government to respond to emergencies. Transfer refers to the use of resources in the government reserve system by the government.[20] However, in many laws and regulations, "requisition" and "transfer" are used interchangeably. Sometimes the word "mobilize" is also used. All these words denote the use of social resources by the government to respond to emergencies. Such a phenomenon continues to exist even after the promulgation of the Public Emergency Law in 2007. We agree with the differentiation of "requisition" and "transfer" in the Law on Prevention and Treatment of Infectious Diseases, and hold that the two words should be used to denote different meanings. This paper studies the government's requisition of social resources. The transfer of government reserve is beyond the scope of this analysis. However, since different choices of wording, "transfer" and "mobilize" may also be used to refer to "requisition", in order to ensure a full coverage of relevant statutes, we searched all usage of "requisition", "transfer" and "mobilize" in the database, and selected entries that referred to "the use of social resources by the government to respond to emergencies" for the purpose of our study.[21]

---

10 of the 1982 *Constitution*: "The State may, in the public interest and in accordance with law, expropriate or requisition land.". Article 10 of the 2004 *Amendment to the Constitution*: "The State may, in the public interest and in accordance with law, expropriate or requisition land for its use and make compensation for the land expropriated or requisitioned". Article 13 of the said statute: "The State may, in the public interest and in accordance with law, expropriate or requisition private property for its use and make compensation for the private property expropriated or requisitioned".

[20] *The Law on Prevention and Treatment of Infectious Diseases*, Article 45.

[21] In legislations, requisition (transfer/ mobilize) are used in difference senses. Some refer to the requisition of social resources; some others refer to the transfer of government reserve materials. When retrieving and examining the provisions, we used several criteria to make a decision on the interpretation. The first criterion is the objects of the verb. For instance, materials of entities and individuals, communication systems of communication enterprises, or the social non-commercial passenger vehicles are obviously social resources. Another criterion is compensation. If there are provisions on compensation, it will be considered requisition of social resources. If it is impossible to judge from the provision itself, we would ask the opinions of relevant agencies to determine the meaning of the provision. For instance, Article 45 of the *Fire Protection Law* provides that as urgently needed by the fire fighting, relevant local people's governments may organize persons and muster necessary materials to assist in the fire fighting. Here "muster" actually refers to requisition.

We found that "requisition" was mentioned in 6 laws,[22] 7 administrative regulations,[23] 3 departmental regulations,[24] 24 local regulations[25] and 25 local government rules.[26] China has central and local emergency plans at all levels and of all kinds. As the plans are too numerous to be analyzed individually, we only choose the national plans and provincial master emergency plans. Among national emergency plans, 8 had provisions on emergency requisition, including the National Master Plan for Public Emergencies, the National Master Plan for Public Health Emergencies, the National Plan for Handling of Urban Subway Disasters, and the National Earthquake Response Plan. Among the 31 provincial and ministerial level emergency master plans, 29 involved government requisitions (except for Liaoning and Shandong Provinces). All the aforementioned laws and regulations and plans that involved emergency requisition totaled 103 instruments.

We also discovered that the term "transfer" was used to refer to requisition in 2 laws,[27] 3 administrative regulations,[28] 3 departmental regulations,[29] 26 local regulations[30] and 15 local government rules,[31] which totaled 49 documents. "Mobilize" was used to mean requisition in 1 law,[32] 1 administrative regulation,[33] 1 department regulation,[34] 7 local statutes[35] and 2 local government rules,[36] totaling 12 instruments.

---

[22] *Property Law, Emergency Response Law, Law on Prevention and Treatment of Infectious Diseases, Martial Law, National Defense Mobilization Law, and Law on National Defense.*

[23] *Regulations on Handling of Destructive Earthquake Emergencies, Regulations on the of Natural Disasters, Regulations on Prevention and Control of Vessel-induced Pollution to the Marine Environment, Drought Control Regulations, Regulations on Forest Fire Prevention, Regulations on Grassland Fire Prevention,* and *Regulations on Nuclear Accidents at Nuclear Power Plants.*

[24] *Rules on Management of Port Operations, Rules on Management of Emergency Preparedness for and Emergency Response to Vessel-Induced Pollution to the Marine Environment,* and *Measures for the Supervision and Management of Security of Postal Services.*

[25] Such as *Regulations of Zhejiang Province on Prevention* and *Control of Geological Disasters.*

[26] Such as *Measures of Gansu Province on Grassland Fire Prevention.*

[27] *Flood Control Law*, and *Pharmaceutical Control Law.*

[28] *Flood Control Regulations, Regulations on Prevention and Control of Geological Disasters,* and *Regulations on Telecommunications.*

[29] *Rules on Management of Road Passengers Transport and Passenger Stations, Regulations on Urgent Handling of Public Health Emergencies,* and *Regulations on Radiation Impact Management of Nuclear Disasters.*

[30] Such as *Flood Control Regulations of Jilin Province.*

[31] *Rules of Heilongjiang Province on Implementation of the Regulations of the People's Republic of China on Flood Control.*

[32] *Fire Protection Law.*

[33] *Regulations on Handling Major Animal Epidemic Emergencies.*

[34] *Rules on Management of Civil Aviation Emergencies.*

[35] *Rules of Gansu Province on Management of Agricultural Machinery.*

[36] *Measures of Hebei Province on Implementation of the Regulation on Handling Major Animal Epidemic Emergencies.*

From the total of 164 laws and regulations[37] retrieved, it could be seen that legislations at every level had formulated provisions on emergency requisition, including the Constitution, statutes, administrative regulations, local government regulations, departmental rules, local government rules, and other regulatory instrument as well as emergency plans, which indicates that a complete legal framework for emergency requisition is in place.

In terms of the time frame, only 21 of the laws and regulations on requisition were adopted before 2003, and most of them were about flood control and drought mitigation. The outbreak of SARS gave rise to a large number of laws and regulations on public health emergencies. In 2003 and 2004, 27 laws and regulations containing requisition provisions were adopted. In 2006 and 2007 when the Emergency Response Law came out, 12 laws and regulations containing requisition provisions were passed. Before 2012, the year 2010 was the time when the largest number of legislations regarding requisition took effect, totaling 21 instruments. The scope of legislations regarding emergency requisition was also expanded from public health emergencies to include natural disasters, martial law, and defense mobilization.

In terms of contents, Property Law and Emergency Response Law made general provisions regarding emergency requisition.[38] Some statutes for special purposes, such as the Law on Prevention and Treatment of Infectious Diseases and the Flood Control Law, laid out principles for emergency requisition compensation in their respective fields. Most of the above-mentioned legislations only had one to two clauses on emergency requisition. The National Defense Mobilization Law was the only exception, devoting one entire chapter to this subject, which was Chap. 10, Requisition of Civil Resources and Compensation.

To further evaluate China's legal framework on emergency requisition, we made an in-depth analysis on the content of the legislations. Emergency requisition concerns a number of basic issues including: who has the requisition power (subjects of requisition); what to requisition (objects of requisition); who should pay compensation for the requisition (subjects of compensation); and how to compensate

[37]The legislations analyzed in this paper are the ones currently effective. If the legislations are amended, this paper will adopt the amended versions. If the text includes both "provisions on requisition" and "provisions on transfer", this paper will analyze the "provisions on requisition".

[38]Article 44 of the *Property Law* provides, "in order to meet such urgent needs as rushing to rescue or providing disaster relief, the immovable or movable assets of entities or individuals may be requisitioned within the limits of power and in compliance with the procedures provided by law." Article 12 of the *Emergency Response Law* provides, "to respond to an emergency, the relevant people's government and its departments may requisition the assets of entities and/or individuals. After use of the requisitioned property or upon completion of handling the emergency, the property shall be returned to the owner in a shall be made." Article 52 of the *Law* provides, "the people's government performing the duty of unified leadership or being responsible for organizing an emergency response may, when necessary, requisition from entities or individuals for equipment, facilities, premises, means of transportation and other materials needed for emergency rescue; may request other local people's governments to support them with personnel, material or financial resources or technology assistance; may require the companies that produce or supply daily necessities and materials for emergency rescue;, and may require the entities that provide medical services, transportation and other public services to do so.".

(procedures). We looked at all the emergency requisition (transfer/mobilization) legislations in five aspects: subjects of requisition; objects of requisition; procedures for requisition; subjects of compensation; and compensation standards. To avoid confusion, we analyzed the statutes using "requisition", "transfer" and "mobilize" separately.

First, among the 103 legislations, 6 laws mentioned "requisition" and all 6 specified objects of requisition; 5 of the 6 prescribed that compensations should be made; 4 of the 6 specified the subjects of requisition; and 2 prescribed procedures for requisition as well as the subjects of compensation. Among the 7 administrative regulations, all of them specified objects of requisition; 6 of them prescribed that compensations should be made; 1 of them stated subjects of compensation; and none of them prescribed procedures for requisition. All the 3 departmental regulations prescribed subjects, objects, and compensation of requisition; none of them prescribed the procedures or the subject of compensation. Among the 24 local regulations, 20 specified subjects of requisition, 19 specified objects of requisition; 15 prescribed that compensations should be made; 2 prescribed procedures for requisition; and 1 stated the subject of compensation. Among the 25 local government rules, 22 specified the subject of requisition; 21 specified the object of requisition; 2 prescribed procedures for requisition; 11 prescribed that compensation should be made, but the subject of compensation was not mentioned. Among the 9 national plans, 6 specified the subject of requisition; 4 specified the object of requisition; 4 stated the subject of compensation; 3 prescribed that compensations should be made; and none of them prescribed procedures for requisition. Among the 29 provincial master plans, 26 prescribed that compensation should be made; 22 specified the object of requisition; 15 specified the subject of requisition; 7 stated the subject of compensation; and 2 prescribed procedures for requisition.[39]

Applying the same method to analyzing legislations using "transfer", we found that 2 specified the subject and object of transfer; 1 prescribed that compensation should be made. All of the 3 central government administrative regulations stated the subject and object of transfer, and none of them provided for procedures and compensation. Out of the 26 local government regulations, 23 specified the subject of transfer; 24 specified the object of transfer; 17 prescribed that compensation should be made; 1 stated the subject of compensation; and none prescribed procedures for transfer. All the 15 local government rules made provisions on the subject and object of transfer; 2 specified the subject of compensation; and 9 stated that compensations should be made.

Moreover, we analyzed the 12 legislations that used the word "mobilize". One law specified the subject and object of mobilization, but did not mention compensation or procedures. One administrative regulation stated the subject and object of mobilization as well as the subject of compensation, and prescribed that compensation should be made. One central government department regulation specified the subject and object of mobilization. Seven local statutes prescribed the subject and

[39]The three department regulations on emergency requisition are specialized provisions. They are different from other legislations and therefore be differentiated from the other legislations.

object of mobilization, as well as the subject and standard of compensation. Two local government rules specified the subject and object of mobilization, and another one stated the subject and object of mobilization, and the compensation subject and standard.

Finally, among all the 164 legislations that we analyzed, 135 specified the subject of requisition (transfer/mobilization), accounting for 82%; 126 specified the object of requisition (transfer/mobilization), accounting for 77%; 105 prescribed that compensation should be made, accounting for 64%; 27 stated the subject of compensation, accounting for 16%; and only 8 prescribed procedures for requisition (transfer/mobilization), accounting for 5%. This indicated that procedures for requisition (transfer/mobilization) were missing in almost all levels and forms of legislation. The subject of requisition was clearly defined, but the subject of compensation was not clear.

We also noticed that in this multi-layered legal framework, the provisions language was very similar to one another. Many statutes appeared to be just a copy or replica of statutes of upper levels.[40] For instance, Article 15 of the Regulations on the Relief of Natural Disasters (a central government administrative instrument) prescribes that "when responding to natural disasters, the local people's governments at and above the county level, or the disaster relief coordination agencies under the people's government, shall have the power, within their own administrative areas, to requisition materials, equipment, means of transport and sites. After the emergency relief is over, the requisitioned materials, equipment, means of transport and sites shall be returned in a timely manner, and compensation shall be made in accordance with relevant government regulations." Article 30 of the Regulations of Zhejiang Province on the Prevention and Control of Geological Disasters (a local government regulation) prescribes that "where materials, facilities, equipment, buildings and land of entities or individuals are requisitioned in need of disaster relief, the requisitioned materials, facilities, equipment, buildings and land shall be timely returned after use. Where the requisitioned materials, facilities, equipment, buildings and land belonging to entities or individuals are damaged or destroyed, compensations shall be made." Article 33 of the Measures for Safety Supervision and Administration of the Postal Service (a departmental rule) prescribes that "to respond to emergencies, postal agencies shall have the power to mobilize personnel and to requisition goods, materials, vehicles, sites and related equipment of postal services and express delivery enterprises, and compensation shall be made in accordance with relevant provisions." Article 13 of the Regulations of Shanxi Province on Earthquake Emergency Recue (a local government regulation) prescribes that "earthquake rescue teams of all regions are obliged to participate in rescue operations of earthquakes, natural disasters, and major accidents. While carrying out their missions, earthquake rescue teams shall have the power to request assistance from relevant entities and

[40]The copying and duplicating issue was first mentioned by Professor Ye Bifeng in the paper entitled *Analysis of Copying or Detailing Rules from the Perspective of Legal Interpretation: Departmental Rules Cannot Provide for Emergency Requisition Compensation*. The paper was submitted at Nanyue Forum of 2011 on Government based on the Rule of Law.

personnel, and relevant entities and personnel are obliged to assist. In need of rescue operations, necessary sites shall be occupied, and materials and equipment be requisitioned, which shall be returned in a timely manner after use; in case that materials were damaged or destroyed, compensation shall be according to relevant government provisions. The above-quoted four statutes were adopted respectively by the State Council, a local people's congress, a department of the State Council and a local government. They were supposed to have their own characteristics. However, apart from some minor differences in wording, their main contents were all copied from the Emergency Response Law.

Due to this kind of coping and duplicating, some important issues in emergency requisition are left unregulated. Although the legal framework is in place, some core elements are still incomplete, ambiguous, or even contradictory.

2. Problems of the emergency requisition legal framework.

Through the analysis above, we realized that the following main problems need to be addressed: ambiguous relationship between the subject of requisition and the requisitioned persons (including entities); lack of provisions on requisition procedures; insufficient means of compensation; and vague compensation standards.

(1) Ambiguous relationship between the subject of requisition and the requisitioned person.

As a general law on emergency response and management, the Emergency Response Law regulates emergency requisition in Article 12 and Article 52. Legal scholars generally believe that the subject of requisition prescribed in the Emergency Response Law is the government rather than government departments.[41] But such provisions were not followed by subordinate laws made afterwards. For instance, the Regulations on the Relief of Natural Disasters of September 1, 2010 (an administrative regulation), prescribes that the local people's governments at and above the county level, or the disaster relief coordination agencies under the people's government, shall have the power to requisition. The Regulations on the Prevention and Control of Vessel-Induced Pollution to Marine Environment promulgated on March 1, 2010, prescribes that the local people's governments at and above the level of a city divided into districts or marine administrative authorities shall have the power to requisition. The Drought Control Regulations of February 26, 2009 prescribes that the flood control and drought relief command agencies of local people's governments shall have the power to requisition. In terms of departmental rules, the Safety Regulatory Measures for Supervision and Management of the Postal Service of February 26, 2009, prescribes that postal administrative departments shall have the power to requisition. There are similar examples in local statutes and local government regulations. Almost all local statutes on implementation of the Drought Control Regulations provide that the flood control and drought relief agencies of local people's governments are the subject of requisition. The Measures of Tianjin Municipality on Response to

[41]Li Fei (ed.), *Explanation of and Practical Guide on Emergency Response Law of the People's Republic of China*, China Democracy and Rule of Law Press, 2007, p. 207.

Public Health Emergencies (a local government regulation) amended and effective on November 8, 2010 prescribes that health administrative and/or relevant departments shall have the power to requisition. The Regulations of Shanxi Province on Earthquake Emergency Rescue released on May 20, 2008, prescribes that earthquake rescue teams and people's governments at and above the county level in earthquake-stricken areas shall have the power to requisition. The above-mentioned legislations are subordinate to the Emergency Response Law. Their provisions on the subject of requisition contradict with that of the Emergency Response Law and should be rendered invalid. However, these legislations mostly regulate emergency response management in specific fields and in practice it's hard to avoid conflicts in application. Since the subjects of requisition at different levels of legislations are confusing, it will bring difficulties when handling emergencies or even cause legal disputes.

The Emergency Response Law and other legislations on emergency requisition do not define the legal relationship between the subject of requisition and the entity/person whose assets are requisitioned. While participating in government emergency response, the requisitioned entity/person might undertake all kinds of work, including official actions, such as assisting the police in keeping order. According to the analysis of the administrative law theories, such situation constitutes administrative entrustment. If the exercise of the entrusted power by the entrusted entity/person causes legal consequences, it shall be borne by the entrusting agency. However, the laws do not provide for the administrative entrustment in emergency response and the scope of power of the entrusting and the entrusted entities. This gives rise to problems in practice. For example, during the 2008 snow disaster in Southern China, the State Grid and other companies in the course of opening up rescue paths damaged farmland, forests, and farm crops while repairing the power facilities in mountainous areas. As there was no provision on administrative entrustment in laws, the companies faced large numbers of civil litigations, including damage claims thereafter.

(2) Lack of provisions on requisition procedures.

The emergency requisition procedures include application, decision, approval, announcement, extension, change, termination, as well as means and duration of requisition. Currently the legislations on emergency requisition only prescribe that the government shall have the power to requisition, and that requisitioned assets shall be returned after use and compensations shall be made. There are few provisions on requisition procedures. The existing ones are too vague. For instance, Article 17 of the Martial Law only prescribes that "a receipt for requisition shall be made out," and other procedures are left unaddressed. The emergency plans are supposed to be more detailed and practical, but few of them specify requisition procedures. The National Master Plan for Rapid Response to Public Emergencies prescribes that "emergency transportation means shall enjoy preferential treatment in terms of arrangement, traffic control and road passage to ensure smooth and safe operation; procedures for requisition of public transportation means in time of emergency shall be established according to law to ensure that supplies and personnel for disaster relief can reach the destination timely and safely." Detailed provisions are also lacking in emergency plans made by departments of the State Council and local governments.

(3) Vague compensation standards.

In the government emergency requisition system, only a few statutes have limited provisions on means of compensation, and most of them just mentioned one means of compensation, namely, monetary compensation. Only the Emergency Plan for Highway Traffic Accidents and the Emergency Plan for Waterway Accidents adopted by the Ministry of Transportation prescribe compensation other than monetary means, but still lack application provisions.

Most relevant legislations prescribe that "compensations shall be made in accordance with relevant provisions of the law", "proper compensations shall be made in accordance with relevant provisions of the State Council", and "corresponding compensations shall be made in accordance with relevant government provisions".[42] However, the "relevant provisions" are non-existent; and the meanings of "proper compensations" and "corresponding compensations" standards are too vague to apply. In practice, the compensations are usually made arbitrarily.

Some regions have begun to experiment with measures to solve this practical problem. So far three local governments have formulated specific rules on emergency requisition, of which two are local government rules and one regulatory instrument. The two local rules are: the Implementation Measures of Hangzhou City on Emergency Requisition (November 1, 2009) and the Measures of Taiyuan City on Requisition of Goods and Sites for Emergency Response (May 1, 2010); and the local directive is the Implementation Measures of Siping City on Emergency Requisition (November 1, 2009). Although these above-mentioned regulations have comprehensive provisions on the subject, object, procedures and compensations related to requisition, they only apply to a specific region. Besides, as the compensation standards vary from region to region, it could easily cause unfairness in their application. Therefore in reality, local legislations cannot solve the problem. We suggest that a uniform emergency requisition system be established through central government legislation.

3. Improvement of legal framework for emergency requisition.
(1) Determining legal rights and limits of the subject of requisition and the requisitioned entity/person.

Worldwide, subjects of requisition usually fall into two categories: the head of the State, and the head of government or government agencies. In some countries like in the U.S., the Property Requisition Act of the United State authorizes that the President in light of "imminent and impending danger" can requisition "any military equipment, supplies, munitions, or component parts thereof, or machinery, tools, materials, and necessary services and arms" for the defense of the United States. The Emergencies Act in Canada authorizes the Prime Minister the power to requisition

[42] Article 32 of *Regulations on Grassland Fire Prevention*, Article 4.12.2 of *National Emergency Plan on Flood Prevention and Drought Control*, and Article 44 of *Regulations of Yunnan Province on Protection of Power Facilities*.

in time of emergency. Other laws designate the government or government departments as subjects of requisition.[43] For instance, in Taiwan, depending on the types of emergencies, subjects of emergency requisition could be the Ministry of National Defense, the Ministry of Interior (central government), Department of Health under the Executive Branch (central government), and (local) governments at county or city level.[44]

Article 52 of China's Emergency Response Law prescribes that the subject of requisition is the people's government that performs the duty of unified leadership or is responsible for organizing the handling of an emergency. Based on the principals of "unified leadership, all-round coordination, categorized control, hierarchical responsibility, and territorial jurisdiction", the local people's government should be the major responsible subject of emergency response. In practice, the duty of unified leadership and the duty of emergency response might be performed by the same local government or by different ones. If the government exercising unified leadership and the government organizing emergency response belong to the same administrative division and are superior-subordinate to each other, in order to facilitate requisition and management of requisitioned property, the people's government responsible for organizing emergency response is more suited to be the subject of requisition. If the emergency and the requisition take place at different regions, the two local governments thus constitute an assistance relationship prescribed by the Emergency Response Law. After consultations between the two governments, or with the coordination of the superior government governing both administrative regions, the requisitioning government shall exercise the power of requisition, and the utilizing government and the requisitioning government shall bear joint liability. If the entities or individuals being requisitioned for properties or labors have complaints about the requisition or compensation, they can file the complaint either with the requisitioning government or the utilizing government.

The law should also further specify the legal relationship between the subject of requisition and the owner of the requisitioned property, especially the rights and responsibilities of the owner, such as reporting to and handing over requisitioned property at the designated place, obeying government arrangement, and fulfilling the assigned tasks. In particular, it should be made clear that the official acts performed by the requisitioned entity/person are entrusted by the government, and therefore the consequences shall be borne by the government. To facilitate public utility entities to participate in emergency response, the government can incorporate the entities into the emergency requisition framework through administrative entrustment, but the legal consequences of requisition should be borne by the entrusting government.

---

[43]While a declaration of a public welfare emergency is in effect, the Governor in Council may make such orders or regulations with respect to the following matters as the Governor in Council believes, on reasonable grounds, are necessary for dealing with the emergency: ...(c) the requisition, use or disposition of property. [Emergencies Act .R.S.C. 1985, c. 8 (4th Supp.)].

[44]See *the Disaster Prevention and Response Act, All-Out Defense Mobilization Preparation Act* and relevant provisions in other laws and regulations.

(2) Exploring diversified compensation means and setting a fair and reasonable compensation standard.

Diversified means of compensation and their combinations depending different situations during requisition, can provide more choices of compensation for the requisitioned entities, thus reaching fairness in a broader sense. Subjects of requisition can make compensations in a variety of ways, in addition to restoration, returning property and money, they can also offer tax waiver or reduction, in-kind compensation, and medical subsidies, as separate or combined form of compensation.

It is generally believed in the world that the principles of compensation should be "fair and reasonable", or "proper", or "according to actual losses". In the United States, requisition compensations must be made in a reasonable and timely manner. The laws prescribe that, without just compensation, private property shall not be taken for public use, and that just compensations shall be determined and made as soon as possible.[45] The government needs to consider many factors in order to determine the amount of just and reasonable compensation, which include the price that would result from fair negotiations between a willing seller and buyer[46]; putting the property owner in as good a position as if the property had not been requisitioned[47]; reproduction cost, loss during requisition, insurance cost, earning capacity of the property before requisition, and its possible future uses. Not all these factors need to be considered when deciding on the amount of proper compensation, for they are affected by relevance, significance, or qualification.[48]

The Supreme Court of the United States usually determines the proper amount of compensation for the loss of the asset owner based on the fair market value. However, if the value of the asset increases significantly as a result of government requisition, the added value will be deducted from the amount of compensation. If the market value of the asset is difficult to determine, the following methods are usually

[45]The 5th Amendment to the *U.S. Constit*ution provides, "…nor be deprived of life, liberty, or property, without due process of law; without just compensation, nor shall private property be taken for public use".

[46]"Just compensation" for vessels requisitioned by former War Shipping Administration pursuant to former section, was the sum which, considering all circumstances, would in all probability result from fair negotiations between an owner, who was willing to sell, and a purchaser, who desired to buy. *American-Hawaiian S.S. Co. v. U.S.*, Ct.Cl.1955; 133 F.Supp. 369; 132 Ct.Cl. 246; War And National Emergency.

[47]"Just compensation" within bareboat charter obligating charterer to pay owner "just compensation" in case of actual or constructive total loss of vessel means the full and perfect equivalent in money of the vessel that was lost and requires that owner be put in as good position pecuniarily as he would have occupied if the vessel had not been lost. *Eastern S. S. Lines v. U. S., D.C.Mass.*1947, 74 F.Supp. 37, affirmed 171 F.2d 589. Shipping 58(3).

[48]Under bareboat charter obligating United States as charterer to pay owner just compensation in case of actual or constructive total loss of vessel, the fair value of vessel after it was declared a constructive total loss was to be determined in the light of reproduction cost, new, depreciated to time of loss, value placed on vessel for insurance, earning capacity of vessel, its possible future uses, and manner in which vessel had been maintained, but each factor was to be subjected to the test of relevancy, competency and weight. *Eastern S. S. Lines v. U. S.*, D.C.Mass.1947, 74 F.Supp. 37, affirmed 171 F.2d 589. Shipping 58(3).

used to evaluate the property: the property sale situation, proceeds estimate, asset replacement, and development cost. In Nicholson Transit Co. v. U.S., the court took into consideration the reproduction cost, the vessel's condition, the date of taking; the age of the vessel, the customary methods of depreciation, the original cost to the plaintiff, the amounts expended upon repairs, replacements and alterations, the general condition of the vessel at the time of taking, the apparent years of remaining useful life, and the probability of greater expenditures for repairs and replacements in the future.[49] The government shall not compensate for consequential damage resulting from requisition. In another case, the U.S. government's requisition in 1942 of ships on which owner had contracted to transport lumber did not result in taking of shipper's property by the United States, though requisition required cancellation of a lumber shipping contract, and damages sustained by shipper as result of cancellation were consequential damages for which no recovery could be had by shipper from the United States.[50]

Japan also adopts the principle of just compensation. Section 3, Article 29 of the Constitution of Japan promulgated in 1946 prescribes that private property may be taken for public use upon just compensation therefore. The State or public organizations must not requisition private property or impose limitations on private property without compensation.[51]

Australia adopts the principle of just compensation and advance payment. Under normal circumstances, compensation for requisition may be paid in advance. If the owner of the requisitioned asset does not apply for compensation and the Minister offers compensation, the advance shall be no less than 90% of the amount of the Minister's offer.[52] In France, the amount of compensation is calculated with the price table provided by the Minister. If there is no price table, it shall be determined by a Provincial Evaluation Committee. The Committee is made up of an equal number of representatives from administrative agencies and from business and agricultural sectors. If the claimant opposes the Committee's decision, a lawsuit could be brought to a regular court.[53]

---

[49] In arriving at a fair valuation of the Fleetwood, the court takes into consideration the reproduction cost, which is found to be $650,000 as of June 17, 1942, the date of taking; and further the age of the vessel, 39 years; the vessel's condition; the customary methods of depreciation, which are valuable as guideposts; the original cost to the plaintiff, the amounts expended upon repairs, replacements and alterations, and the general condition of the vessel at the time of taking; the apparent years of remaining useful life and the probability of greater expenditures for repairs and replacements in the future. *Nicholson Transit Co. v. U.S.*, Ct.Cl.1951, 118 Ct.Cl. 344. War And National Emergency.

[50] Government's requisition in 1942 of ships on which owner had contracted to transport lumber did not result in taking of shipper's property by United States, though requisition required cancellation of a lumber shipping contract, and damages sustained by shipper as result of cancellation were consequential damages for which no recovery could be had by shipper from United States. *Georgia Hardwood Lumber Co. v. U.S.*, Ct.Cl.1948, 78 F.Supp. 808, 111 Ct.Cl. 621. War And National Emergency 14.

[51] Yang Jianshun, *An Introduction to the Administrative Law of Japan*, China Legal Publishing House, 1998, p.606.

[52] § 56, *Land Acquisition* Act. (1989).

[53] Wang Mingyang, *Administrative Law of France*, Beijing University Press, 2007, p. 322.

In Taiwan, compensation standard is determined in the following order: (a) compensation shall be made to the property owner and operating personnel based on the rate set by government bodies; (b) where there is no government rate, compensation shall be made based on the rate set by relevant associations; (c) where there is no government or association rate, compensation shall be determined by the agreement between the government, the owner of the requisitioned property and the operating personnel; (d) where the agreement does not apply, the government shall determine the rate based on the current local price level and the age of the property.[54]In anti-epidemic disease situations where contamination may be involved, the law provides for higher compensation rate to make up for special losses of the owner.[55]

On the standard of administrative compensation, the academia in China has two views. One holds that the requisitioned entity/person should be compensated for "actual losses".[56] The other maintains that the amount of compensation should be determined by the total losses of the victim, and that the long-term impact on the survival and development of the damaged entity/person should be taken into full consideration.[57] We believe that the principle of just and reasonable compensation should be adopted for the requisitioned property and labor. The government should set the compensation standard based on the market value of the property, the reproduction cost, losses resulted from requisition and other relevant factors, and publicize the standard to the public. If the persons concerned have objections towards the compensation standard, they can commission professional agencies to evaluate the property. More specifically, for consumables goods like coal and candles, the loss should be calculated based on the market value at the time of requisition; and for non-consumables such as vehicles and tents, compensation should be calculated based on the market rental price. If the property is damaged, the subject of requisition should be responsible for repairing the property or paying for the repair cost.

[54]Article 4 of *the Regulations of China Taiwan on Reimbursement for Requisition and Transfer for Disaster Response*.

[55]According to Article 4 of the *Operational Procedures and Compensation Methods of China Taiwan for Requisition of Anti-Epidemic Materials,* compensation for requisition of land and buildings shall be 20% higher than the rent of land and buildings in the adjacent area within the same region during the time of requisition. Where requisition of the above-mentioned materials lasted less than 15 days, it shall be counted as 15 days in the calculation of compensations. Where the requisition lasted more than 15 days and less than 30 days, it shall be counted as 30 days in the calculation of compensations.

Article 5: The compensation standard for requisitioned materials other than what is provided in Article 4 shall be determined in the following order: (1) the government rate plus 20%; (2) the market rate over the time of requisition plus 20%; (3) by agreement between the government and the requisitioned entity/person.

Article 6: Where the anti-epidemic materials requisitioned by governments of all levels are consumables, compensation shall be made within 30 days after derequisition.

[56]Jiang Ming'an, "A Study on Administrative Compensation System", *Legal Science Magazine*, issue 5, 2001.

[57]Shen Kaiju, "On the Standard of Administrative Compensation", *Henan Social Sciences*, issue 1, 2005.

As for compensation for lost work income of requisitioned personnel, in theory, there are three standards to choose from: (1) the loss in income due to missed working time; (2) the pay of the position undertaken by the requisitioned personnel during the requisition period; (3) the average pay of staff and workers in the previous year. The first standard may lead to different remunerations for people doing the same work during the requisition period. The second one will be difficult to determine and operate in practice since requisitioned personnel may change positions frequently during the requisition period according to actual needs. The third standard seems easier to apply and relatively fair. Also, because China's State Compensation Law prescribes that compensation for loss in income due to missed working time shall be calculated on the average daily pay of staff and workers in the previous year. Even though State compensation addresses unlawful acts of the State, while compensation for emergency requisition addresses lawful acts of the government in time of emergency, in light of actual conditions in China, it is viable that income remuneration for requisitioned personnel be calculated on the average daily pay of staff and workers in the previous year. For the health and safety of the requisitioned personnel, the requisitioning entities should buy personal injury accident or other insurance for the requisitioned personnel. While making the payment, the subject of compensation should deduct the amount that can be obtained through insurance or other means.

(3) Specifying procedures for emergency requisition and compensation.

The legislations of many countries and regions have detailed provisions on procedures for emergency requisition and compensation. In New Zealand, for instance, Article 90 of the Civil Defense Emergency Response Management Act prescribes that an entity exercising the requisition power must give the owner or person in charge of the requisitioned property a written statement specifying the property requisitioned and to whom the property is to be returned after requisition. In a state of emergency, unexpected situations may arise; for instance, certain property must be requisitioned to save lives, but the owner or person in charge of the property cannot be immediately found. Section (4), Article 90 of the Act prescribes that under such circumstances, the subject of requisition may immediately take control and direct the use of the requisitioned property. To protect the interests of the owner or the person in charge of the property, Section (5) of the said Article prescribes that in the case of Section (4), as soon as it is reasonably practicable in the circumstance, a written statement must be given to the owner or person in charge of the requisitioned property, specifying the property requisitioned and under whose control it has been placed.

In Taiwan, government agencies must abide by the following procedures during emergency requisition: (a) a requisition statement is produced and delivered to the requisitioned entity/person; (b) the requisitioned entity/person shall report to the required agency and deliver the requisitioned items based on the requirements of the notification, and the subject of requisition shall provide the disaster relief badge or issue the receipt certificate; (c) derequisition after use; (d) the requisitioned items are returned and compensations made.[58]

We believe that due to the urgent nature of emergency requisition, its procedures should be simplified. However, the basic requirements for legitimate procedures must be met. The procedures should at least include the following steps. (a) Providing requisition documents. If the conditions make it impossible to provide legal documents and an oral requisition is made instead, remedies should be made afterwards. (b) Filling out requisition forms and specifying the name, quantity, and quality of the property or labor. (c) Informing the ways and time limits of remedies. For the need of emergency response, the enforcement of requisition should not be suspended while the requisitioned person is applying for remedies. (d) Derequisition. After the requisition term is over or the mission is completed, the subject of requisition should decide to derequisition based on the emergency response conditions. (e) Returning the requisitioned property and making compensations. If the value of the requisitioned property cannot be determined, professional appraisal or notary agencies should be commissioned to evaluate the materials, labor, or other

---

[58]Article 15 of *Rules of China Taiwan of Implementation of the Disaster Prevention and Response Act* provides: while the recruiting or requisitioning agency recruits personnel or requisitions property in accordance with Section 1 and Section 3 of Article 31, Section 2 of Article 32, a recruitment or requisition statement shall be provided and delivered to the recruited persons or the owner, utilizer or the person in control of the requisitioned property (hereafter referred to as the requisitioned person). In times of urgent need, the recruiting or requisitioning agency may inform the recruited or the requisitioned person through telephone, fax or other proper means and issue the recruitment or requisition statement later. The aforementioned recruitment or requisition statement may be delivered by coordinating agencies, schools or associations on behalf of the requisitioning agency.

Article 17: the requisition statement shall incorporate the following information: (1) the name, birth date, gender, identity card number, address and other identifiable features of the requisitioned person; if the requisitioned person is a legal person or other groups with a manager or representative, then its name, business address, the name, birth date, gender, identity card number and address of its manager or representative; (2) the purpose, facts, reasons and statutory basis; (3) the name, unit, number and size of the requisitioned item; (4) the region receiving the requisitioned person or property; (5) the duration of requisition; (6) time and place for handing in the requisitioned property; (7) the name of the executing agency and the signature of its chief; (8) document number and date of issuance; (9) the purpose of the administrative execution and remedial methods for objection to the execution, and time limit and the authority receiving the objection.

Article 18: upon receiving the recruitment or requisition statement or notification, the recruited or requisitioned person shall report to the agency or deliver the requisitioned items required on the notification. Upon arrival of the recruited person or receiving the requisitioned items, the disaster response center or governments of all levels shall confer the disaster relief badge or issue the receipt certificate for the requisitioned items, and shall arrange the duties of the recruited persons or utilize the requisitioned properties properly. If the term for recruited person or requisitioned term is over and the recruited persons or requisitioned properties are still needed, the term shall be extended.

Article 19: when the cause for recruitment or requisition ceases to exist, the recruiting or requisitioning agency shall issue a derequisition document and return the requisitioned property. Compensations shall be made within two months of derequisition in accordance with Article 49 of the Act.

Similar provisions can be found in Article 7 of the *Measures on Material Requisition and Personnel Recruitment for Civil Defense*, and Articles 6 and 7 of the *Operational Procedures and Compensation Methods for Requisition of Anti-Epidemic Materials in Taiwan.*

requisitioned items. (f) Issuing certificates for the return of the requisitioned property or compensation documents. The requisitioning entities should provide certificates for the return of the requisitioned property or compensation documents according to actual situations. Where possible the requisitioned property should be returned to the original owner; and if the property cannot be returned, or the property is consumed or damaged, compensations should be made. (g) Making compensations according to law. Requisitioning entities should make compensations based on the legal standard or make up for the shortfalls determined by the appraisal report in cash or through other means, as specified in the compensation documents.

Unlike ordinary administrative requisition, the emergency requisition is prioritized and enjoys simplified procedures. However, even emergency operations should follow the basic principles of the rule of law and strike a balance between efficiency and protecting the legitimate rights of the requisitioned persons. Emergency requisition should also be combined with emergency prevention for better operation. The government should improve the reserve information system, and keep good records of materials, equipment, facilities and human resources in advance and update the information regularly, so that they can be successfully requisitioned when needs arise.

Chapter 8
The Development and Improvement of Administrative Review System

8.1 The Historical Course of Administrative Review System

Administrative review and administrative litigation are two legal ways in which a citizen, a legal person or an organization can sue a government official. Compared with administrative litigation, the pace of development of administrative review is not slow. The Regulations on Administrative Review was issued by the State Council in 1990 and the Administrative Review Law in 1999. Administrative review is free-of-charge and efficient by comparison with administrative litigation. Yet in China, cases of administrative review are fewer than administrative litigation; whereas in other countries, the ratio can be 10:1, or even 24:1. Also at present, 70% of administrative disputes will go to administrative litigation without administrative review, which shows a lack of public confidence in administrative review. In fact, administrative review is an important way for settling administrative disputes, safeguarding people's lawful rights and interests, promoting administration according to law, and achieving social justice. However, its role has been underplayed, as people tend to worry that officials may naturally protect each other. Another factor would be system defects. Estimates show that under the horizontal (region-based) and vertical (profession/industry-based) administrative management system in China, there are about 18,000 agencies handling administrative review, but there are only 1532 professional review officers at three levels of local governments, averaging 0.2 staffing person per agency at the county level who handle 50% of all review cases. Such scattered review power and personnel has become a bottleneck for effective role of administrative review in settling disputes. In practice, some officers don't have any case to handle while in other places some cases cannot be handled for lack of review officers.

© Social Sciences Academic Press and Springer Nature Singapore Pte Ltd. 2018
H. Ma and J. Wang, *Building a Government Based on the Rule of Law*,
Research Series on the Chinese Dream and China's Development Path,
https://doi.org/10.1007/978-981-13-0999-1_8

1. The Era of the Regulations on Administrative Review.

Administrative review system began in "Old China" after the 1911 Revolution. Article 8 of the Provisional Constitution of the Republic of China prescribed that "according to law, people have the right to file a petition with the executive authority and a lawsuit with the administrative court." In 1930, the government of the Republic of China promulgated the Administrative Petition Act, which established the system of administrative petition (i.e. administrative review). According to the Act, if the right of a citizen was impaired by an unlawful or inappropriate act of an official, he or she could petition for revocation or alteration of the penalty. Such petition would have a review and an appeal, and if the party was not satisfied with the result of the appeal, he or she could bring an administrative lawsuit.

The administrative review system of the People's Republic of China was established in the 1950s. In 1950, the Government Administration Council (today's State Council) approved the Measures for Establishing Financial Inspection Agency by the Ministry of Finance. Article 6 of the Measures prescribed that "where the inspected entity has solid reasons to believe that the decision of the inspection agency is improper, it may petition to the superior agency for re-examination. The "re-examination" here in essence was administrative review. That was the earliest form of administrative review in New China. Since then, the scope of administration review has been gradually expanded. The word "review" first appeared in the Organization Rules on the Committee of Taxation Review and the Provisional Regulations on Stamp Tax, both were issued by the Government Administration Council in 1950. In the late 1950s, the administrative review developed in its initial stage with more and more pertinent laws and regulations being adopted. An important feature of administrative review at that time was that the review decision was final, meaning that the party who was unsatisfied could not bring an administrative action. Administrative review system developed rapidly as part of the socialist legal framework building since the Third Plenary Session of the 11th CPC Central Committee (1978), and especially since the late 1980s, and more relevant laws and regulations sprung up. It is estimated that, by the end of December 1990, over 100 laws and regulations regarding administrative review had been promulgated. These statutes were improved not only in legislative techniques and but also in terms of connection and coordination with other pertinent laws and regulations, which helped with administrative disputes resolution and self-constraint within the administrative system. Even so, the lack of a general law on administrative review led to absence of a unified legal basis for the scope, jurisdiction, adjudication, procedure and statute of limitation of administrative review. During this period the number of review cases was small and administrative review system not mature.

On April 4, 1989 the Administrative Litigation Law was enacted, which put the legislation of administrative review law on the agenda. In order to ensure effective implementation of the Law, the Legal Affairs Bureau of the State Council convened ministries, local legislative departments and scholars to discuss the preliminary design and framework of the Regulations on Administrative Review in Wuhan, October 1989. The draft of the Regulations was discussed at another meeting held in Chongqing in November the same year. And the Regulations on Administrative Review was issued by the State Council in 1990 (hereinafter as the Review Regulations). The Articles of the Review Regulations indicated that the legislative body intended the review as an administrative process. The Interpretation of the Regulations on Administrative Review prepared by the Legal Affairs Bureau of the State Council[1] explained that "administrative review refers to the specific administrative act where a review of a petition is conducted when a dispute arises between the penalized party and an administrative agency in the course of exercising the agency's administrative function, and the penalized party petition to the next higher level of the acting agency for review of the disputed specific administrative act." In terms of its nature, the Interpretations pointed out that "administrative review is a regulated supervision act carried out by a higher level administrative agency over its subordinate agency."[2]

The initial implementation of the Review Regulations proved that the prediction of the Interpretation was correct: "the cases of administrative review will far outnumber those of administrative litigation. Among 100% of administrative lawsuits brought before the court could be filed for review by an administrative agency first, and 70% of the cases are required to do so before it can be brought to court".[3] After the Regulations was promulgated the number of review cases increased sharply. Statistics show that, from January 1991 to the end of 1997, there were about 220,000 cases of administrative review, averaging 30,000 a year. For eight years since the release of the Regulations, it played a positive role in the oversight of administration by law and protecting the lawful rights and interests of citizens, legal persons, and other organizations. However, with the development of administrative review and administrative litigation mechanisms, the gap between the two widened, especially in the number of cases handled. Each year there were about 30,000 administrative review cases, and over 100,000 administrative lawsuits. Why did people choose administrative litigation over review despite the cost-effectiveness and convenience of the latter? The academia believed that it reflected the many flaws of the Regulations in its 8 years of practice. The nature of administrative view was not clearly defined and the problems begun to surface shortly after the Regulations was implemented.

2. The Era of Administrative Review Law.

The adoption of the Administrative Review Law in 1999 marked the establishment of an independent system of administrative review in China. And the choice was made not to make the administrative review a judicial process.

On April 29, 1999, the 9th Session of the 9th Standing Committee of the National People's Congress deliberated on and approved the Administrative Review Law of the People's Republic of China (hereinafter as the Law), which took effect on October 1, 1999. In designing of the Law special attention was paid to avoid judicial procedures

[1]Now the Legislative Affairs Office of the State Council.

[2]The Legislative Affairs Bureau of the State Council: *Interpretations to the Regulations on Administrative Review*, China Legal Publishing House, January, 1991, p. 1.

[3]Ibid., p. 163.

in the review process. For instance, applicants have a choice of jurisdiction. Article 12 of the Law prescribes that an applicant, who disagrees with a specific administrative act of an agency under a local people's government at or above the county level, may apply for administrative review either to the people's government at the same level or to the next higher level of the agency. Also Article 15 prescribes that if applicants do not know which agency they should apply to, they can file the review application with the county-level government in the locality of the specific administration act, and this government will forward the case to the relevant agency. Article 5 prescribes that except provided by law otherwise, the decision of the review is final and no appeal. Article 3 prescribes that the reviews will be conducted by the legal affairs unit of the agency without setting up a separate and independent administrative review agency. Article 22 prescribes that administrative review, in principle, shall be done with examining documents in writing only. Article 39 prescribes that an administrative review agency shall not charge any fees to an applicant. In order to emphasize that the review is an internal oversight process of an administrative agency, some provisions in the Review Regulations are not included in the Review Law, such as eligibility of application and jurisdiction It can be concluded that in terms of the structural design, articles and the content, the Review Law intended to highlight the review as an internal supervision mechanism which is different from judicial procedures.

Although both the academia and functional agencies had high expectations for the upgraded administrative review system, its implementation lagged behind of the expectation. Before the Law came into force, applications for review were not many, averaging 30,000 each year. In 1999, the number was 32,170. In 2000 when the law was enacted and promulgated, the review was boosted to the extent that the applications increased to 74,448; and in 2001, the number passed the 80,000 milestone and reached 80,857. However, in the following years, the number stagnated at around 70,000–80,000 per year. Compared with litigation, administrative review seemed to be fairer and more convenient; its scope was broader than litigation; the review covered both legality and reasonableness; and it was free of charge.

In reality, however, the applicants didn't seem to care about these advantages. The number of review was dwarfed by that of administrative litigation, and even more so by grievance complaint letters. This indicated that when people tried to decide how to resolve an administrative dispute, the convenient and practical review mechanism was not a popular choice. The main reason being that applicants assumed that the review agency was the superior body of the same agency disputed, and they might "protect each other" rather than the legitimate rights and interests of the party concerned. What happened in reality proved that to some extent the public concern was justified. The percentage of the review confirming the original decision maintained high, above 50%, which was not improved by implementation of the Review Law. The rate climbed to 60.59% in 2006. The rate of revoking the administrative act was low, about 10%. There were even fewer cases in which the scope of functions of a review agency was altered, with the rate below 10% or around, 5% to more exact.[4]

[4]Statistics derived from *the Past, Present and Future of Administrative Review of China* by Qing Feng, published in *the Review and Prospect of the Administrative Law of China*, the Publishing

The reason being that since the review agency was usually the superior agency to the respondent of the application, it should exercise its supervision power and thus had the responsibility to alter or revoke the administrative act if it was unreasonable. But according to the Administrative Review Law, if the administrative review agency altered the original act, the review agency would become the defendant in an administrative lawsuit. So in practice, in spite of knowing that the act was wrong, the review agency still chose to maintain the original act to avoid becoming a defendant in a lawsuit and would rather let the respondent agency of the administrative review be the defendant, thus more burdens was put on the applicant. Therefore, both the academia and the functional circles believed that the advantage of administrative review did not yield the expected result with the passing of the Law. Many scholars and experts questioned the effect of the Law. Some even held that administrative review was again in a gloomy situation facing a tough choice of becoming stagnated or going forward. The real root cause was the negative effect of excluding judicial procedures from the review process as intended by the Review Law. For example, in some places administrative review agencies were removed or consolidated; many reviewing officers left; and the funding was not secured. Some cases were not handled, revoked or altered as they should be. Such injustice impaired public trust and hindered healthy operation and development of the system. Based on an analysis of the current system, Mr. Fang Jun proposed to establish a quasi-judicial administrative review system, including ensuring independent review, promoting neutral examination, making full use of review advantages and simplifying procedures.[5]

Entering the 21st century, social development demanded for deepening of government reform. How to enhance government's administrative capability and effectively resolve social disputes became an urgent task for the government. In 2003 the new administration of the State Council put forward three basic principles for governance, namely democratic decision-making, administration according to law, and oversight of administration. To meet the requirements by the State Council, governments and agencies at all levels must improve institutional building, enhance administrative law enforcement, and strengthen administrative supervision, so as to increase their administrative capacity and quality. Against this backdrop, on March 22, 2004, the State Council issued the Implementation Program for Comprehensive Promotion of Government Administration by Law. In terms of administrative review, the Program required the following improvement: the Law of Administrative Review be implemented earnestly and the work of administrative review done well; applications filed in accordance with the law must be accepted and handled on the basis of sound legal grounds and sufficient evidence, and through proper procedures so as to ensure a fair decision; unlawful or improper administrative act must be corrected so as to protect the lawful rights and interests of citizens, legal persons and organizations;

House of China University of Political Science and Law, p. 719–744, and *the Law Yearbook of China*.

[5]Fang Jun, On Updated Views and Institutional Reconstruction of Administrative Review in China, the *Judicial Reform of Administrative Review System in China* edited by Zhou Hanhua, Peking University Press, April, 2005, pp. 26–31.

new approaches and measures need to be explored to improve the quality of review; procedures should be simplified for cases where the facts are clear and disputes are minor; capacity-building of review officers need to be enhanced; an accountability mechanism need to be installed to hold the officers accountable in situations such as: applications are not accepted or adjudicated; unlawful administrative act not revoked, corrected or confirmed as it should be; decision is not made within the statutory time limit; and other violations of the Review Law. The Program shed light right on existing problems in the administrative review system.

3. The development of the Implementation Regulations of the Administrative Review Law.

As mentioned above, as social reforms in China entered a crucial stage, many social problems began to surface. A large number of people still voiced their grievance through the complaint petition mechanism. How to effectively solve administrative disputes had become an urgent task for the government.

In September 2006, the General Office of CPC Central Committee and the General Office of the State Council issued Opinions on Preventing and Resolving Administrative Disputes and Improving the Settlement Mechanism, in which specific requirements were made for improving administrative review. On October 11, 2006, the Decision of the CPC Central Committee on Building a Socialist Harmonious Society was approved by the 6th Plenary Session of the 16th CPC Central Committee. According to the Decision, Chinese government should speed up building a government based on the rule of law; strengthen administration according to law; exercise power and carry out functions strictly in accordance with the statutory authority and procedure; improve the accountability system of administrative law enforcement; and upgrade the system of administrative review and compensation.

In December, 2006, State Councilor Hua Jianmin chaired the national conference on administrative review, where new strategic arrangements were laid out under new circumstances. In his speech entitled Strengthening Administrative Review and Promoting Social Harmony, Mr. Hua Jianmin stressed that China was entering a critical period with profound changes in economic and social structure, interest pattern and people's outlook; opportunities for economic and social growth were accompanied by many social problems which took the form of increased administrative disputes; administrative review was an important mechanism to resolve people's legitimate claims in a systematic, legal and effective way.

In order to improve administrative review system as required in the Decision of the CPC Central Committee on Building a Socialist Harmonious Society, efforts were made in summarizing practical experience and making the review process more practical. For this purpose, the Legal Affairs Office of the State Council drafted the Regulations on Implementation of the Administrative Review Law, which was designed to better resolve administrative disputes and move the procedure in the direction closer to some judicial procedures. When answering questions raised by reporters, the spokesman of the State Council Legal Affairs Office summarized the Implementation Regulations on Administrative Review in the following four aspects:

(1) The Regulations prescribes review channel and protection of the lawful rights and interests of citizens, legal persons and other organizations in the provisions as follows: (a) to ensure that administrative review agencies take cases proactively, agencies are required to accept applications for administrative review filed by citizens, legal persons or organizations who deem their lawful rights and interests are impaired by an administrative act, unless the applications are not in compliance with the Administrative Review Law or the Regulations on Administrative Review; (b) to improve the review procedure, the administrative agency of a higher level has the power to order the lower level agency to accept and adjudicate an application where the ground for rejection is deemed insufficient. If the agency still refuses to accept the application, the superior review agency may order the agency to accept it within certain time limit, or directly accepts it by itself; where the application is not in compliance with relevant provisions, the applicant should be notified of the reason for rejection; (c) to safeguard the right to be informed of the citizens, legal persons or organizations where an administrative act may have a negative influence on their rights and obligations, they should be notified of the right to file for administrative review, the review agency, and time limit for the application; (d) the Implementation Regulations specifies the method of calculating the time limit for filing an application, and the information that need to be included in the content of the application.

(2) To improve the quality of case adjudication, the Regulations introduces means of improving hearing, encouraging mediation and settlement, and procedures for suspension or termination of the review. In order to avoid the delay of taking an administrative act, the Regulations specifies the time limit in which the respondent agency must make a new administrative act ordered by the review agency. Also, in order to encourage citizens, legal persons or other organizations to resolve administrative disputes through review and to relieve them of the fear for suing a government official, the Regulations prescribes the restriction of alteration, i.e., within the scope of the review request, the review decision may not put the applicant in a worse situation than the original act or decision.

(3) The Regulations has a special chapter on guidance and supervision of administrative review. It prescribes that people's governments above county level should exercise supervision on their departments and their subordinates on how administrative reviews are handled; that review agencies can propose legal opinions to relevant agencies to correct their unlawful act or remedy the losses; that review agencies can make suggestions on improving certain mechanism and administrative law enforcement; that review agencies above county level should submit a work report to the people's government on a regular basis; that review agencies should file major review decisions to their superior agency for record.

(4) To strengthen the responsibility of administrative review agencies, the Regulations requires that agencies at all levels carry out their duties in an earnest way; encourage the offices of legal affairs within the agencies to handle matters related to review in accordance with the law; and provide, increase and adjust full-time review staffing according to relevant rules so as to ensure that the agency has the capability of handling its case load. The Regulations also requires that government above the county level establish and improve the review accountability mechanism; include

review work into the government target and responsibility system. In addition, the Regulations specifies the duties, functions, and accountabilities of administrative review agencies.[6]

8.2 Problems and Their Causes of Administrative Review Practice

1. The current administrative review situation.

For 30 years since the reform and opening-up, the administration review system has been through ups and downs, from scattered legislation to the release of Regulations on the Implementation of the Administrative Review Law. Great progress has been in terms of using administrative review as an important measure for administrative power oversight and rights relief. However, worrisome problems are still salient in implementation of the Law. Especially in recent years, all kinds of social issues keep rising, which exposes many problems in the administration review system and erodes its healthy development. The main problems are the following:

(1) Dwindling impact and authority of the review system.

The review system has become less well-received by the public in comparison with the popularity it received when the Administrative Review Law was first promulgated in 1999. It is estimated that the applications plummeted from 2002 to 2004. Though, between 2005 and 2007, the number was on the rise in general, it still dropped in many provinces and cities. The numbers reflect many problems in the system, which directly affect the role of administrative review. If the number remains low, the review cannot fulfill its function as a filter for administrative litigation and consequently will overburden the courts; and the dwindling number shows the lack of confidence of the public in the review system, which makes its advantages of being convenient, cost-effective meaningless. The small number also indicates that agencies under most circumstances are passive in their review work, i.e., more complicated and costly procedures have been deployed.[7]

(2) The extremely high rate of confirming the original decisions and its fairness is being questioned with weak credibility.

Figure 8.1 shows that though the nationwide rate of affirming decisions somewhat dropped in the past three years, it still remained as high as above 50%. As a result,

[6]Answers of the Head Official of the Legislative Affairs Office of the State Council to Questions from the Media on the Regulations on Implementation of the Administrative Review Law.

http://www.legalinfo.gov.cn/misc/2007-06/12/content_635680.htm last time retrieved: July 2, 2009.

[7]Liu Xin: Debate on Repositioning of Administrative Review, *Legal Forum*, September, 2011, issue 5, vol. 26.

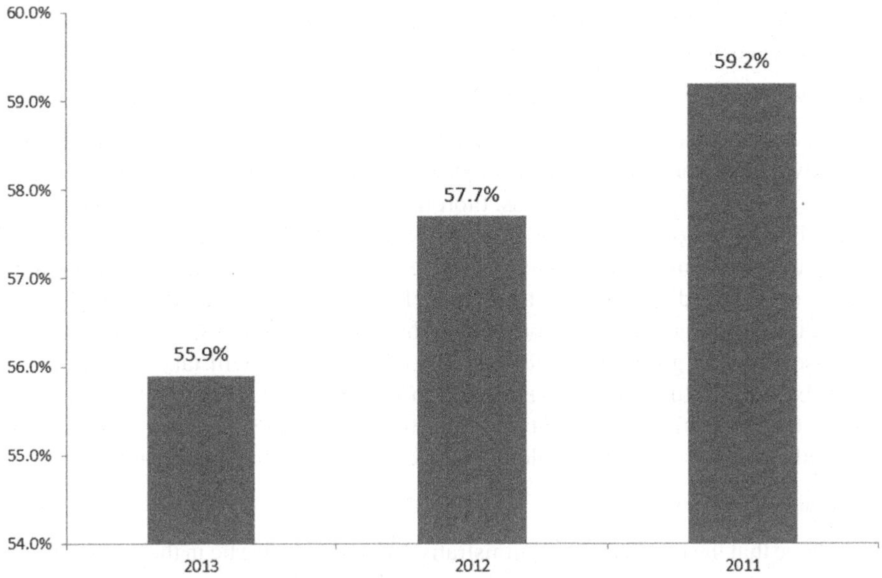

Fig. 8.1 Cases in which the original administrative order is re-affirmed upon review (2011–2013)

people began to challenge the fairness of the administrative review and abandon it as a way of remedy. Besides, over 70% of cases were brought to court without administrative review, which to some extent also reflected that the fairness of review was questioned in people's mind.

(3) The acceptance and handling of review cases unsatisfactory.

On one hand, compared with cases of the first-instance administrative litigation, review cases were smaller in number, so its advantages were not fully tapped. Compared with administrative law enforcement cases, the administrative review cases were even fewer. Meanwhile, the number of applications rejected had been increasing, which showed a lax and passive attitude of the review agencies.[8]

(4) The conflicts and discrepancies between administrative review and relevant systems intensified.

As an important mechanism of resolving administrative disputes, administrative review is only a part of the entire legal framework. The ideal situation would be different mechanisms supplement and coordinate with one another. In practice, however, there are many conflicts between administrative review and other applicable conflict resolution mechanisms, especially with administrative litigation and the court on many issues. How to correctly handle the relation between the review agency and the court has become a serious problem for smooth operation of review work.

[8]Liu Dongsheng: *the Reconstruction of the Administrative Review System*, Doctoral Dissertation at China University of Political Science and Law, April, 2006.

Another problem that merits attention is how to coordinate administrative review with grievance complaint mechanism.

(5) Low efficiency and lagged remedy.

Administrative review is a way for agencies to redress their own wrongdoings. It has a lot of advantages compared with other external supervision and relief mechanisms. In terms of its scope, handling methods, thoroughness of solving a problem, the review mechanism is obviously superior. A sound system of administrative review should be able to resolve most of the administrative disputes. Yet in reality, its strength of quickly solving a dispute did not play out. Influenced by the guiding ideology of administrative management, many agencies handle applications through paperwork. The cases have to go through multiple procedures, and it will take at least half a month before the final decision is issued to the applicant. Meanwhile, during the process of review, the administrative act is still implemented, causing serious delay in remedies, which is most notable in disputes caused by housing demolition.[9]

2. Analysis of Causes.

We believe that the problems in administrative review practice lie in the many flaws in the review system design. In general, the system has adopted excessive administrative means and insufficient judicial means. On the one hand, too much emphasis is placed on internal supervision and efficiency within the administrative system; and on the other, the system ignores procedural requirement of the review mechanism, leading to insufficient protection of the applicant's rights[10]:

(1) Positioning and functions of administrative review still unclear.

The effectiveness of administrative review is largely decided by its positioning pertaining to the procedural and institutional design, which will affect people's choice of whether to engage in the review. Undoubtedly administrative review is a good mechanism of dispute resolution. But it has always been positioned as supervision among different levels of administrative agencies, which stresses dispute resolution mainly through self-policing and self-redress within the system, whereas protecting people's rights is only a by-product of the self-redressing act. Review agencies are not independent and impartial, and the procedures are purely administrative, that is, no prohibition of ex parte communication, no openness and transparency, no cross-examination where all parties are present, and the adjudication is mainly done with paper records. It is the head of the review agency rather than the agency itself that will make the decision, resulting in the phenomenon of adjudication without a decision or a decision made without a hearing. Dispute resolution and internal supervision are not mutually exclusive; rather, they can be supplementary. Review agencies can receive higher-level supervision in the process of dispute resolution. Sufficient understanding of this is crucial to the improvement of the administrative review system.

[9]Liu Xin: Debate on Positioning of Administrative Review, *Legal Forum,* issue 5, vol. 26.
[10]Ibid.

(2) Administrative review agencies lack the independence that they need.

Review agencies at present are within the legal affairs office of a government or within an administrative agency itself, without a uniform independent set of administrative review agencies. The leading official of an administrative agency is in charge. Although review cases are handled by the legal affairs office, which is still an internal division of the agency that just handles specific review matters with no right to make a decision. A decision made in the name of a review agency is actually a decision made by the leading official of the agency. If the official makes the decision based on political considerations rather than from a legal perspective, then the fairness of a decision can hardly be guaranteed. Some local governments are trying to improve such an unreasonable system, and progress has been made. Pilot reform projects of review organizational setup are being carried out in some places and some legal experts and scholars are included as members of the review committee.

(3) Administrative review procedures unsound.

Designed as a model of administrative order, thus procedures of administrative review lack the procedures of hearing, cross-examination and defense which will help the review officer with facts-finding and proper application of the law. For instance, the law prescribes that administrative review is primarily done by examining written documents. Even in the case there are provisions for exceptions, there was no oral hearing with all the parties present confronting each other. And review officers can conduct investigation by ex parte communication with each party separately. All too often, cases requiring oral hearing are those where facts are not clear and controversial. Without face-to-face hearing to examine and cross-examine the parties, facts will remain uncertain; or there will be only unilateral statement of the respondent agency, which makes the review decision more difficult or will lead to an unfair ruling. Moreover, the lack of transparency of the review process will greatly reduce the confidence of the parties and the public in the decisions.

(4) The scope of review too limited.

Currently an internal administrative act is not subject to review; and the challenge to a regulatory instrument has to be together with a specific administrative act and cannot be reviewed separately. Yet as an internal examination mechanism of an administrative agency, the scope of review should be broader than that of the administrative litigation. All cases that are not suited for court adjudication should be covered in the scope of administrative review.

(5) The review mechanism not linking with the process of administrative litigation and grievance complaint.

Administrative review and administrative litigation lack necessary connections between them in terms of scope, applicable legal basis, and the parties involved, which constrains both of their due effect. As the scope of administrative review is rather vague, many cases are pushed to grievance complaints agency. Handling of such complaints is more of a political function, and the relief granted is not as timely and proper as that of administrative review. As for the link with administrative litigation, if administrative review is deemed as a judicial or a quasi-judicial procedure, then the review can be a "pre-trial" and the applicant disagreeing with the decision can bring a lawsuit against the original agency rather than making the review agency a defendant. This is crucial to change the situation of high re-affirming rate of original administrative decisions. Given the reform trend and pilot program, the review panel mostly consisted of independent professionals should not sued; neither should the review agency in name become a defendant in administrative litigation. The practical and institutional flaws of administrative review have everything to do with its incorrect positioning, so it should be the logical starting point of redefining the nature of administrative review

3. The key to the reform: restructuring review agencies.

According to the Administrative Review Law, no special administrative review agency is required for a government and its department to exercise review power, while its legal affairs office is the de facto administrative review body. In practice, there are four types of review entity setups: (a) a division under the legal affairs office is designated as the administrative review office; (b) instead of setting up a special division under the legal affairs office, delegating the power of review to an existing division or office under the legal affairs office, or designating special officers to handle review matters within the legal affairs office; (c) establishing an administrative review committee under the government or a functional department and the committee's office is located within the legal affairs department of that government; (d) setting up a special review body within an administrative agency with the sole function of conducting administrative review without overlapping with other functions. It has an independent legal status and review decision-making authority.

The above-mentioned types of organizational setup show that review bodies in China are scattered and varied without a uniform and centered structure. At present, the first two are the primary review settings, and they are by nature an internal and subordinate part of the administrative agency without independence. The arrangement of the legal affairs office taking charge of administrative review does not meet the requirements of the complex and specialized work of administrative review.

Therefore, most people agree that the breakthrough point of improving the administrative review system must begin with the reform of review agency setup, which is the key task of revising the Administrative Review Law. Only with a fair, independent and specialized administrative review agency can various problems faced in the administrative review work be hopefully solved.

8.3 Reform of Administration Review System and Revision of the Administrative Review Law

(1) Improvement of the administration review system and the revision of the Administrative Review Law.

According to the design of supervision and relief system in China, administrative review is efficient and convenient for the public. It is a normal way of relief and the core of supervision and relief system, so it should play a major role in settling disputes. The severe flaws in the system of administrative review hinder it from performing its function. Instead, grievance complaints and other nonconventional methods have become a more popular choice and the main channel for dispute settlement. In recent years, with rapid economic and social progress, various disputes have increased greatly, and the aforesaid problem has become more salient. Consequently, unprecedented demands from all walks of life are calling for reform of the administrative review system, and putting comprehensive revision of the Administrative Review Law on agenda. The Review Law is an important legal corner stone of the administrative review system. On the one hand, the system reform must be accomplished through revision of the law; at the same time the review system reform is crucial and necessary for improving the Review Law. Therefore, the reform of the system of administrative review should start with revision of the current Review Law. We propose that the Review Law should be revised in the following aspects[11]:

(2) Re-defining the nature of administrative review.

The nature of administrative review involves four theories: the administrative theory, administrative relief theory, administrative judicature theory, and judicature theory. The Review Law defines administrative review as an internal self-correction mechanism within the administrative system, which raises serious challenge to its fairness and hinders the review from functioning as a more specialized and convenient dispute resolution approach compared to litigation. Since administrative review and administrative litigation both adopt the principle of "no complaint, no case", administrative review should be the first rights remedy mechanism for citizens. Otherwise the very purpose for a citizen to apply for a review would be lost. Therefore, remedy for violated rights should be the primary function of administrative review while supervision an intended byproduct in the review process.

(3) Reforming administrative review agencies to make them more independent, professional and authoritative.

Reforming the review system is the very core of revising the Review Law, which will directly affect other related mechanisms. Under the current Review Law the review bodies are scattered within each government and its departments; governments at all levels and all their departments can handle review matters, therefore become the

[11]Wang Wanhua: Several Major Issues in Revising the Administrative Review Law, *Administrative Law Review*, issue 4, 2011.

review agencies. This setup is seriously flawed for lacking of independence and the staff not specialized, which greatly impairs the authority and dispute resolution function of the administrative review system. Hence the revision of the Administrative Review Law must focus on the reform of administrative review agency's setup to solve the problems mentioned above.

(4) Expanding the scope of administrative review.

The review application scope directly affects the scope of the rights of citizens, legal persons and other organizations that applied for review, as well as directly affects to what extent social problems can be solved through administrative review. Therefore, it is also a key issue in revising the Review Law. The current review scope is too narrow and unable to adapt to the changing situation. The scope of review prescribed in the Administrative Review Law corresponds to the Administrative Litigation Law, which is very problematic. Administrative review refers to resolution of administrative disputes by administrative agencies, involving the relations of a superior administrative agency and its subordinate. Administrative litigation refers to resolution of administrative disputes by the court, involving the relations between judicial power and administrative power. To make the scope of these two different dispute resolution mechanisms almost the same would mean that some administrative acts that are not qualified for judicial review also cannot be handled by administrative review, thus citizens, legal persons and other organizations are left without means for remedy. Those cases not eligible for judicial review are not necessarily ineligible for administrative review, so the application scopes should not be exactly the same. All acts by administrative agencies that may affect the legal rights and interests of the interested people should be included into the scope of administrative review. This is an important issue to be considered when revising the Administrative Review Law. The basic idea for revision is to expand the scope of review as broad as possible, especially to include: (a) acts by organizations with public management function to exercise public power; (b) administrative discipline measures by administrative agencies to their staff; and (c) regulations and regulatory directives issued by the State Council.

(5) Improving administrative review procedures.

The system design at the initial stage of administrative review legislation deliberatively separated review procedures from judicial proceedings, which resulted in simplification of review procedures and making them internal measures only. Thus, the lacking of fundamental system guarantee of rational and fair procedure has impaired the functions of administrative review. Therefore, in the revision basic elements of due process should be introduced to so as to safeguard procedural rights of the applicant. Specifically the following procedures should be modified or added when reconstructing the review procedures: (a) adding the provision to allow that the applicant may file a review application either with a review agency, or with the agency that made the original administrative act; (b) adding the provision of recuse; (c) improving facts-finding and evidence presenting means; (d) classifying review procedures into general procedure and summary procedure; (e) abolishing the practice of adjudication by written documents only; adding hearing arguments from the applicant, the agency and the third party; and (f) introducing mediation in a moderate way.

(6) Improving the types of review decisions.

There are many problems in this area. For instance, decisions on dismissing the application for review and on dismissing the requested act of the review are confused; requirements for deciding to revoke or correct an act or declare an act unlawful are not clearly defined; the types of review decisions are insufficient to meet practical demands. Therefore, the key to improve review decisions is to amend and modify the provisions on the types of review decisions to adapt to the complicated circumstances. We specifically suggest: (a) abolishing the decision of affirmation; (b) adding the decision of dismissal of the review request, decision of ordering correction, and decision of situation with specific applicable conditions; (c) in terms of decisions against a unlawful procedure, different types of decisions should be made for different circumstances, including decrees of nullity, revocation, order of supplementation and correction; (d) revising the provision from "administrative review agency directly makes the decision to revoke or alter an act" to the review agency orders the respondent agency to revoke or alter an administrative act; € abolishing the provision of "the decision of administrative review becomes effective upon the time it is served" and, instead, making relevant provisions based on different circumstances.

4. The key to reforming administrative review system: reconstructing the administrative review entity setup.

When the administrative review system was first established, legislators tried to stress the value of independence of administrative review system, by deliberately avoiding the convergence between administrative review and administrative litigation, so as to strengthen its function as an internal supervision mechanism. Therefore, the administrative review body was set up under the framework of the horizontal (region-based) and vertical (profession/industry-based) management system.

Chapter 3 of the Regulations on Administrative Review specially prescribes the jurisdiction of administrative review. Article 11 prescribes that one who does not accept a specific administrative act undertaken by the people's government at or above the county level may file an application for review with the relevant agency at the next higher level or with the people's government of the same level under the following circumstances: (a) there is no immediate higher-level agency in charge of the subject matter; (b) it is provided by law or regulation that the people's government has the jurisdiction. The review application filed against administrative act by a department under the State Council shall be handled by that department.

Article 12 prescribes that a review application filed against a specific administrative act undertaken by any of the local people's governments at various levels shall be handled by the people's government at the next higher level. An application for review filed against a specific administrative act undertaken by a provincial government (including an autonomous region or a municipality under the central government) shall be handled by the same level of government which had undertaken the aforesaid act. Article 13 prescribes that an application for review filed against a specific administrative act undertaken jointly by two or more administrative agencies shall be handled by an administrative agency at the next higher level over the aforesaid two or more administrative agencies. Article 14 prescribes that an application for review filed against a specific administrative act undertaken by a dispatched agency of a local people's government at or above the county level shall be handled by the local government that established the dispatched agency. An application for review filed against a specific administrative act undertaken by an agency by a dispatched agency in its own name according to the provisions of certain laws, regulations and rules shall be handled by the department that established the dispatched agency.

Article 15 prescribes that an application for review filed against a specific administrative act by an organization authorized by the laws, regulations and rules shall be handled by the administrative agency immediately over the said organization. An application for review filed against a specific administrative act by an entrusted organization shall be handled by an administrative agency at the next higher level over the entrusting administrative body. Article 16 prescribes that an application for review filed against a specific administrative act which, according to law, is subject to approval of an administrative agency at a higher level, shall be handled by the administrative agency that makes the final decision unless otherwise prescribed by the law and regulation.

The Administration Review Law has similar provisions on the jurisdiction of administrative review. Article 12 provides that an applicant, who refuses to accept a specific administrative act of the departments under local people's governments at or above the county level may apply for administrative review either to the people's government at the same level or to the same agency at the next higher level. An applicant who refuses to accept a specific administrative act of an administrative agency of a vertical management system, such as the Customs, banks, tax collection, foreign exchange control, or a State security agency shall apply for administrative review to the competent authority at the next higher level. Article 13 prescribes that a citizen, legal person, or any other organization that refuses to accept a specific administrative act of local people's governments at various levels shall apply for administrative review to the local people's government at the next higher level. An applicant who refuses to accept a specific administrative act of an agency at the county government level, which is legally dispatched by a provincial-level government (including an autonomous region), shall file an application to the dispatching government for administrative review.

Article 14 prescribes that a citizen, legal person, or any other organization that refuses to accept a specific administrative act of a department under the State Council, or a provincial-level government (including an autonomous region, or a municipality directly under the Central Government) shall apply for administrative review to the department under the State Council, or the provincial-level government that undertook the specific administrative act. The applicant who refuses to accept the administrative review decision may bring an administrative litigation to a people's court; or apply to the State Council for a ruling, and the State Council shall make a final ruling according to the provisions of this Law.

There has been constant criticism in the academia on the lack of independence of administrative review agency. In the Analysis of the Flaws of the Vertical Jurisdiction of Administrative Review System in China, Liu Heng pointed out that the flaws of the vertical jurisdiction lie in the following aspects: (a) it impairs the fairness of administrative review decision; (b) it is not beneficial to the public; (c) lacking legal basis for administrative organization; (d) weak enforcement of a decision by a superior administrative department; (e) vertical jurisdiction, is difficult in reality; (f) vertical review jurisdiction of large number of specific administrative acts by various government departments is not conducive for the government to learn about and exercise supervision of administrative acts by its subordinate departments in a timely and comprehensive manner, and consequently the function of internal supervision will be hampered; (g) it leads to a more scattered administrative review power with multiple administrative agencies, which increases administrative costs. In addition, due to uneven location of review applications filed, some review agencies are understaffed while others are staying idle. And when eventually the excessive agency is closed, then some new cases will be left with no agency or staff to handle them. The article also pointed out that the key of rooting out aforementioned flaws is to make the review more like a. judicial process and ensure the independence of administrative agencies.

The practice of administrative review proves that the value of administrative review doesn't have to be realized through its separation from administrative litigation, since the two systems can supplement each other. Administrative review has the inherent function of dispute resolution and this unique role is gradually recognized. Therefore, one important measure of improving the review practice is to carry out the pilot program of making the review agency independent and procedures with more "quasi-judicial" features.[12]

In 2008, in order to further improve the administrative review system and its working methods, to enhance the quality and efficiency of administrative review in dispute resolution, to boost its credibility, and to give full play to its role in settling administrative disputes, and to build a government based on the rule of law and a harmonious socialist society, the Legal Affairs Office of the State Council following the directives of the CPC Central Committee and the State Council, decided to launch a pilot program of establishing administrative review committees in eight provinces and municipalities, namely Beijing, Heilongjiang Province, Jiangsu Province, Shandong Province, Henan Province, Guangdong Province, Hainan Province and Guizhou Province.

Actually as early as in 2007, some cities already began to explore establishing such a review committee. A notable example would be the administrative review committee of Harbin City, Heilongjiang Province, which was established in July, 2007, to explore a relatively centralized model of administrative review power. The committee was a review agency authorized by the government to make final decisions on administrative review cases and directly report to chief officials of the city

[12]Liu Heng & Lu Yan, "An Analysis of the Flaws of the Vertical Jurisdiction of Administrative Review in China", *Chinese Journal of Law*, issue 2, 2004.

government. The city administrative review committee consisted of 1 chair, 2 vice chairs, and 18 members. The chair was the executive deputy mayor; and the two vice chairs, one was the director of the city government Legal Affairs Office, and the other was the deputy director of the Legal Affairs Office especially in charge of administrative review work. The members were selected and appointed from law professors, scholars, senior lawyers, legislators, and members of the local Chinese People's Political Consultative Council. Members from outside of the government accounted for 81%, more than half of the total.

Administrative review office under the committee was located in the Legal Affairs Office of the municipal government, where the committee members conducted investigation, reviewed cases and implemented decisions of the committee. Their job responsibilities included: accepting review applications; investigating basic facts; submitting to the committee reports of investigation and preliminary hearing of cases; handling matters decided by the committee; conducting review mediation; and doing related research and surveys.

The committee separated investigation from decision-making, i.e., the review office conducted fact-finding investigation while the committee members voted for the decision. Five to nine members would participate in voting with members outside of the government accounted for over 50%. The committee followed the following procedures in a deliberation meeting: (a) the case investigation team submitted a report on investigation and cross-examination hearing to the committee; (b) committee members reviewed the report and posed questions to the investigation team and the team responded to the questions; (c) members engaged in deliberation and discussion; (d) members filled out the voting opinion form; (e) votes were counted and the decision made by the majority rule. The review decision would be signed by the committee chair and the decision would be issued in the name of the municipal government. If the chair deemed it necessary for the matter to be reconsidered, the chair should instruct the administrative review office to hold another deliberation meeting attended by at least nine members, or a committee meeting with over two thirds of the members present. The deliberation and vote would be made again by the majority rule. The new review decision would be sent to the chair for review and signature. If the chair deemed it necessary for the municipal government to discuss and make a decision, a report would be submitted to the executive meeting of the people's government for a collective discussion and decision.[13]

After the pilot program of the administrative review committee was launched in Harbin City, administrative review cases used to be handled by the municipal government and its departments now were all investigated, deliberated and decided by the review office and the committee by the majority rule, and then sent to the committee chair for approval. The working departments of the municipal government no longer handled administrative review cases.

[13] *The Establishment and Operation of Harbin Administrative Review Committee*, issued on the website of Legislative Affairs Office, the State Council, http://www.chinalaw.gov.cn/article/dfxx/zffzdt/200804/20080400046777.shtml, last retrieved on July 2, 2009.

Unlike the situation in Harbin where the administration power was consolidated, the Beijing municipal government also established an administrative review committee and the first term was composed of 28 members. The municipal government official in charge of legal affairs assumed the position of executive deputy chair of the committee. Besides, 18 people were selected from universities, research institutes, and government ministries in Beijing and became non-permanent members. Such setup was unprecedented. As an administrative review entity of the municipal government, the committee functioned through holding review hearings and plenary sessions. For significant and difficult cases, the committee would hold joint review and joint consultations, and the final decision would be reported to the municipal government.[14]

We have every reason to believe that as the administrative review agency becomes independent; the system will play a bigger role in safeguarding the legitimate rights and interests of citizens, legal persons and other organizations; in settling administrative disputes; and in supervising administrative agencies. The key issues are: how to correctly define the purpose and function of administrative review; how to effectively combine the functions of disputes resolution with supervision of administrative acts; and the undefined purpose of administrative review is a leading constraint on its role to be fully played out.

[14]*The Beijing Administrative Review Committee Established, Joint A Adjudication of Big and Difficult Cases*, http://news.china.com/zh_cn/news100/11038989/20071114/14471553.html, latest retrieved, July 2, 2009.

Chapter 9
Developing and Improving the Administrative Litigation System

9.1 A Historical Review

Before 1949, the Kuomintang (KMT) government did pass and enacted an administrative litigation law. The law came to an end when KMT's rule in mainland China ended. Since the founding of the PRC, development of China's administrative litigation System has gone through the following four stages.[1]

1. The initial stage.

In the early years after the founding of PRC, the Chinese leaders did realize that citizens should have the right to complain against and sue administrative agencies for their misconducts. Article 19 of "The Common Program of the Chinese People's Political Consultative Conference" promulgated on September 29th, 1949, prescribes that "citizens and civic organizations may file complaints with the people's supervisory agency or people's judicial authority against any state agencies or civil servants for misconducts and negligence. In December 1949, the Provisional Organization Regulation of the Supreme People's Court prescribes that an administrative adjudication tribunal shall be set up in the Supreme People's Court. Article 97 of the 1954 Constitution of the PRC prescribes that "PRC citizens have the right to file complaints, either written or oral, with state agencies at all levels against the staff of state organs for misconducts and negligence. Citizens who suffer a loss due to rights infringement at the hand of government civil servants are entitled to compensation." At that time, some legal documents had provisions on administrative litigation. For example, Article 31 of the Rural Reform Law of 1950 prescribes that, after the township government determines a rural person's status, if this person or another disagrees with the determination, he or she could, within 15 days of the decision file a petition

[1] Zhao Daguang, The Development and Experience of Administrative Adjudication in the Past 60 Years, *Law Application*, Dec. 2009.

© Social Sciences Academic Press and Springer Nature Singapore Pte Ltd. 2018
H. Ma and J. Wang, *Building a Government Based on the Rule of Law*,
Research Series on the Chinese Dream and China's Development Path,
https://doi.org/10.1007/978-981-13-0999-1_9

to the People' Court of that county for a ruling. In 1952 the Government Administration Council issued the Rules of Establishing People's Tribunals in the Campaign against Five Illegal Activities, which prescribes that "business owners who disagree with the Thrifty Inspection Committee's determination and treatment of their status (law-abiding, basically abiding, semi–abiding, and semi-non abiding) may appeal to the municipal or county-level People's Tribunal. Similar regulations could also be found in Provisional Regulation on the Inspection of Import and Export Commodities (1953) and Provisional Regulation on Port Management (1954). Article 41 of the Constitution of the PRC of 1982 prescribes that "PRC citizens have the right to criticize and make suggestions to any state agency or functionary. Citizens have the right to file with relevant state agencies complaints or accusation against any state agency or functionary for any misconduct; but false fabrication or deliberate distortion of facts is prohibited. The state agency concerned must investigate the facts and handle citizen's complaint, accusation or report in a responsible manner. No one may suppress such complaint or accusation or retaliate against the citizen who filed the complaint or accusation. Citizens who suffered losses as a result of infringement of their civil rights by any state agency or functionary are entitled to compensation in accordance with the law." Thus, we can see that the Constitution and laws laid down a constitutional foundation for administrative litigation and state compensation system. However, due to absence of specific provisions and administrative adjudication organs in People's Courts, so administrative litigation was non-existent in China then. Therefore, at this stage there were a few sporadic regulations that were not really put into practice.

2. The stage of laws for special purposes.

After the reform and opening up, the reconstruction of legal system began. Administrative litigation began to be practiced in China in accordance with some laws for special purposes and regulations. For example, the Election Law of 1997 prescribes that People's Courts have jurisdiction over the cases regarding the list of voters. The Law on Income Tax of Foreign Enterprises of 1980, Economic Contract Law of 1980 of and the Regulation Concerning Land Requisition for State Construction of 1982 all prescribe that People's Courts have jurisdiction over administrative disputes. And in practice, some courts actually handled administrative disputes.

3. The stage of the Civil Procedural Law.

On March 8th, 1982, Civil Procedural Law of the PRC (Provisional) was released. Section 2, Article 2 of the Law prescribes "that the Law herein governs administrative litigation adjudicated by People's Courts according to law", which provided specific legal grounds for adjudication of administrative disputes and laid the basic foundation for the establishment of administrative litigation system of New China. Thereafter more and more special statutes provided for court jurisdiction over administrative disputes. By 1989 when the Civil Procedural Law was passed, around 130 special statutes and regulations prescribed that administrative lawsuits could be filed with the people's courts. A large number of the administrative disputes involved public security penalties and land issues. In October 1986, Wuhan Intermediate People's Court of Hubei Province and Miluo County-level People's Court of Hunan Province, taking the lead, set up administrative tribunals. In October 1988, the Supreme People's Court also established an administrative tribunal and the local courts followed suit.

Since 1980s, legal scholars began to explore the possibility of establishing an independent administrative litigation system. They held that based on actual situation and China's development needs as well as other countries' experience in this area, it's high time for China to enact an administrative litigation law. This recommendation was accepted by the legislative body and a task force was set up to work on legislation of administrative litigation.

4. The stage of the Administrative Litigation Law.

Controversies did not impede legislative work. On April 4th, 1989, Administrative Litigation Law of the PRC was passed at the Second Plenary Session of the Seventh National People's Congress. It was a milestone in the reconstruction of China's administration according to law, and marked the official establishment of administrative litigation system in PRC. Compared with other laws, Administrative Litigation Law suffered unimaginable difficulties in its implementation. According to the daily brief of August 1990, from the Secretariat of CPC Central Committee Office, over 2000 township-level officials in a certain area threatened to resign before the Administrative Litigation Law took effect. However, despite the obstacles, the administrative litigation system survived and developed rapidly in the past two decades. The scope of administrative disputes heard in People's Courts continued to expand and now covers almost all fields in administrative management. The types of administrative disputes kept increasing and so far there are over 50 varieties of administrative litigation cases.

Since Administrative Litigation Law was adopted, the Supreme People's Court has issued more than 20 Interpretations, 16 judicial guidance directives and over 200 responses concerning application of the laws. Table 9.1 shows the currently effective and important Interpretations of the Supreme People's Court:

The Judicial Interpretations listed in Table 9.1 provided much needed guidance for proper implementation and adjudication practice of the Administrative Litigation Law. Their contents and contributions could be summarized as follows: (1) they included detailed and operational provisions on the scope of accepted cases, forms of ruling and judgment and other relevant administrative litigation procedures, e.g. Interpretation by the Supreme People's Court for Several Issues Regarding the Implementation of Administrative Litigation Law; (2) they helped set up a comprehensive evidence system in administrative litigation, including types of evidence, burden of proof, and rules of examination and cross-examination, e.g. Provisions of the Supreme People's Court on Issues Regarding Evidence in Administrative Litigation; (3) they specified the legal grounds for adjudication and application of laws in administrative disputes, e.g. Provisions of the Supreme People's Court on Issues Regarding Handling Administrative Cases of International Trade, and Provisions

Table 9.1 Currently effective and important interpretations of the Supreme People's Court

Date of release	Title	Content
May 6, 1996	Interim Litigation Rules Governing the Processing of Compensation Claims by the People's Court Compensation Commission	Procedures on case filing acceptance, adjudication, investigation and hearing, and enforcement of judgment
May 6, 1996	Interpretations of Several Issues Regarding the People's Courts' Implementation of the State Compensation Law of PRC	The scope of state compensation, major actions, qualification of compensation recipients, compensation-providing agencies
April 29, 1997	Provisions of the Supreme People's Court on Issues Regarding the Processing of Administrative Compensation Cases	The scope of case acceptance, jurisdiction, parties to the lawsuit, acceptance of lawsuits, trials and decisions
March 10, 2000	Interpretation by the Supreme People's Court of the Issues Regarding the Implementation of Administrative Litigation Law of PRC	Scope of case acceptance, litigants, evidence, jurisdiction, acceptance of lawsuits, trials and decisions
September 21, 2000	Interpretations by the Supreme People's Court of the Issues Regarding Judicial Compensation in Civil and Administrative Litigation	Scope of judicial compensation, types of enforcement measures, unlawful preservative measures, denial of compensation in accordance with the law
February 21, 2001	Interpretations by the Supreme People's Court on Jurisdiction over Administrative Cases Regarding Property Management Right of State-owned Assets	Administrative litigation regarding property rights determination of state-owned assets shall be handled by the competent court according to the situations specified in this document
February 7, 2002	Interpretations by the Supreme People's Court on Jurisdiction Assignment for Administrative Penalty Cases involving PRC Customs Law	Lawsuits filed challenging administrative penalties imposed by the Customs shall be heard by a local court with jurisdiction in accordance with relevant provisions of the Administrative Litigation Law
October 1, 2002	Provisions of the Supreme People's Court on Evidence-Related Issues in Administrative Litigation	Allocation of burden of proof, time limit for producing evidence, requirements for evidence production, obtaining, preserving, examination and cross-examination, and verification and acceptance of evidence
October 1, 2002	Provisions of the Supreme People's Court on Issues Regarding Hearing Administrative Cases of International Trade	Types of cases, jurisdiction, and adjudication
January 1, 2003	Provisions of the Supreme People's Court on Issues Regarding Applicable Laws in Deciding Anti-Subsidy Administrative Cases	Scope of case acceptance, parties of the lawsuit, court with jurisdiction, adjudication and decision

(continued)

Table 9.1 (continued)

Date of release	Title	Content
January 1, 2003	Provisions of the Supreme People's Court on Issues Regarding Law Application in Hearing Anti-Dumping Administrative Cases	Scope of case acceptance, litigants, court with jurisdiction, adjudication and decision
September 5, 2003	Provisions of the Supreme People's Court on Issues Regarding People's Courts Hearing Personnel Dispute Cases of Non-Profit Public Entities	Subject matters of cases regarding personnel disputes between a non-profit public entity and its staff
February 1, 2008	Provisions of the Supreme People's Court on Issues regarding Jurisdiction for Administrative Cases	Jurisdiction of Intermediary People's Courts, actions required if basic-level courts fail to perform duties, and calculation of adjudication time limit
February 1, 2008	Provisions of the Supreme People's Court on Issues Regarding Withdrawal of Administrative Lawsuit	Details regarding during litigation the defendant agency corrected its specific administrative act and the plaintiff applies to withdraw the lawsuit
January 4, 2010	Provisions on Issues regarding Handling of Administrative Permit and License Cases	Details regarding lawsuits against permit/license issuing agency's non-action, the defendant, evidence obtaining and other related issues
November 18, 2010	Provisions of the Supreme People's Court on Issues Regarding Housing Registration Trials	Acceptance and adjudication of cases concerning housing registration agency's acts such as registration, inquiry, and copying registration records
March 18, 2011	Interpretation of the Supreme People's Court on Issues Regarding Application of the State Compensation Law (I)	Application of the Revised State Compensation Law
August 13, 2011	Provisions of the Supreme People's Court on Issues Regarding Administrative Cases of Government Information Disclosure	Acceptance of filing, burden of proof, adjudication and judgment of government information disclosure cases
September 5, 2011	Provisions of the Supreme People's Court on Issues Regarding Rural Collectively-Owned Land Administrative Cases	Acceptance of filing and adjudication of administrative actions involving rural collectively-owned land
February 15, 2012	Provisions of the Supreme People's Court on Acceptance of State Compensation Cases	Requirements of the acceptance of filing and adjudication of state compensation cases
April 10, 2012	Provisions of the Supreme People's Court on Application for Compulsory Enforcement of Decisions on Compensation for Requisitioned Properties on State-Owned Land	Requirements and procedures of compensation for requisitioned properties on state-owned land

of the Supreme People's Court on Issues Regarding Law Application in Hearing Anti-Dumping Administrative Cases.

9.2 Achievements and the Current Situation of Administrative Litigation in China

1. Achievements since the implementation of the Administrative Litigation Law.

Achievements have been made in establishing and improving China's administrative litigation system in the following aspects.

(1) Establishing, for the first time, the legal system of common people suing government officials. This is a departure from the traditional notion that officials are superior to commoners. This system makes citizens and the government equal before law and subject them equally to the judgment of the court. In the course of the 23 years since the Administrative Litigation Law took effect, the number of administrative disputes has increased, and the scope of accepted cases widened. In particular, the Interpretation for Issues Regarding the Implementation of Administrative Procedural Law issued by the Supreme People's Court in 2000 to a certain extent expanded the scope of the cases to be accepted for filing and adjudication.
(2) Safeguarding the legitimate rights and interests of the objects of administrative acts. Through investigation of the challenged administrative act, administrative litigation could effectively stop infringement of unlawful administrative acts on the objects of administrative agencies. And administrative litigation cases, enormous in number and diverse in types, has enhanced people's rights awareness and concept of litigation. The public has become more aware of protecting their legitimate rights and interests.
(3) Overseeing power-exercising of administrative agencies and promoting administration according to law. Administrative litigation is highly effective in ensuring that administrative acts comply with the law. Once the administrative acts are judged unfavorably by the court, the administrative agencies and the staff will be held accountable. Under such pressure, administrative agencies and their staff will strengthen self-discipline and improve their competency in administrative law enforcement. Through administrative litigation, lawful administrative acts are affirmed and encouraged and unlawful acts are redressed in a timely manner.
(4) Ensuring economic security and social stability. Since the establishment of administrative litigation system, China has been experiencing significant transformation with intensified social conflicts, which will undermine social stability if not dealt with properly and timely. From this perspective the development of administrative litigation in China has played a positive role in understanding people's living conditions, solving their complaints, remedying their losses, and removing the source of people's sufferings. Therefore, the

administrative litigation "offers a new and good way for resolving conflicts among the people and proves to be an indispensable mechanism for maintaining long-term stability of the country."[2]

(5) Accelerating the continued improvement of administrative law system. The birth of Administrative Litigation Law served as a catalyst to bring out a bulk of administrative statutes: the State Compensation Law, the Administrative Penalty Law, the Administrative Review Law, the Legislation Law, the Administrative Permits Law, and the Administrative Mandatory Enforcement Law, are all passed and released under the background of Administrative Litigation Law which has greatly accelerated the improvement of administrative law system in China.

(6) Promoting academic studies of administrative jurisprudence. The establishment of administrative litigation system in China has directly promoted the prosperous development of academic studies on administrative jurisprudence. Theories of subjects of administrative law, administrative acts, and administrative procedures are all closely related to the practice of administrative litigation. Administrative disputes provide abundant materials for academic studies. Meanwhile, the highly convincing decisions rendered by the judges, under the guidance of active judicial power and by applying jurisprudence and principles of administrative law, have broadened the vision of scholars and the scope of academic studies.

2. An Overview of Administrative Litigation.

From 1988 to 2012, the people's courts at all levels in China handled administrative disputes, totaling over 1,900,000 at the first-instance hearing, around 470,000 at second-instance hearings and around 40,000 cases for judicial review (re-trial) (see Table 9.2).

After Administrative Litigation Law took effect in 1990, the number of administrative lawsuits grew rapidly from less than 10,000 before 1989 to over 20,000, doubled the yearly average. In over 20 years since 1988, administrative litigation cases increased steadily from over 8000 in 1988 to over 136,000 in 2011, which was around 17 times growth. The Law played an important role in settling administrative disputes and protecting the legitimate rights and interests of the citizens. Yet it did not lead to anticipated "blowout" of administrative disputes. Great imbalance still exists among courts in different areas. Lots of administrative disputes occur in developed regions, while courts in less developed areas sometimes need to look for cases.

3. Problems of Administrative Litigation in Resolving Social Conflicts.

Since its establishment in 1989, administrative litigation has played a significant role in settling administrative disputes and resolving conflicts between administrative

[2]Luo Haocai, A Great Achievement in Democracy and Legal System Construction: the 10th Anniversary of the Promulgation of the *Administrative Litigation Law*, http://www.chinalawedu.com/news/21601/21712/148/2004/12/ma177919293416121400260233_145881.htm.

Table 9.2 Number of administrative disputes heard by People's Courts at all levels, 1988–2012

Year	Cases accepted for first-instance trial	Cases closed for first-instance trial	Cases accepted for second-instance trial	Cases closed for second-instance cases	Cases Accepted for judicial review	Cases closed for judicial review
1988	8573	8029	2356	2218	489	447
1989	9934	9742	2908	2888	564	551
1990	13,006	12,040	3432	3325	602	538
1991	25667	25,202	6930	6708	1181	1031
1992	27,125	27,116	8334	8273	988	914
1993	27,911	27,958	7426	7584	1154	1162
1994	35,083	34,567	7699	7672	1345	1332
1995	52,596	51,370	9694	9536	1628	1512
1996	79966	79,537	11,454	11,365	1885	1910
1997	90,557	88,542	12,754	12,684	2230	2184
1998	98,350	98,390	14,330	14,220	2432	2339
1999	97,569	98,759	18,045	18,072	3182	3001
2000	85,760	86,614	19,743	19,404	2746	2918
2001	100,921	95,984	22,536	22,149	2967	2875
2002	80,728	84,943	27,674	27,649	1797	1867
2003	87,919	88,050	25,134	25,045	1833	1801
2004	92,613	92,192	27,495	27,273	1850	1852
2005	96,178	95707	29,448	29,176	1894	1780
2006	95617	95,052	28,956	29,054	1950	1870
2007	101,510	100,683	29,986	29,964	1098	2035
2008	108,398	109,085	32,920	31,366	1543	1521
2009	120,312	120,530	32,643	32,981	1358	1405
2010	129,133	129,806	35,334	35,188	1448	1578
2011	136,353	136,361	33,479	33,440	1564	1519
2012	129,583	128,625	32,549	32,584	1277	1287
Total	1,931,362	1,924,884	483,259	479,818	41,005	41,229

agencies and the public. But some existing problems are hindering the function of administrative litigation.[3]

(1) A small number of administrative agencies are still resentful regarding administrative litigation and reluctant to cooperate in hearings. When a party files a lawsuit, some administrative agencies and their staff do not treat the plaintiff properly or participate in the litigation. Instead, some even interfere with the

[3]Ma Huaide, Mitigating Social Conflicts and Administrative Litigation System, *Chinese Cadres Tribune*, 2011, issue 3.

adjudication. A judge once commented in his paper that in China administrative litigation faces myriad difficulties and the root cause is that judicial power is trumped by administrative power and remains relatively weak. Some agencies still do not understand or accept why the court is legally authorized to examine their administrative acts. They express resentment, refuse to cooperate and sometimes even engage in obstruction of justice.

(2) Per capita number of administrative disputes is very low. Interested parties need to enhance awareness of administrative litigation; besides they lack trust for the judicial system.

The principle of "no complaint, no trial" has also been adopted by administrative litigation, so litigation can only be initiated by the interested party whose rights are infringed. Since the adoption of the Law, administrative litigation cases are very few and it is very hard to sue administrative agencies. The per capita number of administrative disputes is extremely low, which does not mean that administrative agencies are very competent or that they rarely infringe upon the legitimate rights and interests of citizens. Judging by the astronomical number of grievance complaint letters, calls and visits received by the grievance petition agencies at various levels, the small number of administrative disputes does not mean that the total number of administrative disputes is low; rather, it is due to the fact that lots of disputes are not filed with the courts. One of the causes is the low rights and litigation awareness of the potential plaintiff. China has a long history of self-sufficient natural economy where people were under strong influence of the clan rule and Confucian culture, which led to the lack of rights awareness and litigation concept among the public. Another important reason is that, at present, judicial corruption is serious and worsening, resulting in people's distrust in courts and administrative litigation system.

(3) Administrative adjudication is obstructed and judges are not independent.

Over 20 years of administrative litigation practice suggests that judicial organs are actually controlled by multiple non-judicial forces. The judicial power has an obvious tendency of being controlled by administrative and local authorities. There is a popular saying in judicial practice, that "choosing a right court is half of the winning battle". China still has a long way to go to achieve independence for the courts and the judges. Not only external environment of administrative adjudication needs to be improved but also within the court system support needs to be provided to enhance independence of adjudicatory bodies and judges.

(4) Trial quality needs to be improved.

Despite of impressive progress, many problems still exist in the adjudication of administrative disputes, such as many cases that should be accepted by court are actually rejected; it is common for the court to decide cases beyond the time limit;

lawsuit withdrawal rate is too high and majority appeared to be "abnormal withdrawal; and improper application of laws is also common.

(5) Administrative litigation system needs to be further advanced.

Administrative Litigation Law has been implemented in China for more than 20 years and during this period the Supreme People's Court has issued quite a few Interpretations and Provisions to improve the system. However, since the Law has not been revised, many problems cannot be solved from the source. They include: the purpose of administrative litigation not clear; the scope of case acceptance too narrow, the scope of protected rights and interests not sufficient; and the level of first-instance trial court too low. Besides, under the current system public interests administrative lawsuits are not accepted, and provisions on the defendant of an administrative litigation after administrative review are not reasonable.

These problems make it very difficult for the court to adjudicate the cases fairly and independently. The cost of the plaintiff to bring an administrative lawsuit is very high in terms that the party is faced with many non-legal risks when challenging the powerful local government and its subordinate agencies. So, some of them would rather pick other routes such as through grievance complaint petition to a higher level or making a group incident or mass disturbance to attract attention. They seem to believe that "the more trouble you make the more attention you get." This way not only the original conflict is not mitigated; it may trigger even more serious social unrest.

9.3 Improvement of the Administrative Litigation System and Revision of the Administrative Litigation Law

The administrative litigation system has played an important role in promoting administration according to law, safeguarding the legitimate rights and interests of the interested party, resolving administrative disputes, and maintaining social stability. However, as the society develops, this Law needs to be revised to meet ever-changing social requirements.

1. Purposes of administrative litigation.

Article 2 of the Administrative Litigation Law provides that the purpose of the Law is protecting the legitimate rights and interests of citizens, legal persons and other organizations, and safeguarding and overseeing the exercise of administrative power by administrative agencies in accordance with the law. In practice, two problems exist with the said provision.

First, it puts too much emphasis on ensuring administrative agency's exercise administrative powers in accordance with the law and weakens the purpose of protecting the legitimate rights and interests of the interested party.[4] As a result, in practice, some courts refuse to accept cases that should be accepted, or fail to dismiss the cases that should be dismissed. This also becomes an excuse used by the Party and government leaders for interfering with administrative litigation. In some places, the court even consults with the Party and government organs on the acceptance, hearing and judgment of cases. Second, the said provision neglects the function of administrative litigation in settling administrative disputes. Consequently, some courts refuse to accept administrative disputes in order to avoid conflicts that might be caused by the litigation.

Some scholars, therefore, propose to add resolving administrative dispute as a purpose of administrative litigation, and even a top priority,[5] with the ultimate purpose as protecting the rights and interests of citizen, legal persons and other organizations.[6]

2. Scope of case acceptance.

The scope of accepted cases has been the most controversial issue in the theory and practice of administrative litigation. Particularly since China entered historic transformation, various social conflicts have been on the rise. More courts are trying to avoid their duty of administrative adjudication by declaring that the case concerned is beyond the scope of case accepted, thus failed to protect the legitimate rights and interests of interested parties. With the growing demand for widening the scope of accepted cases, in March 2000 the Supreme People's Court issued the Interpretation on Issues Regarding the Implementation of Administrative Litigation Law. The Interpretation defines the scope of accepted cases by means of generalization and exclusion by enumeration. In other words, it provides a specific enumerated list of matters that the scope of accepted cases does not cover. As long as the dispute is not on the exclusion list, the interested party is in principle permitted to file an action with the court. Although it is controversial whether the Supreme People's Court has gone beyond the scope of accepted case prescribed by the Law, the direction in which the efforts were made should be affirmed.

Despite persistent and strong calls for the expansion of the scope of accepted cases in administrative litigation, in reality, the number of administrative disputes has stayed stubbornly small, never accounting for more than 2% of the total cases handled by the court.[7] By comparison, the number of grievance complaint letters,

---

[4] Ma Huaide, Problems of the *Administrative Litigation Law* and Suggestions for its Revision, *Legal Forum*, Sept. 2010.

[5] Guo Xiujiang, Overview and Outlook on the Purpose of the Administrative Litigation Law: Dynamics of Legality Review and Administrative Dispute Resolution, *Review and Outlook on China's Administrative Litigation Law*, China University of Political Science and Law Press, Dec. 2006, p. 804.

[6] Ma Huaide, Protecting the Rights and Interests of Citizens, Legal Persons and Other Organizations Should be the Fundamental Purpose of Administrative Litigation, *Administrative Law Review*, issue 2, 2012.

[7] Guo Xiujiang, Review and Outlook on the Purpose of the Administrative Litigation Law: Dynamics of Legality Review and Administrative Dispute Addressing, *Review and Outlook on China's*

calls and visits totaled close to 20 million, which was 20 times the number of administrative review and administrative litigation cases combined. Therefore, expanding the scope of accepted cases in administrative litigation and improving judicial capability are of great significance for protecting the legitimate rights and interests of the interested party and overseeing the exercise of power of administrative agencies.[8] The academia has suggested the following amendments for the scope of cases accepted: using the method of generalization in defining the scope of acceptance; replacing administrative acts with administrative disputes as the criterion for acceptance; and listing for exclusion the types of disputes that are not suitable for administrative litigation.

3. Parties to administrative litigation.

Parties to administrative lawsuits are the subjects in administrative litigation. The qualifications for being a plaintiff or defendant, in particular, are directly related to whether the party could obtain remedies through administrative litigation. In the Administrative Litigation Law, there are two Articles regulating the qualifications of a plaintiff. Article 2 provides that "if a citizen, a legal person or any other organization considers that his/her/its legitimate rights and interests have been infringed upon by a specific administrative act of an administrative agency or its staff, the party shall have the right to bring a suit before a people's court in accordance with this Law". Here "consider" is a subjective criterion, which is hard to apply in practice and it has resulted in many controversies concerning the qualifications for a plaintiff in an administrative lawsuit. In fact, plaintiff qualifications are closely related to the scope of accepted cases. Some courts use "personal right and property right" prescribed in Article 11 of the Law as a standing requirement to reject someone to be the plaintiff. They insist that the plaintiff should be the person against whom the specific administrative act is directed at, which impeded the interested party to seek remedy of infringed rights through administrative litigation. To follow the general tendency of relaxing restrictions on plaintiff qualifications, the Supreme People's Court, in its Interpretation in 2000, clearly defines plaintiff as citizens, legal persons and other organizations whose interests are legally connected to the administrative act that the lawsuit is filed against. Another problem closely related to plaintiff qualifications is the public interest administrative litigation. In academia, there are controversies over which organizations can, on behalf of the public, bring a lawsuit against an administrative act that has harmed the general interest of the public. Some suggest that the Procuratorate should shoulder this responsibility, and others suggest that the law should expressly designate some social organizations for this matter. No consensus has been reached. The issue also needs urgent attention when revising the Law. Otherwise, the qualification requirements for plaintiff will remain incomplete and the public interests cannot be fully protected.

Administrative Litigation Law, China University of Political Science and Law Press, December 2006, p. 804.

[8]Ma Huaide, Improving Administrative Litigation System to Promote Social Dispute Resolution, *Legal Information*, Aug., 2011.

Defendant is defined on the basis of the theory of administrative subjects. Due to the complicated administrative management system in China, it is rather difficult to determine the defendant in an administrative litigation. In many situations, the actual administrative actor is not the defendant. The Interpretation of the Supreme People's Court attempts to clarify the definition of defendant in administrative litigation on the basis of the administrative subject theory. Unfortunately, the defendant definition has become even more obscure. In order to make it easier for the interested party to exercise the right to litigation, the requirements for defendant determination should be simplified in the revised version of the Law. Some scholars suggest that "whoever did the act shall be the defendant", which seems like a simple solution.

4. Jurisdiction of administrative litigation.

Jurisdiction of administrative litigation cases includes level of jurisdiction, regional jurisdiction, and jurisdiction by order. When the law was drafted, the drafters believed that jurisdiction system should facilitate lawsuit initiation of the interested party and improve the court's efficiency in handling cases. Generally speaking, a basic-level court in a place where the case occurs would make the jurisdiction easy for the parties to file a case, make an answer, conduct investigation, collect evidence and implement the judgment. Also, jurisdiction of administrative disputes should be consistent with criminal and civil cases. As for the level of jurisdiction, the Law prescribes that basic-level courts are the first-instance court of administrative disputes by default. In China, courts are set up according to geographical administrative divisions. Personnel decision and financial supply of courts are controlled by the same-level administrative division. When an administrative agency is sued, to avoid losing the case, the defendant agency often tries to influence the judge from independently exercising the adjudicatory power through power connections. Basic-level courts are under absolute control of the local administrative power. In practice, the court usually exits as a department of the local government. The administrative ranking system is applied in the management of the court; yet the ranks of court officials are half-level inferior to their counterparts of other government agencies. The court is also controlled by the local government in terms of personnel, finance, and material supplies. In the Party organization, the ranking of Party representatives of the courts is much lower than their counterparts of the local government. Moreover, with highly localized control, the court, is reduced to a tool of local protectionism, undermining unified judicial standard by the rule of law. Under the current judicial system, when a county or higher level people's government is the defendant, the basic-level court is rarely able to avoid interference and obstruction from the administrative agency, which greatly undermines justice. Therefore, how to ensure independence of the court to uphold justice is the important objective for the reform regarding jurisdiction level in administrative litigation. The Supreme People's Court, in an attempt to suppress judicial localization, has through its judicial interpretations designated more intermediary courts as the first-instance court of administrative disputes. The academia also put forward some solutions from different perspectives, such as further narrowing down the jurisdiction scope of the basic-level court; upgrading the level of regional jurisdiction; expanding the scope plaintiff's choices of regional jurisdiction; setting up circuit administrative tribunals; and establishing special administrative courts. The objectives of the above are to promote fair adjudication; to make it easier for the parties to participate; and to reduce the litigation cost and burden.

5. Types of judgment in administrative litigation.

The current Administrative Litigation Law prescribes four types of the first-instance judgment, namely "affirming", "revoking", "performing" and "altering" It also specifies requirements for the application of each type of judgment. These judgments, especially "affirming" and "revoking", and their application requirements, for the first time set up the systematic criteria for deciding the legality of administrative acts, which has played a positive guiding role in building the administrative law system in China. However, the four types of judgment are basically centered around administrative acts and neglect the claims of the plaintiff, therefore encountered some difficulties in practice. The Interpretation of the Supreme People's Court on the Law incorporates the claim of the party in the judgment consideration and adds another two types, i.e., "legality declaratory judgment" and "dismissal of the litigation request". This to a certain degree makes up for the deficiency of the provisions in the Law.

However, as administrative adjudication further develops, the said six types of judgment fall short of meeting the needs of various kinds of administrative disputes. The amended provision still cannot effectively resolve administrative disputes, and shows their limits in safeguarding the legitimate rights and interests of citizens and the public interest. The problems are two folds: First, some types of judgment do not match the purpose of administrative litigation. For example, as for the relationship between the "affirming" judgment and the judgment of "dismissing the litigation request", when deciding the dispute between the object and subject of an administrative act, the court, as an adjudicator, only needs to dismiss the case if the administrative act is found lawful and reasonable; it is not necessary for the court to reinforce the legal effect of the administrative act by "affirming" the judgment.

Second, the existing types of judgment are not suitable for new kinds of litigation, such as public-interest litigation, litigation between administrative agencies, and litigation regarding the parties' status.[9] Thus, social demands are not met and judicial

[9]Public-interest litigation is an action filed by citizens against unlawful practices of an administrative agency for matters that are not directly related to the citizens' own rights or legal interests but in order to safeguard public interests. Citizens should be permitted to file an action for special disputes concerning public laws. Litigation between agencies refers to an action in which the court, through legal procedures, settle the disputes between administrative subjects over the allocation or exercise of power. Such disputes should be settled by the court so as to ascertain power allocation, to prevent agencies from overstepping the boundary of their powers or abusing powers, to reduce disputes caused by power overlapping, and to improve management efficiency. Litigation of parties is an action for declaring or establishing the legal relations between parties. It is an action with one side of the said relation as the defendant and it is concerning legal relations in public law. Litigation of parties is important for settling disputes between parties over administrative acts.

resources are wasted. The academia suggests providing additional types of judgment for those new litigation; expanding the scope of accepted cases; and increasing the types of administrative litigation. Some other issues are also covered in the discussion regarding revision of the Law, such as procedures of administrative litigation, the third-party litigation, coordination between civil and administrative litigation, and coordination between administrative review and administrative litigation.[10]

6. Statute of limitation of administrative litigation.

The statute of limitation of bringing an administrative lawsuit is prescribed mainly in the Administrative Litigation Law and relevant Interpretations of the Supreme People's Court. The Administrative Review Law also includes some relevant provisions. The following problems could be found in those provisions: (1) administrative efficiency is over emphasized and the statute of limitation is too short. (2) The provisions are vague. There is only one Article in the Administrative Litigation Law regarding the statute of limitation, which fails to cover complicated circumstances in practice. For instance, in case of non-service of the administrative decision to the concerned party, what kind of limitation is proper and for how long; also in case that the decision is served but the party is not informed of the right to litigation, how should the time limit be calculated. (3) There are conflicts among these provisions. Although the Administrative Litigation Law and judicial interpretations do not have many provisions regarding the statute of limitation, and the ones they do have are contradictory to each other. The first one is the starting date, which the Law and the Interpretation have different ways of calculating. The second is that the statute of limitation for administrative review inherently contradicts the statute of limitation for administrative litigation. Article 9 of the Administrative Review Law provides that citizens may apply for administrative review within 60 days from the date when they are aware of the administrative act concerned. On the surface, the statute of limitation for administrative review seems irrelevant to the statute of limitation for administrative litigation. However, they are inherently related and even contradictory with each other. Since the statute of limitation for administrative review is obviously shorter, so if the party has an option to choose either review or litigation, they may initiate litigation even after the statute of limitation for administrative review is over. However, according to the existing laws, in some cases the party must apply for administrative review first before initiating an administrative lawsuit, and if the statute of limitation for review is over, then the party also loses the chance of litigation. This will deprive the party's right for judicial remedy and undermines the legal principle that the parties should have equal time and opportunity for obtaining legal remedies. The statute of limitation for administrative review is apparently shorter than that for administrative litigation. In cases where administrative review is a required prerequisite for administrative litigation, then the party who exceeds the statute of limitation for review will not be able to file for litigation. (4) The basic provisions of statute of limitation are defective without suspension or extension of limitation.

[10]Ma Huaide, Improving the Administrative Procedure Law and Categorization of Administrative Litigation, *Jiangsu Social Sciences*, issue 5, 2010.

Considering the flaws in current legislation and practical problems, we make the following suggestions on revising the statute of limitation for administrative litigation: (1) change the current cumbersome and impractical limitations to one year starting from the date when citizens, legal persons or other organizations become aware or have reason to know about the administrative act that has infringed their legitimate rights and interests. Where a real estate is involved, the longest protection term is suggested 20 years from the date when the administrative act is committed, or 5 years for other administrative acts from the date when the administrative act is committed. (2) Adding provisions on extension and suspension for the statute of limitation for administrative litigation, which is an important matter that should be specified in the Law.[11]

7. The key to improving administrative litigation is the reform of administrative adjudication system.

The report of the 18th National Congress of the CPC points out that the rule of law is the basic way of state governance and administration; it is imperative to ensure that laws are made scientifically, enforced strictly, justice administered impartially, and everyone abides by the law; more importance needs to be attached to the rule of law in state governance and social management. Secretary-General of the CPC Xi Jinping directs that fairness and justice should be felt by people in every single case. The 24-year-old Administrative Litigation Law has contributed, to a certain extent, to settling administrative disputes, but with economic and social development and the increased disputes, the Law can no longer meet the new demand of establishing a government by the rule of law and requires immediate modification.

(1) The current situation of China's administrative adjudication system.

The practice of administrative litigation has exposed that main challenges facing the administrative litigation lie with particular problems in the administrative adjudication system, which have greatly hindered its function. The problems are: (1) it is very hard to avoid outside interference, which seriously undermines the fairness of adjudication. (2) Enforcement of the judgment has become a serious challenge. (3) The low-efficiency of adjudication makes it hard to ensure its quality. (4) Judicial authority is lacking, especially in administrative adjudication.[12]

(2) Reform choices.

The problems discussed above make it difficult for administrative litigation to play its role in overseeing administrative power and resolving administrative disputes. Therefore reform is imperative. At present, three reform plans have been proposed. First, designating higher-level courts to hear administrative disputes; increasing choices of

[11] Ma Huaide, Problems of the Administrative Procedure Law and Suggestions for Its Revision, *Legal Forum*, Sept. 2010.

[12] Ma Huaide, The Purposes of the Reform of Administrative Adjudication System: Setting up Administrative Courts, *Law Application*, July 2013.

jurisdiction and designated jurisdiction; relatively centralizing adjudication power; allowing the plaintiff to choose a third-party court jurisdiction; upgrading the hearing court level: when a government is sued, the plaintiff has the right to request the court at one-level higher than the defendant agency to hear the case.

Second, on the basis of the existing administrative adjudication system, set up administrative tribunals and circuit tribunals under the Supreme People's Court and the provincial high people's court, for the advantage of the specialty and timeliness of the tribunals. They are convenient for the parties to attend; can resolve the situation where the basic-level court refuses to accept the case; enforcement agency delays in taking action; and the administrative agency refuses to implement the judgment.

Third, following the example of continental law countries and establish specialized administrative courts to handle administrative disputes.[13]

(3) Establishing administrative courts.

As the current administrative adjudication system is in an all-round crisis situation, a systematic structural reform must be adopted. The first and second proposals mentioned above, though practical, could not solve the fundamental problems. The purpose of reform is not to treat the symptoms but to cure the root cause; therefore, the only way out for the reform is to set up an independent set of administrative courts that is vertically under the supervision of the Supreme People's Court. This way not only the control of local governments and judicial localization can be rid off, but also the court can effectively adjudicate some highly specialized administrative disputes over intellectual property, tax, and land. At the same time, the system can oversee all levels of governments to exercise administrative power by law, and ensure that the central government's administrative decrees are carried out without obstruction. In addition, this kind of system is conducive to enhancing judicial fairness and efficiency through relatively centralized adjudication power. It is also helpful for judges to accumulate experience in administrative adjudication and therefore improves the quality of case handling.

Under the current legal framework, the Constitution and the Organic Law of the Courts do not cause obstacles to the establishment of administrative courts. With the rich experience gained in administrative adjudication for many years, setting up administrative courts does not require a large amount of additional personnel, financial and material resources; nor will it produce great backlash against the existing administrative adjudication system or suffer cultural impediment. The system design of the administrative courts should include the following.[14]

(1) The organizational structure can be set up with three levels of courts — the High Administrative Court, Appellate Administrative Courts, and Ordinary Administrative Courts, with the second-instance judgment as the final decision. In terms of hierarchy, only the Supreme People's Court will set the relatively independent High Administrative Court as the court of last resort for administrative disputes. Both

[13]Ibid.

[14]Ibid.

Appellate Administrative Courts and Ordinary Administrative Courts are directly under the administrative court system. All levels of administrative courts are independent in terms of organizational relationship, separate from the people's courts at various levels and not subordinate to any of them. Each province, autonomous region and municipality will have an appellate administrative court and several ordinary administrative courts. The establishment of administrative courts will avoid geographical overlapping, changing the existing pattern that court jurisdiction covers the same area as administrative jurisdiction.

(2) The duties, powers and the scope of accepted cases of administrative courts. After setting up administrative courts, the scope of accepted cases in administrative litigation should be expanded. Administrative courts may review internal administrative acts and abstract administrative acts as long as it is necessary for judicial power to impose restriction.

(3) The personnel of administrative courts will be composed of a president, vice president and several judges. The President of the High Administrative Court shall be nominated by the President of the Supreme People's Court and appointed by the Standing Committee of National People's Congress. All other personnel shall be appointed by the Standing Committee of NPC according to the nomination of the President of the Supreme People's Court. The president, vice president, and judges of appellate administrative courts and ordinary administrative courts shall be nominated by the President of the High Administrative Court, and appointed by the Standing Committee of National People's Congress. The qualifications for judges and the source of judge selection should be strictly controlled so as to guarantee the high quality of the judges.

(4) Institutional guarantee of administrative courts. To make sure that administrative courts can exercise adjudicatory powers independently and avoid interference of administrative agencies, the expenditure of administrative courts shall be totally funded by state revenues instead of revenues of local governments. Management of personnel, finance and assets shall be exclusively controlled by the High Administrative Court. Budgets and plans for establishment expenditure and personnel shall be gathered and sorted out by the High Administrative Court and submitted to the legislature NPC through the Supreme People's Court instead of being controlled by administrative agencies. Matters, such as formulation of budget, management and allocation of funds, and hire and fire of, may first be provided by the revised Administrative Litigation Law, and thereafter by a specialized organic law of administrative courts. Besides, institutional guarantee should be provided to ensure independence of judges in administrative courts.

All in all, the reform of administrative adjudication system is critical to the reform of administrative litigation system and the judicial system as a whole. Setting up administrative courts is an essential approach to reform administrative adjudication system. Thus administrative courts can fundamentally overcome the deficiencies in the administrative adjudication system, as well as offers a feasible solution for China's judicial reform.

Chapter 10
State Compensation and Government Accountability

10.1 The History of State Compensation System

In a democratic political system, the government is but a part of the society and does not have privileges. It is a special legal person that serves the public interest and the people and it is endowed with rights and capacity to stand in legal relationship with other entities. If and when the government infringes upon the rights of citizens through the act of its agencies, it ought to compensate the victim just like any other legal persons and entities. The State compensation system is a showcase of state accountability. Before the 1870s, the State was exempted from legal liability under the rule of state immunity. Thereafter the state liability system was first introduced in Europe in the form of compensation for wrongful convictions. After WWII, the State compensation system became common worldwide. The earliest provision on State compensation in China was in the draft Constitution of 1934. Its Article 26 provides that "civil servants who infringe on the people's freedom and rights shall be punished and held liable both criminally and civilly. In addition the victim can make claims for compensation from the State in accordance with the law." In December, 1946, the Constitution Assembly of the Nationalist Party (Kuomintang) adopted the draft Constitution, symbolizing that the Republic of China officially recognized the State compensation system. Prior to the founding of the People's Republic of China, the Chinese Communist Party (CPC) also adopted infringement compensation of public officials in revolutionary base areas. For instance, Article 10 of the Human Rights Protection Regulations of Shandong Province adopted during the War against Japan's Aggression provides that "government functionaries who infringe on people's freedom and rights shall be punished and held liable both criminally and civilly. In addition, the victim can claim compensation according to law." Since the founding of the People's Republic of China, China's State compensation system has undergone the following four stages.

© Social Sciences Academic Press and Springer Nature Singapore Pte Ltd. 2018

H. Ma and J. Wang, *Building a Government Based on the Rule of Law*,
Research Series on the Chinese Dream and China's Development Path,
https://doi.org/10.1007/978-981-13-0999-1_10

1. Establishment of Constitutional Principles for State Compensation (1954–1985).

In January 1954, the Provisional Regulations for Harbor Management of the People's Republic of China was adopted. Its Article 20 provides that "if the port authorities forbid vessels to depart from the port on no legal ground, the vessel owner can claim compensation for direct damages and reserve the right to sue the port authorities."

Article 97 of the 1954 Constitution provides that "people have the right to be compensated for the loss caused by public officials' infringement of their rights." This was the first time that the State compensation system was recognized by New China's Constitution. But the 1975 and 1978 versions of the Constitution did not mention State compensation. The 1982 Constitution provides in Section 3, Article 41 that "people have the right to be compensated according to law for the loss caused by government agencies' and public officials' infringement of their rights". This resumed the State compensation provision of the 1954 Constitution and provided constitutional basis for the state compensation system.

2. Applicable Civil Compensations (1986–1989).

Article 121 of the General Rules of the Civil Law provides that "if a government agency or its personnel, while performing its duties, encroaches upon the lawful rights and interests of a citizen or legal person and causes damages, it shall bear civil liability." In the tort system, this Article is usually referred to as the tort liability of the government agency; and civil law scholars regard it as one of the special tort liabilities. Even though the provision in the General Rules of the Civil Law was unsophisticated, it, for the first time, gave citizens the right to claim for State compensation. After that, courts in China began to accept and hear cases on State compensation under the civil procedure, marking the beginning of China's practice on State compensation.

Following the General Rules of the Civil Law, some specific laws also included provisions of State compensation. Article 42 of the Regulations on Administrative Penalties for Public Security passed in 1986 provides that "public security organs shall acknowledge their mistakes to those who are wrongly punished and return the fines and confiscated property; where the legal rights and interests of those punished are infringed upon, compensation shall be made for the loss." Article 54 of the Customs Law (1987) provides that "if the Customs causes damage to any inward and outward goods or articles while examining them, it shall compensate for actual loss from such damage."

3. Administrative Compensation as a Distinct Category (1989–1994).

The Law of Administrative Procedure promulgated in 1989 made the first attempt to separate State compensation (administrative compensation only) from the civil law compensation. With the form of administrative compensation litigation, the Law of Administrative Procedure actually solved several core substantive problems in State compensation, shaped up the system, and laid a solid foundation for the State Compensation Law. Article 67 of the Law of Administrative Procedure provides that a citizen, a legal person or any other organization who suffers damage because of the infringement of the party's lawful rights and interests by a specific administrative act of an administrative agency or its personnel, shall have the right to claim compensation. If a citizen, a legal person or any other organization makes a separate claim for damages, the case shall first be handled by an administrative agency. If disagrees with the decision of the administrative agency, the party may file a suit in a people's court. Mediation is applicable in compensation litigation.

Article 68 of the same law provides that if a specific administrative act of an administrative agency or its personnel infringes upon the lawful rights and interests of a citizen, a legal person or any other organization and causes damage, the administrative agency shall be liable for compensation. After paying the compensation, the administrative agency shall order its personnel who committed intentional or gross mistakes in the case to bear part or all of the damages.

Article 69 of the same law provides that the compensation shall be paid as expenditure of the government budget at various levels. The administrative agency responsible for causing the compensation may be ordered to bear part or all of the damages. Specific measures shall be formulated by the State Council.

Roughly at the same time when the Administrative Procedure Law was passed, the Standing Committee of the National People's Congress assigned its Legislative Affairs Commission to study and draft the State Compensation Law. The Work Report of the NPC Standing Committee (1991) stated that six laws need to be drafted and the State Compensation Law was one of them. In 1993, the CPC Central Committee proposed to establish accountability and compensation mechanism for unlawful exercising of power in the document entitled the Decision of the CPC Central Committee on Certain Issues in Establishing a Socialist Market Economy.

4. Comprehensive Setup of State Compensation (1995–present).

The draft State Compensation Law was submitted to the 8th NPC Standing Committee for deliberation in 1993, and the State Compensation Law of the People's Republic of China was adopted at the 7th session of the Standing Committee of the 8th National People's Congress on May 12, 1994 and came into force on January 1, 1995. It marked the establishment of a relatively comprehensive and systematic State compensation system in China. Along with the Law of Administrative Procedure, it plays an important role in protecting the right to claim State compensations of citizens, legal persons and other organizations and ensuring that State organs abide by laws when excising powers.[1]

The main provisions of the State Compensation Law are as follows: (1) the Law follows the principle of liability for violation of the law. Under this principle, the State shall only be liable for compensation when an administrative agency or its functionaries, in exercising their administrative powers, infringe upon the lawful rights and interests of citizens, and thereby causing damage to them. This is an objective principle of single liability. It distinguishes State compensations from State remuneration. State compensation is based on unlawful acts, while State remuneration

[1] *The Work Report of the NPC Standing Committee* by Tian Jiyun at the 3rd session of the Standing Committee of the 8th National People's Congress on March 11, 1995.

refers to lawful acts. (2) The Law incorporates administrative compensation, criminal compensation, and judicial compensations in a comprehensive way. It also combines substantive law with procedure law by defining the scope of State compensation and setting the standard, procedures and method of calculation of compensations. (3) The State Compensation Law specifies procedures for administrative compensation and criminal compensation respectively.

The State Compensation Law not only improved the state legal liability system, but also provided system safeguard for citizens' rights. But the implementation of the Law was not satisfactory. Some even mocked it by calling it the "Law of No Compensation from the State." To respond to the call for change from all directions the Law was revised by the Decision on Revising the State Compensation adopted on April 29, 2010 at the 14th session of the Standing Committee of the 11th National People's Congress and it took effect on December 1, 2010. The 29th session of the NPC Standing Committee made the second revision in 2012 and it came into force on January 1, 2013.

10.2 Revision of the State Compensation Law

The second revision focuses on the issues that emerged since the promulgation of the State Compensation Law. Its purpose is to provide full remedy to the victim, protect the legitimate rights and interests of citizens, legal persons and other organizations, and ensure that the State organs exercise their powers in accordance with the law. The revised State Compensation Law makes the following innovations:

1. Evolving from single liability for violation of the law to a diverse State compensation liability system, expanding the scope of compensation, and further clarifying the State liability for compensation.

There are several principles for determining the liability, such as liability for violation of the law and liability for mistakes. Since liability for violating the law is relatively clear and objective, so it was adopted by the 1995 State Compensation Law. Article 2 of the original version of the Compensation Law provides that "where State organs or State functionaries execute their functions and powers in violation of the law and thus infringe upon the legitimate rights and interests of citizens, legal persons and other organizations, and thereby causing damage to them, the victims shall have the right to claim State compensation in accordance with the law." This single liability principle suggests that if and only if the act of State organs or State functionaries, in performing official duties, violate the law, infringe upon the legitimate rights and interests of the citizens, legal persons and other organizations, and cause harm to them, then compensation should be made for the harm. If the official act does not violate the law, even if they cause damage, the State shall not bear the compensation liability. Although this principle to some extent is justified, its drawbacks are becoming increasingly conspicuous. For instance, sometimes it is difficult to set the criteria for "violation of the law". Under this principle, damage caused by factual acts, by administrative acts excluded from administrative litigation, and by public facilities cannot be included in the scope of State compensation.

Section 1, Article 2 of the revised Law provides that where the State organ or its functionary in performing its duties infringes upon the lawful rights and interests of citizens, legal persons and other organizations, and thereby causing damage to them, the victim shall have the right to claim State compensation in accordance with this Law. Compared with the original provision, the new version deleted the term "in violation of the law", which indicates that liability has evolved from single liability for violation of the law to a diverse liability system. This change further expands the scope of State compensation. For example, Section 3 of Article 3 and Section 4 of Article 15 of the original Compensation Law provides that if a State organ or its functionary uses or instigates violence such as beating, and thereby causing bodily injury or death of a citizen, the victim is entitled to compensation. In the new State Compensation Law, Section 3 of Article 3 provides that using or instigating or indulging violence such as beating and abuse, and thereby causing bodily injury or death to a citizen, such situation is under the scope of administrative compensation. Section 4 of Article 17 provides that citizens who have been subject to torture, bodily injury or death as a result of the use of violence such as beating by a government functionary or instigated or indulged by a functionary are entitled to criminal compensation. The new version of the law makes violent behavior such as beating and abuse by instigation or indulgence by a government functionary eligible for compensation. Article 17 of the new State Compensation Law also provides that if after the arrest the criminal charge is dropped or not prosecuted; or the person is found not guilty in the original trial, or found innocent in a retrial through the procedure of trial supervision, but the original sentence has been executed, the person is still entitled to compensation. In other words, as long as the person is found not guilty in a retrial, compensation should be made to the victim, whether or not the judge had fault or violated the law in the original trial. In terms of criminal compensation, the new Law combines, liability for violation of the law and consequence liability. The State is liable not only for illegal detention, but also for legal detention that exceeds the time limit and for wrongful arrest.

The new Law has made some improvements over the original version, but objectively speaking, the liability system for State compensation is still a work in progress. Based on different situations, the principle of accountability of official duties with or without fault need to be established to ensure that all violations of the citizens' legitimate rights and interests are compensated with proper remedy.

2. Raising Compensation Payment Standard and Adding Compensation for Emotional Sufferings.

The State compensation standard set by the original State Compensation Law was quite low. This was mainly because when the law was made, the financial resources of the State were rather limited. As a result, only direct losses specified in the law were recoverable. The revised Law makes more specific provisions on the compensation standard. (1) The compensation standard for the right to life and health is raised. Article 34 provides that, where a bodily injury is made, medical expenses, nursing cost as well as lost income due to missed working time shall be compensated. Daily compensation for lost income shall be assessed according to the State average daily pay of staff and workers in the previous year, and the maximum shall be five times of the said average yearly pay. Here nursing cost is added to the compensation. In the case of partial or entire loss of ability to work, medical expenses, nursing cost, disability aids cost, rehabilitation expenses, and disability compensation shall be paid. The disability compensation shall be determined in accordance with the degree of lost work ability based on the disability scale set by the State. The maximum amount of compensation for loss of work ability shall be twenty times the State average yearly pay of staff and workers in the previous year. In the case of total loss of work ability, living expenses shall also be paid to persons who cannot work but have been supported by the disabled. The added compensations by the new Law include nursing cost, disability aids cost, rehabilitation cost, cost for continued treatment and other necessary expenditures incurred due to the disability. (2) Compensation standard for property right is recognized as part of the indirect loss. Article 36 provides that for returned fines, confiscated money, unfrozen deposits and remittance, interests shall be paid based on the bank deposit rate over the same period. (3) The greatest improvement of the new Law is adding the provisions on mental injury. Article 35 provides that a State organ or its functionary's violation of law may not only infringe upon a citizen's personal freedom and the right to life and health, but also may cause mental injuries. Therefore, the revised Law provides that in the case of mental injury, the State shall eliminate the negative effects, restore reputation of the injured party, and make an apology; if the infringement causes serious consequence, appropriate solatium shall be paid by the State.

3. Simplifying the State Compensation Procedures and Defining the Burden of Proof.

Under the original Compensation Law, the first procedure for compensation is to confirm infringement. The prerequisite of demand for compensation is the confirmation from the judicial organ for wrongful detention, wrongful arrest, miscarriage of justice, or other unlawful acts committed when executing their functions and powers. In practice, such organs liable for compensation often deny or delay the confirmation with various excuses. When claimants appeals to a higher authority they seldom get satisfactory results. This actually deprives the claimants' right to compensation. Since the handling of criminal cases involves more than one judicial organ including the police, the procuratorate and the court, the confirmation process can be very cumbersome and it is often used as a means to avoid compensation. As a result, the State compensation procedures are obstructed, and the rights and interests of victims undermined.

The revised State Compensation Law removes the confirmation procedure and reduces the steps in the application for compensation. When designing specific procedures, the revised Law emphasizes more on the responsibility of liable organs. Under the new Law, when a claimant applies for compensation, the State organ liable shall, make a decision within two months from the date of receiving the application. If payment is not made within this period, or if the claimant is not satisfied with the amount of compensation, the claimant may apply for administrative review to the next higher level of the liable agency. And if the claimant disagrees with the review decision, a compensation request can be filed with the compensation commission of the court. This offers a procedure safeguard of the claimant's right to legal remedy.

The revised Law partly strengthens the liable State organ's burden of proof. According to Article 15, where a citizen dies or loses the ability to act when the person is detained or personal freedom restrained due to compulsory administrative measures by a State organ liable, this organ shall provide evidence to prove whether there is a causal relationship between its conduct and the death or loss of ability to act of the citizen.

4. Improving the Compensation Payment System to Guarantee Payment.

As there were no specific provisions in the original Law regarding the compensation payment mechanism, there was no legal safeguard for the payment of compensation. The current practice is that once the compensation liability is determined, the liable organ shall advance the compensation, and then applies to the financial authority of the same level for reimbursement. There had been quite a few compensation payment problems during the decade after the State Compensation Law was first implemented. Some relatively poor regions' budgets did not have State compensation expenditure. Although the Measures of the State Council on the Management of the State Compensation Expenses provided that compensations shall be advanced by the liable organ first and then be reimbursed by the State budget. But in practice, due to budget reform in recent years, the budget of each agency is increasingly meticulous, and many State organs had no fund for the advance. The revised State Compensation Law improves the payment mechanism by providing that the State compensation expenses should be included in the budget of all levels. The claimant can apply for compensation to the liable organ with the proper legal document such as a written decision or mediation agreement on compensation. The liable organ is obligated to apply to the finance department for compensation payment within seven days upon receiving the claimant's application, and the relevant financial department shall make the payment within fifteen days after receiving the payment application.

10.3 Responsible Government and the Development of Administrative Accountability System

In its narrowest sense, government liability refers to the negative legal consequences borne by the government organs and their functionaries for unlawful exercise of power. The established State compensation system is one form of State liability, where the State is held accountable for damage caused to the legitimate rights and interests of citizens, legal persons, and other organizations. This system has played a positive role in safeguarding people's rights, overseeing State organs and their functionaries, and raising the legal accountability awareness of the State and the government. Yet the social development and further understanding of government liabilities have made it clear that the State compensation system cannot cover all legal liabilities of the government.

The government infringement liability for compensation has been aggravating since the mid 20th century, which is manifested in the following aspects: the scope of government compensation liability has been expanded to covering almost all domains of administrative management; a liability determining system has been established combining liability without fault, liability for consequences and liability with fault; the criteria for compensation have been relaxed; the compensation standard has been raised; and the remedial function strengthened. The development of the government liability system to some extent facilitates the expansion of governmental functions. In the context of building a government based on the rule of law, forming an all-round understanding of government liability and regulating government liability through legislation becomes all the more important. Government responsibility should be understood in a broader sense, including the government's social responsiveness, obligation and legal liability. It demands that the government be able to respond to the social demand and take positive measures to fulfill the needs and interests of the public justly and efficiently.[2]

Responsible government is an inevitable trend in the development of modern democracy and provides the basic foundation for a just and efficient government. To establish a responsible government, the first step is to regulate government responsibility through legislation. In accordance with the Constitution of the People's Republic of China, the mandatory responsibility of the government includes safeguarding the rights of citizens, protecting public interests, maintaining public security and public order, and improving the environment. Secondly, the government should execute its functions and powers justly though ways mandated by the law and fulfill its legal obligations. Thirdly, to ensure the fulfillment of government responsibility, an accountability system should be established under strict oversight, which should include both the State compensation system as the government responsibility as well as the administrative accountability system for liability of individual officials.

The development of State compensation and administrative accountability system in China gives rise to the concept and system of responsible government. Administrative accountability, especially accountability of officials, helps strengthen the building of a responsible government. The idea of accountability of officials in China can date back to the remarks made by Deng Xiaoping in the Expanded Meeting of the Political Bureau of the CPC Central Committee on August 18, 1980. He instructed that "the officials should shoulder their responsibilities instead of evading them, and those who derelict their duties should be held accountable." In fact, the earliest case of accountability of officials took place in the same year, when the drilling ship Bohai 2 sank and the then Vice Premier Kang Shi'en was recorded a major demerit. Kang Shi'en was the highest-ranking official that has been held accountable for administrative failures. In the twenty years that followed, more administrative accountability cases happened, but they caught little public attention. Since the year 2000, with

[2]Zhang Chengfu, On Responsible Government, *China Renmin University Journal*, issue 2, 2000.

increased production safety accidents, accountability received renewed attention. On April 21, 2001, the State Council issued Provisions of the State Council on Investigation for Administrative Accountability for Extraordinarily Serious Safety Accidents. On August 9, 2002, the General Office of the CPC Central Committee and the General Office of State Council released the Interim Measures of Administrative Accountability for Causing Incidents Involving Adding Extra Burden for the Farmers. During the outbreak of Severe Acute Respiratory Syndrome (SARS) in 2003, Zhang Wenkang, the then Minister of Health and Meng Xuenong, the then Mayor of Beijing, were held accountable for hiding information about the epidemic outbreak and for failure to respond. This led to a nationwide accountability drive.[3]

The accountability system is an important part of the State political system and the State oversight ability. A sound and effective accountability system is an importance sign for a mature country under the rule of law. Therefore, improving the accountability system and establishing a responsible and transparent government based on the rule of law has becomes a fundamental objective for reforming the modern administrative system. Compared with Western countries, the administrative accountability system in China still needs to be improved. This calls for efforts on both the macro and micro levels.

1. The development of responsible government and administrative accountability system depends on the design and operational status of other related systems. Therefore, analyzing relevant factors and improving the relevant systems become all the more essential for promoting the development of administrative accountability system in China.

(1) Enhancing legal literacy of administrative personnel, regulating the exercising of state power and keeping it in check. The Report to the 18th National Congress of the CPC asserts that in the course of reform, promoting the rule of law is the greatest consensus. Rule of law runs through the whole process of reform and development and covers all areas of the economic, political, cultural, social, and ecological progress. Rule of law not only provides strong support for all reforms but also is a consensus reached in the process of deepening reforms and promoting scientific development. It must be maintained in the long term and become the basic approach of governance of the Party and the way of thinking of leading officials.[4] Leading official should set a good example for others in this respect. Civil servants should abandon the idea of rule of man, enhance their legal awareness, and get used to "rule of law" way of thinking and acting, which is critical to forming the belief system of the rule of law.[5]

In addition, to achieve the goal of establishing a moderately prosperous society in all respects and building a government based on the rule of law by 2020, the means of regulating the State power and keeping it in check become all the more important.

---

[3]Shi Shuwei, Current Situation and Path Choice Concerning the Administrative Accountability System in China, *Guangming Daily*, Oct. 15, 2010.

[4]Ma Huaide, Rule of Law Is the Greatest Consensus about Future Reform and Development, http://www.legaldaily.com.cn/bm/content/2012-11/14/content_3982765.htm?node=20737.

[5]Ma Huaide, How to Cultivate the Belief of Rule of Law, *People's Forum*, issue 16, 2013.

The Report of the 18th National Congress of the CPC and remarks of government leaders thereafter all emphasize that the basic idea for realizing this goal is to regulate the State power and keep it in check through system building. Whether in reforming the governance structure or in improving the Party's leadership role, or whether in combating corruption or in declaring the government transparency and ensuring no organization or individual is above the law, the common theme is restraining the State power and keeping it in check. This is critical to promoting the rule of law and building a responsible government.[6]

(2) Improving institutional checks for power and reforming administrative law enforcement mechanism.

First, in terms of the anti-corruption legal framework, China has promulgated the Criminal Law, the Law on Administrative Oversight, and the Implementing Regulations for the Administrative Oversight Law and other statutes. It also issued many policy directives. These are large in number and cover almost all areas in which corruption may occur. Even so, corruption is still rampant. This may be attributed to the absence of key legal framework for exercise of power, such as procedure regulation for major decisions-making, the status of government information disclosure regulation not high enough in the legal hierarchy, and no legal basis for human resources management.[7]

Second, access to legal remedies and power oversight need to be improved.

(a) Redefining the role of discipline inspection and supervision. For a long time, the discipline inspection and supervision organs of all levels have cooperated with the administrative agencies in carrying out safety inspection, joint law enforcement inspection, efficiency supervision, and supervision on online administration services. However, some problems have emerged in this process. The most important one is that the disciplinary organs undertake a lot of work beyond their statutory duties. As a result, the principle of functions mandated by law is violated. Sometimes the disciplinary organs are even sued when supporting the work of law enforcement organs for lack of legal ground in their actions. Therefore, the role of discipline inspection and supervision should be properly defined, and the statutory powers and duties of the disciplinary organs should be specified. The disciplinary organs should execute their powers and perform their duties in keeping with the Law on Administrative Supervision. Only in so doing can they exercise proper supervision and play a better role in building a responsible government.[8]

(b) Removing obstacles in administrative review and administrative litigation and improving judicial credibility. The Report of the 18th National Congress of the CPC claimed judicial credibility as an important part of building a moderately

[6]Ma Huaide, The Key to Build a Law-Based Government, *Integrity Culture Studies*, issue 4, 2013.

[7]Ma Huaide, Three Laws Need to Be Made to Combat Corruption from the Root, Renmin.com, http://theory.people.com.cn/n/2013/0227/c112851-20620675.html.

[8]Ma Huaide, On the Role of Inspection and Supervision by Disciplinary Organs, http://www.e-gov.org.cn/news/news006/2014-02-07/147590.html.

prosperous society in all respects. As Xi Jinping put it, "we should deepen reform of the judicial system and ensure that the judicial and procuratorial powers are executed independently and impartially in accordance with the law, so that the people can see justice in every judicial case." The influence of local and administrative authority over judicial functions should be removed, and the role of judicial power in overseeing and restricting administrative power should be restored.[9]

(c) Redefining the functions of grievance complaint letters and visits. Instead of being used to settle disputes, grievance complaints should return to their original function of supervising government work through the voice of people's sentiments.[10]

To build a responsible government, China should also reform the current administrative law enforcement system, which is required by the Decision of the CPC on Major Issues Concerning Comprehensive Deepening of the Reform. There are many problems in this regard based on the Constitution, the administrative organization laws, relevant regulations, and the law enforcement practice. The most conspicuous ones include stratified enforcement, dislocation of power from responsibility, weak foundation, poor collaboration, muddled boundaries, overlapping functions, self-serving practice, insufficient supervision and absence of accountability.[11]

As the administrative law enforcement system has not yet been fully straightened out, problems such as difficulties and conflicts in enforcement, nonfeasance, selective enforcement and entrapment have triggered strong public concern. These problems not only undermine the authority of law enforcement and reduce its efficiency, but are also inconsistent with the goal of building a government based on the rule of law. In recent years, many regions have been experimenting with administrative law enforcement reform measures. Yet few of these reforms and experiments produced satisfactory results. The main reason is that many problems are institutional and cannot be solved at the grassroots level. Top-down design is needed to address the root cause, to find a way out of the current dilemma and to lay a firm foundation for the building of a responsible government based on the rule of law.

2. The administrative accountability system has its unique features. In addition to providing a sound institutional environment through reforms at the macro level, the responsible government and administrative accountability also need to be fine-tuned at the micro level.

(1) Transforming from internal accountability to external accountability.

Currently China practices the internal accountability system, which means Party cadres are held accountable by Party organizations and administrative officials held

[9]Ma Huaide, The Key to Improving Judicial Credibility, *People's Judicature: Application*, issue 9, 2013.

[10]Ma Huaide, Be Vigilant to the Phenomenon of Believing in Grievance Petitions Rather Than the Law, *Study Times*, Jan. 25, 2010, p. 005.

[11]Ma Huaide, Establishing a Comprehensive, Authoritative and Standard Administrative Law Enforcement System, *China Party and Government Official's Forum,* issue 12, 2013.

accountable by administrative agencies. The Inner-Party Supervision Regulations (for trial implementation) released on February 18, 2004, has provisions on inquiry and questioning, dismissal or replacement. Regulations of the Communist Party of China on Disciplinary Actions specifies the disciplinary actions for Party cadres who committed nonfeasance and malfeasance. The Outline for Promoting Administration by Law in an All-Round Way issued in April, 2004 provides that integration of power and responsibility should be a basic principle for governance based on the rule of law. It also has provisions on the decision-making accountability system, the administrative law enforcement accountability system, and improving the administrative review accountability system.

The Law of People's Republic of China on Civil Servants promulgated on January 1, 2006 specifies the conditions under which the civil servants shall be accountable to their higher authority, as well as resignation and dismissal of civil servants, thus further strengthening the administrative accountability system. During the 4th Session of the 10th National People's Congress on March 5, 2006, Premier Wen Jiabao, in the Report on the Work of the Government, proposed that the administrative accountability system be established and perfected, and that the government's execution ability and credibility be enhanced. In 2008, for the first time, administrative accountability was incorporated in the Working Rules of the State Council and Priorities for the State Council's Work. And in July 2009, based on the practice in recent years, the CPC Central Committee released the Interim Provisions on the Implementation of Accountability System for the Party and Government Leaders.

However, both the general principles of accountability in modern administrative work and China's past experience of public administration indicate that a single accountability and activation mechanism alone is not sufficient for multiple varieties of accountability. To give full play to the role of the accountability system, China should gradually shift towards external accountability system with the people's congresses as the mainstay plus involving public participation. Article 3 and Article 128 of the Constitution provides that the administrative organs, judicial organs, and procuratorial organs are created by the people's congresses and to which they must answer. In accordance with Article 41 of the Constitution, "citizens of the People's Republic of China have the right to criticize and make suggestions to any State organ or functionary; citizens have the right to make complaints, to press charges against, or to make informative report about any State organ or functionary for violation of law or dereliction of duty." In practice, however, if the people's congresses are to exercise this power endowed by the Constitution and the laws, the means of supervision and accountability still needs to be confirmed through legislation, which include special investigation, inquiry, dismissal and vote of non-confidence. Meanwhile, based on the belief that citizens are the ultimate subject of external accountability, procedures for the public to activate the accountability mechanism needs to be established.

(2) Shifting from an ad hoc emergency accountability to a long-term standing system.

In the past, leading officials were only held accountable after major safety accidents had taken place. Now the administrative accountability system has become a permanent institutional feature. Apart from the above-mentioned documents issued by the CPC Central Committee and the State Council, departments under the State Council and local governments have also adopted provisions on administrative accountability based on their own functions and duties. Regulatory instruments about accountability have been introduced in a dozen fields such as railways, transportation, forestry, fire prevention, land resources, education, finance, health, industry and commerce, cultural relics, insurance, construction, quality control, and the People's Bank of China. At the local level, by July 2009 twenty-eight provinces, municipalities and autonomous regions had made rules or regulations concerning administrative law enforcement accountability or responsibility, accounting for 90% of the total.[12] Forty-three larger cities had made such rules or regulations, accounting for 86% of the total. Among the 43 larger cities, 24 of them codified the system through rules or regulations, and the remaining 19 codified it through regulatory instruments.[13]

At the National Work Conference on Governance based on the Rule of Law in 2010, the then Premier Wen Jiabao emphasized the need for strictly enforcing administrative accountability. He said that accountability should always be maintained regardless of the person, time or location in question. If defiance of orders or prohibition, nonfeasance, malfeasance and other wrongful administrative acts cause major liability accidents or serious violation of administrative law in a region or a department, relevant leading officials or even the executive leaders should be held liable, so as to make sure that government organs and their personnel execute their powers and duties properly. Meanwhile, more research should be done on legislation of administrative accountability to improve the relevant legal system.

(3) Moving from accountability for violation of law to all-round accountability.

In the past, only unlawful acts such as abuse of power or overreaching one's authority were held accountable, whereas omission to act was largely neglected. As a result, some officials were reluctant to perform their duties for fear of making mistakes. Currently, the scope of accountability is expanding from "having faults" to "omission to act". In addition to making more detailed provisions on accountability for fault, the dimensions of accountability for omission to act should be further explored. Criteria for administrative accountability for omission to act should be incorporated in the accountability system. An all-round accountability system encompassing political responsibility, legal responsibility and moral responsibility should be established.

Promoting administrative accountability system and building a responsible government is essential for deepening reform of the administrative system, enhancing the concept of government based on the rule of law, and fulfilling government duties. It is indispensable for governing for the people, governance based on the rule of law, adopting the "scientific outlook on development", and developing a correct attitude toward merits and achievement. It is also crucial for building a harmonious society

[12]Xinjiang Uyger Autonomous Region, Zhejiang Province and Jiangsu Province did it through regulatory instruments.

[13]Larger cities with no regulations on administrative accountability or responsibility system are Lhasa, Xining, Tangshan, Baotou, Anshan and Handan.

and a service-oriented government. To sum up, responsible government and administrative accountability system will continue to play an important part in China's future development. Great efforts should be made to improve the current administrative accountability system and build a responsible government.

Bibliography

1. The Organic Law of the State Council, effective in Dec., 1982.
2. Interim Regulations Concerning the Procedures for the Formulation of Administrative Rules and Regulations, effective in April.
3. Notice of the State Council General Office Concerning the Improvement of Administrative Regulations Promulgation Work, issued in May (1988).
4. The Legislation Law of the People's Republic of China, effective in July, 2000.
5. *Notice on Reducing the authority of the administrative examination and approval over the Investment in Fixed Assets and Simplifying the Examination and Approval Procedures*, March 30, 1997.
6. *Decision of the CCCPC on Some Major Issues Concerning Building Socialist Market Economic System* (passed by the Third Plenary Session of the 14th Central Committee of the Communist Party of China on Nov. 14, 1993).
7. *Proposals of the Central Committee of the Communist Party of China on the Outline of the Tenth Five-Year Plan for National Economic and Social Development*, approved at the Fifth Plenary Session of the 15th Central Committee of the CPC on Oct. 11, 2000.
8. *Decision of the Central Committee of the CPC on Enhancing and Improving the Construction of the Work Style of the CPC*, approved by the Fifth Plenary Session of the 15th Central Committee of the CPC on Oct. 11, 2000.
9. Notice of the General Office of the State Council on the Establishment of the Leading Group of the Reform on the System of Administrative Examination and Approval of the State Council, No. 71, issued by the General Office of the State Council, 2001.
10. Decision of the State Council on Canceling Administrative Examination and Approval for the First Batch of Items (State Issuance (2002) No. 24).
11. Decision of the State Council on Canceling Administrative Examination and Approval for the Second Batch of Items (State Issuance (2003) No. 5).
12. Decision of the State Council on Canceling Administrative Examination and Approval for the Second Batch of Items and Transforming the Management Mode of Some Items Subject to Administrative examination and approval (State Issuance (2003) No. 5).
13. Decision of the State Council on Canceling and Adjusting Administrative Examination and Approval for the Fourth Batch of Items (State Issuance (2007) No. 33).
14. Decision of the State Council on Canceling and Adjusting Administrative Examination and Approval for the Sixth Batch of Items (State Issuance (2012) No. 52).
15. Decision of the State Council on the Matters Including Canceling and Delegating Administrative Examination and Approval for a Batch of Items (State Issuance (2013) No. 19).

© Social Sciences Academic Press and Springer Nature Singapore Pte Ltd. 2018
H. Ma and J. Wang, *Building a Government Based on the Rule of Law*,
Research Series on the Chinese Dream and China's Development Path,
https://doi.org/10.1007/978-981-13-0999-1

16. *The Administrative Permission Law*, effective in 2004.
17. *Kunming Interim Measures for Protection of Groundwater Resources*, issued in 1983.
18. *Measures for Examination and Approval of Foreign Investment*, issued on Aug. 23, 1992.
19. *Rules of Heilongjiang Province on Implementation of the Regulations on Transformation of Operational Mechanism of the State-owned Industrial Enterprises*, issued on Dec. 23, 1992.
20. Rules of Jinan City on the Reform of the Administrative Examination and Approval System (2001).
21. Rules on Shandong Province on Administrative Examination and Approval (2001).
22. Rules of Xining City on Administrative Examination and Approval (2002).
23. Rules of Shenyang City on Administrative Examination and Approval (2002).
24. The Constitution of the Republic of China of 1947.
25. The Constitution of the People's Republic of China of 1954.
26. The Constitution of the People's Republic of China of 1975.
27. Regulations on the Rural Five-Guarantee Work, effective in 1994.
28. Social Insurance Law of the People's Republic of China, effective in 2011.
29. Public Assistance Law of the People's Republic of China (draft open to comments).
30. The Law of the People's Republic of China on the Protection of the Rights and Interests of the Aged, effective in 2013.
31. The Law of the People's Republic of China on the Protection of the Minors, effective in 2007.
32. The Law of the People's Republic of China on the Protection of the Rights and Interests of the Disabled People, effective in 2008.
33. The White Paper on the Socialist Legal System with the Chinese Characteristics, issued on Oct. 27, 2011.
34. The Law of the People's Republic of China on the State-Owned Assets of Enterprises, effective in 2009.
35. Administrative Procedure Rules of Hunan Province, effective in 2008.
36. Shanghai High People's Court, "Studies on Legal Issues concerning Government Information Disclosure", *Administrative Law Enforcement and Administrative Adjudication* compiled by the administrative division of the Supreme People's Court, People's Court Press, vol. 1, 2008.
37. The Constitution of the People's Republic of China of 1982.
38. The Law of the People's Republic of China on Prevention and Treatment of Infectious Diseases, effective in 2004.
39. The Fire Protection Law of the People's Republic of China, effective in 2009.
40. Regulations of China Taiwan on Reimbursement for Requisition and Expropriation for Disaster Response.
41. *The Operational Procedures and Compensation Methods of China Taiwan for the Requisition of Anti-Epidemic Materials.*
42. *Rules of China Taiwan of Implementation of the Disaster Prevention and Response Act.*
43. *The Operational Procedures and Compensation Methods of China Taiwan for Requisition of Anti-Epidemic Materials.*
44. *Implementation of the Emergency Response Law*, the speech of State Councilor Hua Jianmin at the conference on November 13, 2007.
45. Answers of Officials at the LAO of the State Council to the Questions from the Media on *the Regulations on the Implementation of the Administrative Review Law*, July, 2009.
46. The Work Report of the NPC Standing Committee by Tian Jiyun at the 3rd session of the Standing Committee of the 8th National People's Congress on March 11th, March 11, 1995.
47. *The Interpretations to the Regulations on Administrative Review* made by the Legislative Affairs Bureau of the State Council , China Publishing House, Jan. 1991.
48. Deng Xiaoping, Emancipating the Mind, Seeking Truth from Facts, Looking Ahead in Unity, *Selected Works of Deng Xiaoping*, vol.2, People's Publishing House, 1978.

49. Wang Yongqing, *The Textbook of the Law of Administrative Permission of the People's Republic of China*, China Legal Publishing House, 2003.
50. Yang Jianshu, *The General Analysis on the Administrative Law of Japan*, China Legal Publishing House, 1998.
51. Chen Xinmin, Principles of the Administrative Law of China, China University of Political Science and Law Press, 2002.
52. Wong Yuesheng, *The Administrative Law*, China Legal Publish House, 2002.
53. Wang Zhirong, *the Fundamentals of Information Law*, China Legal Publishing House, 2003.
54. Li Fei (ed.) *Explanation and Practical Guide on Emergency Response Law of the People's Republic of China*, China Democracy and Rule of Law Press, 2007.
55. Yang Jianshu, An Introduction on the Administrative Law of Japan, China Legal Publishing House, 1998.
56. Wang Mingyang, Administrative Law of France, Beijing University Press, 2007.
57. Qing Feng, "the Past, Present and Future of Administrative Reconsideration of China", *the Review and Prospect of the Administrative Law of China*, the Publishing House of China University of Political Science and Law, 2006.
58. Guo Xiujiang, "Overview and Outlook on the Purpose of the Administrative Litigation Law: Antithesis and Unity of Legality Review and Administrative Dispute Settlement", *Review and Outlook on China's Administrative Litigation Law*, China University of Political Science and Law Press, 2006.
59. Hu Zhenjie, *et. al.*, *Questions and Answers Regarding Practical Knowledge of the Law of Administrative Permission,* Economy and Management Press, July, 2006.
60. Zheng Chuankun, Yi Xuezhi, Liu Jian, "Studies on the Construction of the System of Relatively Concentrated Administrative Permission Power", *The Forum of Constitutional Law and Administrative Law,* vol. 3, edited by Wen Zhengbang, China Procuratorial Press, 2007.
61. Zhao, Chunling, et al., *The Welfare System and Promotion Step by Step of the Social Security in Our Country*, China Business Press, 2008.
62. Carol Harlow (U.K.) & Richard Rawling (U.K.), *Law and Administration*, translated by Yang Weidong, et al., The Commercial Press, 2005.
63. Leon Duguit, *The Transformation of the Public Law*, translated by Zheng Ge, etc., Liao Hai Press & Chunfeng Literature and Art Press, 1999.
64. Hartmut Maurer (Germany), The General Theories of the Administrative Law, translated by Gao Jiawei, Law Press China, 2000.
65. Cheng Zhongmo, Genera Principles of the Administrative Law (II), San Min Book Co. , Ltd., 1997.
66. Liu Yantao, Studies on Relief Administration, Shandong People's Publishing House, 2006.
67. Jerry L. Marshaw (U.S.), *The Due Process in the Administrative State*, Translated by Shen Kui, Higher Education Press, 2005.
68. Wang Xixin, *Public Participation and Administrative Process: A Framework for Theoretical and Institutional Analysis*, China Democracy and Law Press, Dec. 2007.
69. *2001–2012 Report on China's Administrative Transparency*, Law Press, 2013.
70. Murakami Takenori (Japan), "Issues on Relief Administration", *The Great Modern Administrative Legal System*, vol. 1, ed. by Ogawa Ichiro, Yuhikaku Publishing Co.,Ltd., 1983.
71. Cheng Mingxiu (Taiwan), *Administrative Acts and the Theories of Legal Relations*, New Sharing Culture Enterprise Co. LTD., 2005.
72. Sun Naiyi (Taiwan), "The Protection of the Reliance benefits of the Beneficiaries in the Social Welfare Administration: Lessons learned from the German Social Administrative Procedure Act", *Furen Law Review*, issue 37, June, 2009.
73. Fang Jun, ed., *The Judicial Reform of Administrative Reconsideration System in China* edited by Zhou Hanhua, Peking University Press, April 2005.

74. 2011年3月.Shan Chunchang, *Emergency Management*: *Operational Model and Practice with Chinese Characteristics,* Beijing Normal University press, March, 2011.
75. Wan Pengfei, *Emergency Management Laws in the United States, Canada and the United Kingdom*, Beijing University Press, April, 2006.
76. Ying Songnian, "The Outline of the Law-based administration", *China Legal Science*, issue 1, 1997.
77. Wu Jing, Ten Concentrated Clearing up of Rules and Regulation, *People's Daily*, 13th ed. , March, 28, 2007.
78. Yang Jianshun, The Aims of the Governmental Function Transformation and the Rationales of its System, *China Legal Science*, Issue, 6, 2006.
79. Zhang Wei, "The Transformation of the Governmental Functions from the Perspective of the Administrative Approval System", Thesis of Degree of Northwest University, 2012.
80. Wang Li, "The Administrative Permission Law and the Transformation of the Governmental Functions", *Journal of Zhengzhou Party School of the Central Committee of CPC*, vol. 3, 2005.
81. Yang Jingyu, "On the Administrative Permission Law of the People's Republic of China (Draft): at the 29th Plenary Session of the Standing Committee of the 9th National People's Congress", *The Communique of the Standing Committee of the National People's Congress,* issue 5, 2003.
82. Li You, "From 'Examination and Approval System' to 'Approval System': Theories and Practice of the Reform in Enterprise Registration System of Shenzhen Special Economic Zone", *Economy of Special Economic Zone*, issue 5, 1993.
83. Tang Xiaoyang, "Reforming the administrative examination and approval System and Normalizing Government Examination and Approval: the Enlightenment Gained from the Reform of Guangdong Province and Shenzhen City on the System of Examination and Approval", *Journal of Guangdong Administration Academy*, vol. 3, 2000.
84. Xia Changyong, "The Reform of the Administrative Examination and Approval System to be Intensified: Remarks of He Yong, the Deputy Team Leader of the State Council Work Leading Group of the Reform of the Administrative Examination and Approval System", *China Daily*, Jan. 9, 2003.
85. Ma Huaide, "Suggestions on the Reform of Administrative examination and approval System", *Legal Daily*, p. 12, Oct. 16, 2013.
86. Qiao Xiaoyang, "The Report of the Law Committee of the National People's Congress on the Revision of the Administrative Permission Law of the People's Republic of China (Drafted) : at the 31 Meeting of the Standing Committee of the 9th National People's Congress on Dec. 23, 2002", *The Communique of the Standing Committee of the National People's Congress*, issue 5, 2003.
87. Li Shasha, "The Development of the Administrative Service Center and Construction of the System of Relatively Concentrated Administrative Permission in China", *Journal of Shenyang Carders*, 2011, vol. 13, issue 4.
88. Li Lu, "On the Creativity of the System of Relatively Concentrated Administrative Permission Power and the Perfection of Legislation", *Journal of Socialist Theory Guide*, Sept., 2010.
89. Qing Feng, The Sketch and Theoretical Analysis of the Reform of the System of Administrative Law Enforcement, *Journal of Shanghai University of Political Science and Law*, 2007, issue 1.
90. Yan Erbao, Reflections on the Provision of Government Benefits: Case Study on the German Administrative Laws of Germany and Japan, *Studies on the Administrative Law*, 2010, vol. 3.
91. He Zhengrong, The Development of the Provision of Government Benefits and the Responses to the Theories and System in the Administrative Law, *Academic Forum*, 2007, vol. 11.

92. Jiang Bixin, "How do Studies on the Science of Administrative Law Respond to the Practice of the Service-Oriented Government?", *Modern Legal Science*, 2009, vol. 3.
93. Luo Wenyan, "Service-Oriented Government and the transformation of the Administrative Law: from the Perspective of the Idea of 'Good Governance'in the Administrative Law", *Studies in Law and Business*, 2009, issue 2.
94. Jin Chendong, "On the Principle of the Administrative Law Reservation", *Zhe Jiang Social Science*, issue 1, 2002.
95. Luo Wenyan, "Service-Oriented Government and the transformation of the Administrative Law", *Studies in Law and Business*, issue 2, 2009.
96. Huang Xuexian, "Studies on the Issues Regarding Applying the Principle of Law Reservation to the Provision of Government Benefits", *Jianghai Journal*,issue 6, 2005.
97. Ying Songnian, The Prospect of Chinese Administrative Procedural Legislation, *China Legal Science*, vol. 2, 2010.
98. Zhou Chong, "Increasingly Transparent Examination and CSRC's Advocacy of "the Disclosure of In-Process Information", *Shanghai Securities News*, p.02, March 28, 2012.
99. Chen Zhuo, *Studies on China's Legal System on Government Information Disclosure* (D), Dissertation of Fudan University, 2008, page 27–28.
100. Gao Xiaoping, "Achievements and Development of the Emergency Management System with Chinese Characteristics", *China Administrative Management*, 2008 (11), p. 20.
101. Jiang Bixin & Shao Changmao, "The Reform of Sharing Right, the Provision Procedure of Government Benefits and the Administrative Reform", *Administrative Law Review*, issue 4, 2009.
102. Chen Shuwei, "Enhancing the Capacity Building for Urban Emergency Response Management in China", *Journal of Tianjin Administrative College*, May, 2007.
103. Zhong Kaibin, Peng Zongchao, "Emergencies and the Establishment of Capital Urban Emergency Collaboration System", *Beijing Social Sciences*, 2003(4).
104. Tang Yalin, Guolin, "From Governed by Class System to Co-governance—A Historic Study on the Governance Model of the People's Republic of China", *The Academic Circle*, 2006(4), p. 62.
105. Jiang Ming'an, "A Study on Administrative Compensation System", *Legal Science Magazine*, 2001(5).
106. Shen Kaiju, "On the Standard of Administrative Compensation", *Henan Social Sciences*, 2005(1).
107. Liu Xin: "Debate on Repositioning of Administrative Review", *Legal Forum*, September 2011(5), vol. 26.
108. Liu Dongsheng: *the Reconstruction of the Administrative Review System*, Doctoral Dissertation at China University of Political Science and Law, April, 2006.
109. Liu Heng & Lu Yan, "An Analysis of the Flaws of the Vertical Jurisdiction of Administrative Review in China", on *Chinese Journal of Law*, 2004(2).
110. Zhao Daguang, "Development and Experience of Administrative Adjudication in the past 60 Years" , *Law Application*, Dec. 2009.
111. Luo Haocai, *A Great Achievement in Democracy and Legal System Construction: the 10th Anniversary of the Promulgation of the Administrative Litigation Law*, Dec. 2008.
112. Ma Huaide, "Resolving Social Conflicts and Administrative Litigation System", *Chinese Cadres Tribune*, issue 3, 2011.
113. Ma Huaide, "Problems of the Administrative Litigation Law and Suggestions on Its Revision", *Legal Forum*, Sept. 2010.
114. Ma Huaide, "Protecting the Rights and Interests of Citizens, Legal Persons and Other Organizations Should be the Fundamental Purpose of Administrative Litigation", *Administrative Law Review*, issue 2, 2012.
115. Ma Huaide, "Improving Administrative Litigation System to Promote Social Dispute Settlement", *Legal Information*, Aug., 2011.

116. Ma Huaide, "Improving the Administrative Litigation Law and the Categorization of Administrative Litigation, *Jiangsu Social Sciences*, issue 5, 2010.
117. Ma Huaide, "The Purposes of the Reform of Administrative Adjudication System: Setting up Administrative Courts", *Law Application*, July 2013.
118. Ma Huaide, "The Key to Improving Judicial Credibility", *People's Judicature: Application*, 2013(9).
119. Ma Huaide, "Be Vigilant to the Phenomenon of Believing in Grievance Petition and Visits Rather Than the Law", *Study Times*, Jan. 25, 2010, p. 005.
120. Ma Huaide, "Establishing a Comprehensive, Authoritative and Standard Administrative Law Enforcement System", *China Party and Government Official's Forum*, 2013(12).
121. Zhang Chengfu, "On Responsible Government", *China Renmin University Journal*, 2000 (2).
122. Shi Shuwei, "Current Situation and Path Choice Concerning the Administrative accountability system in China", Guangming Daily, October 15, 2010.
123. Ma Huaide, "How to Cultivate the Belief of Rule of Law", *People's Forum*, 2013(16)
124. Ma Huaide, "The Key to Build a Law-Based Government", *Integrity Culture Studies*, 2013 (4).
125. Shen Lutao, Zou Shengwen, "Coping with Disasters Calmly: An Overview of China's Emergency Plan Framework", *Xinhua News Agency*, Beijing, Feb. 25, 2005.
126. "Ten Backpackers Come to Rescue Five Teachers Trapped on a Cliff at Night", *Beijing Youth Newspaper*, Nov. 28, 2007, B1.
127. Ma Huaide, "Rule of Law is the Greatest Consensus about Future Reform and Development", http://www.legaldaily.com.cn/bm/content/2012-11/14/content_3982765.htm?node=20737.
128. Ma Huaide, "Three Laws Need to Be Made to Combat Corruption from the Root", http://theory.people.com.cn/n/2013/0227/c112851-20620675.html.
129. Ma Huaide, "On the Role of Inspection and Supervision by Disciplinary Organs", http://www.e-gov.org.cn/news/news006/2014-02-07/147590.html.
130. Jiang Ping, "Legislation on "Citizens Suing the Government", *Remembering of the Reform*, http://www.caijing.com.cn/2008-04-11/100056231.html.
131. Li Chunhui, Why Is It Wrong to Construct Security Houses on the Expenses of the Housing Provident Fund?, http://money.163.com/special/focus479/.
132. Shenzhen Social Security Bureau Charged of Entrapment for Committing Inspection by Its Workers Pretending to be Patients, *Yangcheng Evening*.
133. *Sun Rongfa v. Hangzhou Municipal Bureau of Land and Property Management*, 2010 Zhe Hang A. A. No. 92.
134. *Luo Juxin v. Hongzhou Municipal Bureau of Land and Property Management*, 2010 Zhe Hang A.A. No. 93.
135. Emergencies Act .R.S.C. 1985, c. 8 (4th Supp.).
136. The Fifth Amendment to the Constitution of the United States.
137. American-Hawaiian S.S. Co. v. U.S., Ct.Cl.1955, 133 F.Supp. 369, 132 Ct.Cl. 246. War And National Emergency 14.
138. Eastern S. S. Lines v. U. S., D.C.Mass.1947, 74 F.Supp. 37, affirmed 171 F.2d 589. Shipping 58(3).
139. Nicholson Transit Co. v. U.S., Ct.Cl.1951, 118 Ct.Cl. 344. War And National Emergency.
140. Georgia Hardwood Lumber Co. v. U.S., Ct. Cl. 1948, 78 F.Supp. 808, 111 Ct.Cl. 621. War And National Emergency 14.
141. Lands Acquisition Act. § 56. (1989).

The manufacturer's authorised representative in the EU is Springer Nature Customer Service Centre GmbH, Europaplatz 3, 69115 Heidelberg, Germany. If you have any concerns regarding our products, please contact ProductSafety@springernature.com

Printed and bound by CPI Group (UK) Ltd, Croydon, CR0 4YY
30/09/2026
02225444-0009